Dollar Swap
Fintech
make 800%

(Assets Market Rotation Investing Formula)

Pentagon Investing Method

Copyright Notice

Dollar Swap
Fintech
make 800%

(Assets Market Rotation Investing Formula)

Pentagon Investing Method

The subtitle:

Tears of Japan

Published by Sohn DaeShig

Library of Congress Control Number
LCCN: 2024900197 (Paperback)
ISBN: 979-11-392-1736-0 (Paperback)
ISBN: 979-11-392-1737-7 (Hard cover)
ISBN: 979-11-392-1738-4 (eBOOK)

Contact Information: **sohn2738@naver.com**

About the author(Korean):

The author was born in 1953. He was born during the Korean War and has experienced Korea's political, economic, social, and cultural development from the 1960s, when Korea was at its most difficult, to the present, when Korea has entered the developed world. He has been investing in stocks and apartments for more than 50 years.

In September 2011, after fulfilling his duties as a PD specializing in current & cultural affairs at KBS public broadcaster in korea for 30 years, he began to write financial(fintech) books professionally by gathering his own investment experience and the materials he researched in his spare time. He has written about seven books on financial technology.He is a licensed broker and has completed the CRO course.

Bibliographies: Author Sohn DaeShig's main books

1) Jan. 2, 2018. (A financial secret handbook that only passes on to children, 390pages) Korean Edition

2) Apr. 2, 2018. (Tears of the Japanese, 261pages) Korean Edition

3) Mar. 22, 2019. (Rent investors are stupid investors, 371pages) Korean Edition

4) Aug. 10, 2021. (The Fall of Wealth, 298pages) Korean Edition

5) Dec. 1, 2021. (Tears of Korean, 424pages) Korean Edition

6) Sep. 1, 2023. (Wealth Creation, The Hidden Story, 499pages) (How to start investing at age 60 and succeed) Korean Edition

Prologue

Financial experts say that long term investments in stocks and apartments make everyone rich.
But 99% of the people who invested in the long term failed.
In fact, it makes them worse.
So, does that mean Mr.Big Investor was lying when he said he was successful with long term investments?
No!
He's an American!
We are non-Americans.

They should invest differently.
Investors all over the world have been investing in blue chip stocks for the long term, thinking that if they just do it like Mr.Big Investor, they'll be successful, and they're all screwed.

Now, people living outside the U.S have to do things the un-American way when it comes to investing in stocks and apartments. The same goes for the 7.5 million overseas Koreans.

This is because the difference between American and non-American returns is miraculous, up to 800%, which means you can easily earn 8 times more by simply swapping dollars.

The reason why many people fail in their long term investments in stocks and apartments is because they don't do the necessary Dollar Swapping.

Stocks and apartments must be Dollar Swapped once in business cycle. Of course, U.S residents can't do this. Therefore, they can't earn 8 times as much money.

On the other hand, any non-U.S resident can make 8 times as much money as a U.S resident simply by doing a Dollar Swapping. It's a once-in-a-decade opportunity.

Why should I do it?
When should I do it?
How do I make 8 times as much money?
We'll get to that later.

It can be explained as a Pentagon investing method with FRED evidence. So, depending on where you live, your approach to investing in stocks and apartments should be completely different.

The reason Mr.Big Investor, a U.S resident, has always succeeded in long term investing in blue-chip stocks is the same reason we have always failed in long term investing in blue-chip stocks. If you don't live in the US, you shouldn't invest in stocks or apartments for more than 2~3 years.

For non-U.S residents to succeed in the five asset markets (stocks, apartments, dollars, deposits, and government bonds) we need to swap for dollars when stocks are at their most expensive, but we didn't know that.

If you don't live in the U.S, you should swap your stocks and apartments for dollars when stocks and apartments are at their most expensive.If you don't, your investment returns will typically drop by 50 to 90 percent during major market downturns or economic crises, wiping out your profits.

But for investors around the world, everyone who followed Mr.Big Investor's advice and invested in blue-chip stocks for the long term was screwed.

How ironic. That's why it's time to shatter the myth of Mr.Big Investor's long term investing success with the Pentagon Investing Method, the first market-cycle investing formula.

Mr.Big Investor's success in long term investing in value stocks such as consumer staples and low PBR stocks is a myth, a misinterpretation and misinformation.

Therefore, it is time to wake up from this myth of long term investing and realise the reality: Mr.Big Investor's long term investments have actually resulted in drastically reduced returns.

It's just that Mr.Big Investor was misled into thinking that investing for the long term increased his returns. It's time for all of us to wake up from the illusion that all we need to do is invest for the long term. We should always remember that, as the book's subtitle suggests, long term investments in stocks or APTs will ruin everyone.Despite what Mr.Big Investor thinking and doing.

Because money always seeks profit, it always goes through five stages, in this order: stocks, apartments, dollars, deposits, and government bonds. One business cycle usually takes 10 years.

Of course, it can be shorter, but it doesn't matter. You just need to invest in the right order. Depending on their trade dependency, each country will have a slightly different timeframe for an upturn, but in South Korea, if the balance of payments is in the black for a year(In the case of the U.S., a widening balance of payments deficit),the stock market will slowly start to rise.

Six months later, apartments start to rise, and for the next three to four years, both stocks and apartments continue

to rise steadily. Then, one day, the stock market suddenly plummets due to the government raising interest rates to cool down the overheated economy or an economic crisis that no one knows about.
In response, the dollar, which has hit rock bottom, begins to surge, and governments begin to raise interest rates to cool the overheated economy.

This causes the dollar to rise further, and stock prices crash further to match. Six months after the stock market crash, apartment prices start to fall as well.

This is the cyclical investment cycle pattern of the five major assets market in Korea, which has been repeated in every economic cycle for more than 30 years, and it is always the same movement. In other words, there is a regularity. Therefore, this regular cyclical investment cycle pattern can be formulated. Sell stocks and buy dollars when stock prices start to crash.

Six months after the stock market crashes, apartments start to crash as well. The dollar rises steadily and then at some time starts to fall.

When the price of the dollar starts to fall, you sell the dollars and sign up for a term deposit with an interest rate that has risen a few times.

The Pentagon investing method is based on the idea that you should invest in the following five assets in a rotating order.

It is an investment principle that states that you need to invest in the order of rotation of assets to succeed. As money chases profits, there is a way for money to go around and around, and this is the cycle pattern of the asset market.

The author first summarized this as the market cycle investing formula. It is a new financial investment theory that the author calls the Pentagon investing method because the investment cycle resembles a pentagon.

Along this path, money circles the same assets in the same order for about two years every 10 years. This creates a regular and ever-recurring pattern of rotation among the five main financial assets.

When you formalise this into a method, it becomes the ultimate financial formula. Because it's the same sequence every time, it tells you the order in which the money goes around the asset you're investing in, and when it enters and exits.

This regularity and repetitive cycle pattern is the Pentagon investing method, the first cyclical investment cycle pattern in the financial market, the Dollar Swapping financial formula.

When you make money by FinTech, it's very easy to make money when you have a certain investment formula.All you have to do is follow the formula.To create an investment formula, all you have to do is find a cyclical pattern that has a certain regularity to it and turn it into a formula.

Then it becomes too simple for anyone to get rich.No one will lose money and everyone will be rich. The world becomes a paradise for the rich.

Mr.Cyclic, the master of the "Principle of Market Cycles," could not create a formula for buying and selling stocks because he could not find a market cycle in individual stocks. He looked for cycle patterns in all things that change, especially in stock prices.

Mr.Big Investor and his friend have always trusted Mr. Cyclic, but individual stock prices don't change regularly, so it's no wonder he couldn't find a regular cycle pattern in the stock market. Just as you can't tell which way a frog is going to jump, it stands to reason that there can't be a regularity or cycle pattern to the movement of stock prices.

However, the author, a former KBS(Korean Broadcasting

System) PD specialising in current & cultural affairs, who has been investing in stocks and apartments for 50 years and researching and investing for 30 years, approaches the financial markets from a macro perspective, unlike Mr.Cyclic, and comes up with some surprising results.

Contrary to what the experts say, I was trying to understand why, contrary to what the experts say, anyone who invests in stocks or apartments for the long term is doomed.

I was studying the cyclical investment cycle patterns among the five asset markets: stocks, apartments, dollars, deposits, and government bonds.

Any country, when the price of a stock or apartment is at its highest, the dollar exchange rate is at its lowest. Therefore, selling stocks or apartments at this time and swapping them for dollars will maximise your return on investment.

This is because stocks and apartments and the dollar move in opposite directions.This is the basic principle of the author's diamond dollar investment method.

Dollar Swapping alone would yield a return of about 800%. But the author was the first in the world to realize that since no one was Dollar Swapping, long term investors were losing money.

One day stocks are at their highest prices, and then all of a sudden the dollar starts surging nearly 100% and stocks drop 50~90% or more, causing a crash. Apartments have always risen, fallen, or rebounded with a lag of six months or so from stocks.

In other words, no one has ever been able to figure out what to do about the fact that stocks and apartments have always gone up in price over the long term, only to revert back to almost the same level after a major decline.

In addition, when rotating between the five major assets for financial planning, stocks, apartments, dollars, deposits, and government bonds, investors should follow the order of rotation for each asset to maximize returns.

Investors also didn't know that the timing of rotation between assets is also important to maximize returns by investing in line with changes in exchange rates and interest rates.

And, we didn't rotate between the five major asset markets in the order of investment. In particular, not only did we not do Dollar Swapping transactions with stocks and apartments that generate large returns in a short period of time, but they also did not rotate between assets, too.

we also didn't make any timely investments according to the changing situation.So the more they invested in the long term, the more they were screwed. This was an amazing discovery.

In other words, we found the hidden meaning of the old Korean proverb, "Money always goes round and round(in pursuit of profit)," and the hidden meaning of the old elders who said that this proverb also includes the meaning of "Money always goes round and round in the same way.

It was the Pentagon investing method that formulated the idea that money should be invested in the same way and in the same order to maximise profits in every economic cycle, which comes around every 10 years.

Mr.Cyclic took a micro approach, looking for repetition or regularity in stock prices, and found no consistent cyclical pattern in stock market prices.

Taking a macro approach, the authors find that there are regularities and cyclical patterns in the order and timing of investments in the five major asset markets.

As a result, the author's Pentagon Investing Method is the world's first formula for cyclical wealth across five asset markets. So the Pentagon investing method, the new cycle law of asset markets, became the market cycle investing formula.

While researching why long term investing ruins everyone, I stumbled upon a recurring pattern of financial cycles and timing among the five major asset markets: stocks, apartments, dollars, deposits, and government bonds. I realized that there is a double meaning to the old saying "money goes around, money comes around".
In other words, I discovered, theorized, and formulated a regular "cycle pattern" between the five major asset markets that always repeats itself when investing. This is the Pentagon investing method.

So
By now, readers of this book know that the Pentagon investing method has made it so easy to double or 8x your money in 10 years. Making money is now a very easy thing to do.

This is because the author has created a formula that allows investors to rotate their investments in a timely manner, and anyone can become rich. If you include government bonds and Dollar Swappings, you can get up to 16 times the return on your investment, too

The detailed mechanics of how it works, from investing in stocks immediately after a year-long surplus in the balance of payments to the order in which investments are rotated through the business cycle, are described in [Chapter 11].

The Pentagon investing Method can be applied to any era, any country, and anyone. It simply reflects the fact that different countries may experience slightly different cycles and pro-cyclical investment patterns depending on their dependence on trade.

Only this book has all the answers, including the order and timing of investments in stocks, apartments, dollars, savings, and government bonds. The conclusion is that you should never invest in stocks or apartments for the long term, and we'll explain why in detail.

First of all,
This book will thoroughly review why U.S residents and non-U.S residents should invest differently — why U.S stock investing should be different from non-U.S stock investing — and discover new ways to invest so that all investors can succeed.

The dollar is at the centre of this bizarre phenomenon, where people in the U.S succeed in long term investments, while those outside the U.S fail in long term investments. In short, it's because of the dollar.

Secondly,
Countries are trade-dependent ratio, meaning that

their domestic economies are driven by the growth or decline of trade. So investment starts with the balance of payments, or current account surpluses and deficits.

However, the impact is not immediate, but rather lasts for about a year before the money is circulated and has a significant impact on asset markets.

The trade surplus or deficit determines the volume of domestic currency, and the money has a direct impact by increasing or decreasing the volume of currency by about nine times through the credit creation process of banks.

This money eventually flows into the stock market and apartment market to make more money.Investors in this book should also take advantage of this opportunity to increase their wealth.

Third,
All the books in the world are written from an American perspective.It is in the United States that capitalism blossomed in earnest, and the flower of capitalism is undoubtedly stocks, followed by real estate such as apartments.

Capitalism developed in the United States first, and the world's financial books were written by Americans first. People simply translated or adapted them, so event ually all financial books were written from an American perspective.

In other words, outside the U.S, the dollar is the most important investment asset, but from an American perspective, the dollar is just cash.That's why there is such a big difference in the returns of Mr.Big Investor and investors from other countries.

There are hundreds of financial books on the market. If you want to move away from the American perspective, you'll end up writing essay-style financial books like the Chinese and Japanese do, which means you'll end up with books that don't have a point.

Therefore, this book, subtitled: Tears of Japan 'Why everyone who invests in stocks or apartments for the long term is doomed in the end?' is the first book to properlyy analyze the world's financial techniques from a non-American perspective and summarize the basics of new investments.

Investing the way we used to do was a disaster, with stocks and apartments going up and then down, and the final result was always a 50~90% loss. So investors, including financial experts, became believers in Mr.Big Investor, who was successful in long term investing, and they followed him to succeed, but they failed every time.

This is the responsibility of financial experts who failed to properly analyze the reasons and countermeasures. This book is the first to correct that.

Now, i will explain that to be successful, U.S residents must follow the four-step Pentagon investing method and non-US residents must follow the five-step Pentagon investing method.

The difference between how a U.S resident invests and how a non-U.S resident invests must be significant because the dollar is in the middle.

This is the difference between American and non-America n stock investing. A wise investor in any country and in any era should never forget this, especially in times of economic downturns, financial crises, and economic crises. The techniques in this book are the sole property of the author.

Fourth,
As an investor who has been investing for about 50 years, and as a researcher who has studied finance in detail for 30 years, I have always been frustrated that I had to start investing without a good finance book.

So I wanted to provide my children and other investors with a macro view of financial theory that goes beyond the hundreds of financial books on the market. This work is a synthesis of all the piecemeal financial knowledge and research reports that have been floating around, creating a way for anyone to succeed in investing.

If anyone should do it, it's the author, a retired PD who worked as a professional PD for KBS's current affairs and liberal arts program for 30 years. I've always thought that being a station PD doesn't require you to know more and be smarter than others.

This is because the author has always thought that it is a job that requires knowing a lot of subject matter experts and bringing them together when necessary to synthesise their opinions and come to a good conclusion.

There are many excellent economists, analysts, equity research institutes, and investment advisory firms in Korea, and research reports are often published. Among them, Sailer's important research on the 33 year relationship between the balance of payments and stock apartments is detailed in his book.

Next, there are reports that on leaded stocks by Dr Kim Hyun-jin of KB Investment & Securities, who analysed Korean leaded stocks for 30 years, which were very helpful in writing this book.

In addition, William O'Neill's research on calculating the probability of past leaded stocks in the United States becoming leaders again was also helpful.

However, these economists and researchers do not combine their research reports into a new investment thesis by adding more studies or combining them into one.

Therefore, all studies become fragmented studies. There is no synthesis. The author has always wondered: why don't they expand their thinking and do extended research? Is it because of their egos?

This is where the author has the opportunity to create and synthesize a new theory.

By analyzing the graphs of changes in domestic dollar prices and interest rates for each country in Korea and Japan over the past 40 years, as well as the relationship between stocks and apartments, the relationship between these three major research results and the main financial assets of FRED is clearly organized and proven.

The relationship with the main assets of financial wealth is clearly organized and proven.

The first step is to use Japanese data such as the yen-dollar exchange rate, the Nikkei index, and the housing index published by FRED, but adjust the time period and the spacing of the graphs in FRED so that they can be compared on the same date.

For Korea, where there is a lot of data and easy to access, you can use the Korean won-dollar exchange rate, the KOSPI index, and the housing index from FRED to analyse the relationship between the data.

Afterwards, it is a good idea to compare and examine the results between Korea and Japan.It is safe to say that all of the author's results have gone through the process of comparing and verifying the data results between Korea and Japan. Unfortunately, there is an absolute lack of data on housing in both Korea and Japan.

In any case, this is the strongest evidence and the basis for the theory. If anyone can tie it all together and add a little bit more to existing theories and create new ones, I thought it would be me, a broadcaster PD with 30 years of interdisciplinary work and good results.

The author's experience of investing in stocks and apartments for 50 years and meticulously documenting and organizing them for 30 years has also been very helpful in tying them together, organizing them, regularizing them, and theorizing them.

Not to mention that I've always wondered, "Why am I not as successful as I think I am when I invest the way the experts say I should?".

Now, after reading this book and investing a few times, I believe that every investor should be able to invest in assets market regardless of the cyclicality of the economy. The Pentagon investing method, the world's first market-cycle rotation formula is not just a piece of financial knowledge.

It is a comprehensive financial technique. It explains the sequence of cyclical investments in five asset markets: stocks, apartments, dollars, deposits, and government bonds, as well as when to invest and when to exit.

Children and the elderly can invest at any time and succeed, and the probability of success is always greater than 95%.

If you invest in ETFs according to the dollar average method [Special Appendix 2], your returns will be somewhat lower, but your success will be more certain.

This is because it is the result of the author's formula that combines the regularity of 30 years of statistics with a cyclical investment cycle pattern.

This is the world's first market-cycle cyclical investment method, and the first time we've tested it against the predicting of the Pentagon investing method, it's 100% correct.

Even the author was surprised.

The cycles were correct down to the year, month, and day. This is the power of statistics and the power of formulas.

Now, with the author's Pentagon Investing Method, it is possible to accurately predict the cyclical investment cycle pattern, a pattern that even Mr.Cyclic could not create or guess, in every cycle.

In the future, we believe that this formula will be able to accurately predict the timing and percentage change of apartment prices more than 90% of the time. Because it's a formula….

The author's Pentagon approach to investing makes it simple to time asset market cycles. It's a time when anyone can succeed by following the formula.

By simply investing according to the first cyclical investment cycle pattern, the Dollar Swapping wealth formula, and the Pentagon investing method,

Koreans will be among the best in the world in terms of investing in wealth, no matter what era or country they live in.

The first thing you need to do is figure out when each country's trade dependency ratios affects its stock market. Then, if you can figure out when real estate, such as apartments, moves, you can start investing according to the Pentagon investing method in any country.

Fifth,
Both non-U.S and U.S residents can earn another two to three times the return on their investment by investing in government bonds at the end of each business cycle. If you are a U.S resident, the four steps to investing in Treasuries will allow you to take advantage of the huge arbitrage gains when interest rates plummet.

I wonder if Mr.Big Investor, who is said to be successful by investing in stocks for the long term, is rotating into government bonds. Judging by his long term investments in consumer staples stocks, I doubt he does.

In short, this book is a general investment theory on Dollar Swapping with stocks and apartments for non-residents of the United States under the current stock and apartment capital gains tax regime. It is a basic book on dollar investing that can multiply your wealth by 2~8 times just by Dollar

Swapping.

Furthermore, it is the world's first market-cycle rotation investment formula and a detailed explanation of the Pentagon investing method.

In addition, it is the first book to summarize everything about the dollar, including dollar investment techniques and matters related to dollar management.

Jan. 4, 2024
Pangyo in Korea

Table of Contents

Announcement.

As stated in the author's bio, the writer is not an economist, analyst, or researcher at a securities firm or economic research institute. Nor is he a professor of economics or other related subjects.

The writer was born at the end of the Korean War, one of Korea's most difficult periods. The Korean War ended on July 27, 1953, and the writer was born on November 1, 1952(solar calendar) I'm a war child.

As an ordinary citizen who has to live his economic life as a Korean, not as an economist, he has seen and participated in the process of Korea becoming a developed country through political, economic, historical, and cultural changes, from his childhood in Korea to now, after Korea joined the 3050 Developed Countries Club.

I also retired on September 30, 2011, after 30 years of broadcasting, producing, and directing as a producer specializing in current affairs for KBS Television, so it is likely that I have seen and heard at least as much as others who have lived the same number of years.

And due to family circumstances, I was forced to enter the harsh financial market before others, so I have been investing in stocks and apartments for 50 years. In the beginning, I always lost money, but for about 30 years, I studied finance technology, read professional books, and collected and analysed brokerage reports.

As a result, I realised that investors, including myself, were getting screwed over by bad or misleading financial advice. As a former journalist, it's something I wanted to do something about, so I wrote this book.

However, there is one problem with the writer's attempt. As I mentioned earlier, the author is neither an expert in the field nor a professional investor in the industry. Of course, it is true that he has been investing professionally for about 30 years while studying and analysing cause and effect.

There are many professional investors who have made a fortune overseas, such as Mr.Big Investor, Mr.Cyclic, and Andre Kostolani. It's hard to write a book that does go beyond their theories and invesments.

Furthermore, the author will look like a scribbler to investors. However, the authors were able to create several theories that were completely different from theirs.

The most important is the Pentagon investing method, which is an adaptation and evolution of the Diamond

Dollar investment method. The theory that all investments should be thought of, invested, and recovered in terms of dollars is a fact of the Diamond Dollar Investing Method. Almost all of the author's investment theories stem from this.

This book explains why and how to swap stocks, apartments, for dollars. The difference is the Diamond Wealth Dichotomy, which protects your wealth perfectly, and the Pentagon investing method, which increases your wealth by up to 16 times.Even the diagnosis of Long term Deflation(LTD) and how to get out of it is explained here.

The Diamond Dollar Investing Method is a theory that Americans who use the U.S dollar as their everyday currency may or may not know about, even though he is a Nobel Prize winner in economics, but it is now a theory that makes you half an economist if you don't know it — a fundamental investment theory that is so important to Americans and non-Americans alike.

South Korean President Park Chung-hee once argued that we should do a "Korean-style democracy". It will show that there is a difference between the American way of investing and the non-American way of investing in order to make investments like this successful.

There is one important issue on the writer··· is the author's words credible in light of his experience and abilities··· and that is the use of experiments and empirical economics. Almost 100% of the author's claims are verified by FRED's long and short term graphs for various countries, including Korea, so you can trust him 100%.

Finally, if you're still skeptical of the author's theories, you can test them out for yourself by investing 10% of your assets in the Pentagon Investing Method.

If you're a U.S citizen, you must follow the four-step Pentagon investing method, and if you're a non-US citizen, you must follow the five-step Pentagon investing method.

However, it should be noted that the contents of this book are based on the current interest rates of the Korean and U.S Feds, as well as their unique systems and other figures.

But, if you think about it, I don't think it will be a problem for you to apply the figures according to your own country and start a fintech business in any country or at any time.

*** I've edited it to make it easier to read, with lots of white space, as well as some deviations from grammar, as much as possible, like the Korea Beauty.**

Chapter 1) Why everyone who invests in stocks or apartments for the long term is doomed in the end?

Everyone wants to be rich, just as banks make a fortune by lending nine times their deposits through credit creation.

However, very few people succeed in creating wealth by investing their salary and other earnings.
Not only university professors, but also PhDs in economics and business administration will never become rich unless they study financial techniques separately.They are just like everyone else.

This is because fintech is a different field from major and must be studied separately.
But now, after reading this book, anyone can become rich. You'll discover financial techniques you didn't know or knew in reverse.

In other words, everyone would be screwed if you didn't understand the hidden stories that no one told you and rotate your investments in stocks, apartments, dollars, deposits, and government bonds in that order.

If you don't Dollar Swap your stocks or apartments and just invest for the long term, you'll be screwed because the price of your stocks or apartments will drop by less than half every time after the cycle has passed to the next asset market.

American vs. Non-American Stock Investing Methods

Since the dollar is always just cash to Americans, U.S residents like Mr.Big Investor can't and shouldn't swap dollars. Therefore, Americans should follow the four-stage rotation cycle pattern of the American method of investing in stocks.

Non-Americans should invest in the five-step rotation method, which involves swapping stocks and apartments for dollars.

People who don't live in the United States, i.e., non-U.S residents, should invest according to the Pentagon's five-step formula, the first market-cycle cyclical investment formula advocated by the author, if they want to get rich.

Outside the U.S, the dollar is one of the most important assets, as it can change rapidly in price at times. Therefore, stocks and apartments are the most important assets.
Therefore, stocks and apartments should be Dollar Swapped. Let's explain the reasons in turn.

First, let's look at how the price of stocks and apartments changes when the dollar exchange rates.Let's look at the actual changes when the KRW-dollar exchange rate increases and when the KRW-dollar exchange rate decreases.

[Figure 13] is a graph showing the relationship between the Korean won exchange rate, the KOSPI index, and the real house price index over a 42 year period(1981~2023), taken from U.S Federal Reserve data.

The top graph shows the start date of the KRW-dollar exchange rate and the middle graph of the KOSPI index is artificially aligned with the start date of January 1, 1981. The housing index at the bottom, on the other hand, has a start date of July 1, 1981. six months later.

This is because the Korean housing index usually does not start moving until six months after the Korean won-dollar exchange rate and the KOSPI have moved.

Therefore, if you draw a vertical dotted line anywhere in [Figure 13], you can see the KOSPI index and the housing index, which correspond to the KRW-dollar exchange rate on that day, and the price of stocks and apartments on that day. Among them, the housing index should be recognized as the same date, although there is a time difference of 6 months.

When the won-dollar exchange rate rises

From vertical dotted line ⑧ to vertical dotted line ① in [Figure 13] in the next chapter, the graphs show that stocks and apartments plummet while the dollar surges.

[When the KRW-dollar exchange rate graph at the top of vertical dotted line ⑧ in [Figure 13] is at its highest, the KOSPI in the middle and the housing index at the bottom are almost at their lowest prices.

The vertical dotted line ① is December 1997, when Korea was in the IMF situation. Let's not forget that the vertical dotted line ① at the bottom of the graph, which shows the housing price situation, is around June 1998! That's six months earlier.

When the won-dollar exchange rate falls

December 1997, vertical dotted line ① is the peak of the won-dollar exchange rate, and the trough is vertical dotted line ⑤.

You can also see that stocks and apartments soar during the period from ① to ⑤ as the dollar falls back into place. This is a good time to swap stocks and apartments for dollars, i.e., Dollar Swapping.

When the exchange rate is rising, you should sell your stocks and apartments and buy dollars.

When the exchange rate goes down, you can clearly see that selling dollars and buying stocks and apartments will make you a lot of money.

If there were analysts, brokerage firms, investment firms, etc. who took advantage of this opportunity, they would already be very rich.Very few investors took advantage of this.

This is true phenomeno around the world. This book will guide you on how to take advantage of them and become very rich.

In [Chapter 15], I explain in detail how you can easily achieve profits of up to 800% by utilizing dollar fintech. The vertical dotted line ③ shows the KRW-dollar exchange rate during the 2008 subprime crisis, the KOSPI index, and the housing index.

Mr.Big Investor is an American, and so the dollar is just cash to him, so he can't do Dollar Swapping. And he has no reason to do Dollar Swaps.

He is known for his success by investing in stocks for the long term.Therefore, he would not have rotated funds into government bonds, which is step 4 of the Pentagon investing method.

So, although he would lose some money, it seems that he was often half successful with his long term investments. He seems to have covered the ups and downs of stock prices by holding essential stocks for a long time.
The process of earning 8x returns can only be achieved by dollar wapping. Because he's a U.S resident, Mr.Big Investor would not have been able to do this.

We're non-Americans, we didn't know about the Dollar Swapping process. We learned indirectly from Mr.Big Investor that if you invest for the long term, you'll be successful. Mr.Big Investor has always been a long term investor in blue-chip stocks and apartments.
Naturally, half of the price of the property and stocks that went up always went down again, so he lost that much in every 1 decade.

Anyone can lose or gain 800% in Dollar Swapping. We lose or gain about 800% in the process of Dollar Swapping. The return on the Dollar Swap is far greater than the profit on the other four assets together, so we've been making a losing investment all the time.
This is because the difference in return between Dollar Swapping and not Dollar Swapping can be as much as 8x.

Leading stocks change almost every time the bull market goes down

When the dollar returns to normal prices after a spike,

the main stock indexes generally return to their normal values. But individual stock prices usually don't.
In particular, it's almost impossible for a leading stock to recover. This is because after a major decline, the leading stocks usually change.

In other words, individual stocks that were once leaders rarely return to their previous highs before the crash.
The probability of finding them is only one-eighth, or 12.5%, according to William O'Neill's 55 year analysis of the leading stocks in bull markets in the U.S, whether the Dow or the Nasdaq, from 1953 to 2007.

Leading stocks typically rise for three to four years.
They can go up by as much as 4 to 20 times, and when they go down, on average, they fall by 50% to as much as 90%.

This is based on about 30 years of analyzing Korea's leading stocks. How do thematic ETFs, which include leading stocks, perform?
Thematic ETFs are those that include leading stocks or leading industries.

12 years after investing in 'theme-type ETF··· ant investors lost an average of 17%" is an article from the Chosun Ilbo on October 10, 2023.

Since it is an ETF composed of only theme stocks ETFs in industries that belong to the leading stocks, let's compare it with the results of previous research reports on Korean leading stocks.I think theme-type ETF can go up to 2~3 times and go down proportionally.

Nevertheless, the long term 12 year holding performance is minus 17%. So the answer is, "Don't hold stocks for the long term.ETFs didn't come into existence until 2002, so we don't have a study that analyzes thematic ETF in the category of leading stocks, but here are the results.

In the case of stocks, the author seems to be able to forgive long term investments on the condition that you only invest in staples of daily necessities, new drugs, superconductors, etc. For the same reason, U.S residents can invest on apts for long term.

However, they do not invest in cyclical investments according to the Pentagon Investing method(i.e., cyclic investment in the order of the five fintech assets: stocks, apartments, dollars, deposits, and government bonds), so the returns will be less than expected.

In conclusion, even if a U.S resident makes a long term investment in an apartment, the return will be minimal because it is not a assets market cycle cyclic investment. However, necessity stocks that don't lead the markets often find themselves at or near their peak while the market turns up again.

That's why Mr.Big Investor doesn't invest in growth stocks, which are usually the leading stocks of the day, but in value stocks, which are mostly necessities like Coca-Cola, Kraft, and Heinz, and low PBR stocks like BofA and Chevron. And it's also why he hasn't gotten screwed.

So far, he hasn't lost big money by investing long term in blue-chip stocks and not rotating into other assets like savings or government bonds. In other words, his returns may have been cut in half or more, but that's why he didn't go broke.

But now, unlike before, Mr.Big Investor has a whopping 51% investment in Apple, which is a leading, growth, and necessity stock.

It's been reported that Mr.Big Investor has been buying short term government bonds lately.
Short term government bonds are like cash or deposits. The author sees his cash accumulation as a way of preparing himself for the long term deflation that the author believes is already upon the world in 2016.

So far, it appears that Mr.Big Investor does not rotate his cash or deposits into long term government bonds.

This is the final rotation step of the four-step Pentagon Investing Method that is required for U.S residents.

In any case, Mr.Big Investor doesn't swap his cash, savings for long term government bonds, which means he's always missing out on the opportunity to make a big 2x return. As of end of October 2023, he is said to be holding around 200 trillion in cash. The results of the 30 year analysis of Korean stocks will be similar in the US.

Cisco Systems, the symbol of the bursting IT bubble, was the number one stock on the Nasdaq in 2000. After the IT bubble burst, its stock price dropped by more than 90%. This is the brilliance of a leading stock and the horror of a broken leading stock.

In other words, lead stocks go up 3~4 years, 4~20 times, and drop 50~90% on average in a major bear market. So if Mr.Big Investor is 51% invested in Apple, which is a leading and growth stock, he should follow the four-step Pentagon investing method because he is investing in the United States.

In a massive bear market, when all stocks, including leading stocks, are down, Mr.Big Investor should sell all of his stocks, including Apple, and invest in a savings account for a period of time.
Then, when interest rates go down, he has to swap all

of his savings into government bonds according to the Pentagon Investing Method, otherwise he too will be affected by the crash of the leading stocks.

The world is in the middle of a major bear market and a long term deflation, so we'll see, and we'll all know.
He's never been so heavily invested in one or two stocks as he is with 51% of his portfolio in Apple, and since he lives in the U.S, he can't Dollar Swap.

By avoiding growth stocks and focusing on consumer stocks, Mr.Big Investor was able to avoid the downside effects of a major bear market, which would typically result in a 50~90% drop in stocks.
Nowadays, he invests about 51% of his portfolio in growth stocks like Apple, which is not the same as in the past. But he is a good investor.

Dollar Swapping is not required or possible in the US. So a simple long term investment in stocks could have been a successful investment strategy in the US.

However, his long term approach to investing in stocks was successful with significantly reduced returns. It's half the success of the battle.

But now, as long as you know the Pentagon Investing Method, you should know that no matter how good blue chip stocks are in the U.S or outside the U.S, simple long term stock investing should be avoided because it is a disastrous investment method.

Naturally, the author's views differ from those of Mr.Big Investor.

You should not do diversified investments in stocks. You should invest concentratedly in the leading stocks. When you invest in stocks, you should be focusing on the growth stocks of the time and enjoying 4~20x returns in 3~4 years. It is not a diversified investment as you know it. Instead of being diversified investments, you should concentrate on leading stocks in a bull market.

However, if the stock market turns into a major bear market, you should start rotating your investments according to the cycle pattern of the asset market.

You should rotate your investments money, and take the all the investment gains of each asset.

Rotation investments should be necessary for reasons such as a spontaneous stock market correction, a government interest rate hike, or an exchange rate spike.

The Pentagon investing method clearly summarizes this sequence.

It is an investment method that rotates between assets market in the following order: stocks, apartments, dollars, deposits, and government bonds.

Fintech is a combination of the words finance and technology, usually translated as 'financial management'. It generally means the transformation of financial services and industries through the convergence of finance and IT.

It is sometimes abbreviated as "FinTech". It usually means financial management techniques taught in MBA programs. Imagine if Mr.Big Investor sold all of his blue-chip stocks during the Great Recession and invested in the 4-step Pentagon Investing Method!

Suppose you sold all your stocks, invested in deposit, and then invested in long term government bonds every business cycle.

Then, when interest rates fell, he would sell the bonds and buy back the necessity stocks he had owned, over and over again for many years, dozens of times, and he would have made more than 100 times his current wealth.

Because he's older, his investments would have been much more frequent than the average person's.
It's no secret that investing in long term bonds, usually 20~30 years, is much more favorable than shorter-dated

government bonds for earning market gains.

Mr.Big Investor is now buying short term government bonds and investing in cash and cash equivalents.
He seems to recognize that the world is facing either a short term deflation or a long term deflation and is doing his best to keep cash on hand,

I think we're in the middle of a long term deflationary period and it's just a pause in deflation, so I think long term government bonds are a much better investment going forward. However, it is not the time to invest in long term government bonds yet. This is the time to park your money in deposits.

This is because you will need to move into government bonds when interest rates peak and the period of high interest rates ends, i.e. when Higher for Longer is over.

Apartments are somewhat more favorable than stocks because they don't have a leading stock concept.
However, apartments rarely have a leading stock concept, such as a leading apartment, so they usually rise to their full value by the time the next bull market comes along, which is about 8~10 years after a major decline.

This is one of the reasons why investing in apartments is somewhat more favorable than investing in stocks.

However, if a new apartment complex is built in a new popular neighborhood, it may not be the same one that drove the last rise.

Stocks rarely recover their value from a drop. Apartments more often recover their peak prices over time.

This fact shows that investing in ETFs, which are baskets of stocks, is more favorable than investing in individual stocks when investing in stocks for the long term.
Therefore, it is wiser to invest in KODEX200 ETF, KODEX 200TR ETF, TIGER U.S S&P500 ETF, etc. rather than individual stocks such as Samsung Electronics.

Also, since January 2016., the world has been in a long term deflation. Soon, domestic dollar prices will drop over a long period of time, like Japan's lost 30 years.

In a long term deflation, stocks, apartments, and gold, which are inversely correlated to the dollar, become directly proportional to the dollar. It's the exact opposite of the traditional movement.

Thus, all property in the world is expected to fall, so apartments, stocks, the dollar, U.S stocks(TIGER U.S S&P 500 ETF), gold and silver are all expected to fall.
Unless you're an American, the time to start investing or rotating your money is slightly different depending on

your country's trade dependency, but everyone should always rotate money with assets market cycle cyclic investment in any country, and the order is the same if you're not Americans.

The increase or decrease in money supply due to a trade surplus or deficit has a roughly ninefold effect on money supply through the credit creation function of banks. Therefore, the domestic economic impact of trade dependence must be taken into account when investing. So far, I've explained that U.S residents should invest in the U.S way and non-U.S residents should invest in a completely different way.

Dollar Swapping is not possible for U.S residents, but it is essential for non-U.S residents.Again, this is because assets that have passed the cyclical investment pattern sequence usually drop by more than half their increase in price each time.

In every crisis, every crash, the dollar always soars and stocks and apartments drop by 50~90%, so Dollar Swapping is a must.

If you are a U.S resident, you should follow the 4 steps and if you are not a U.S resident, you should follow the 5 steps. We have already explained in detail that non-Americans are doomed if they invest in stocks or apartments for the long term without Dollar Swapping.

[Figure 13] clearly shows the inverse relationship between the price of the dollar, i.e. the KRW-dollar exchange rate, and the price of a stock apartment. Anyone in any country, except for residents of the United States, can grow their wealth by more than eight times in 10 years by rotating their investments in five Pentagon-style steps.

Inflation in the midst of long term deflation

The world is in the midst of a brief period of inflation in a long, long deflationary period.
In other words, two to three years from now, we'll be entering the final stage of the Pentagon's five-step investment process, which is to invest in government bonds.

The theory of investing in financial technology, or fintech to be more precise, has hardly changed over the years.
This is because everyone wants to get rich, and the decision-making process and results of human greed are always the same in the past, present, and future.
However, this is after everyone has accepted the first market cycle investing formula and Pentagon investing method.

The Egg Theory Is Dead, Now the Pentagon Investing Method

It's important to note that Andre Kostolani's Egg Theory, which has captivated investors for some time, is now completely invalidated by the creation of the Pentagon Investing method.
This is because Andre Kostolani's egg theory was created in a closed economy, and in an open economy where trade dependence and imports and exports are the most important factors affecting a country's economy, his egg theory doesn't fit the reality.
In particular, he never thought of Dollar Swapping. This is the crucial error of the Egg Theory.

Investing in stocks for the long term will only make you more screwed

If you're a non-resident of the United States who doesn't use the dollar as your everyday currency, you may not have realized that stocks and apartments require Dollar Swapping as part of the three-step Pentagon Investing Method to succeed.

U.S residents, including Mr.Big Investor, have been successful in investing for the long term without Dollar Swapping, although their returns are diminished.
Instead, they should avoid investing in the most popular growth stocks and focus on blue-chip stocks in necessities that are less price sensitive.

Historically, non-Americans did not swap stocks or

apartments for dollars, but simply made long term investments in stocks and apartments.

Meanwhile, non-Americans do not Dollar Swap stocks or apartments, they simply invest for the long term in a single sector, so even if the lead stock hits the jackpot, in some cases their profits drop by as much as 90% and everyone is screwed.

This is why Mr.Big Investor succeeds in long term investing and non-Americans always fail in long term investing. Mr.Big Investor and other Americans are using the American way of investing in stocks, and the way we have been doing it is the non-American way of investing in stocks.

From now on, non-U.S investors should always follow the non-U.S Pentagon investing method. This means that in step 3, you should Dollar Swap your stocks and apartments!

The dollar is a safe haven in a normal economy and becomes a monster in a crisis.
It can also become a bull market dollar and then a safe haven dollar with a stable exchange rate. It also drives the price of stocks, apartments, gold, oil, etc. up and down.
People living outside the United States can increase their wealth by up to 800%, or 8 times, by simply Dollar

Swapping stocks and apartments.

Let's recap.
A) Stocks and apartments always crash when the dollar soars!
B) As the dollar falls to its normal price, stocks and apartments always continue to rise.

This happens in every country in the world, in every era, except for the United States.
Therefore, these Facts can be theorized. Using this fact, I created the first market-cycle cyclical investing formula called the Pentagon Investing Method. Investing in government bonds is the final step in the cycle that everyone should do, whether they are a U.S resident or non-resident.

Government bonds rise in price when interest rates slowly begin to fall as recessions or economic crises ease, so when interest rates fall, you can close your savings account and buy government bonds.

If you are investing in government bonds and there is an economic crisis and foreigners sell them, the price of government bonds drops and the dollar rises sharply. At this point, you should sell your bonds and buy dollars. When the crisis starts to calm down, you can sell the falling dollar and buy back the government bonds. After that, market interest rates continue to fall.

Again, even swapping government bonds for dollars produces huge short term gains of around 2~3x. If you organize these phenomena properly, you will be able to derive a new investment method, the first cyclical investment cycle pattern of Dollar Swapping, by yourself, and thus the Pentagon Investing Method was born.

In conclusion, it is important to remember that anyone who is a non-resident of the United States and invests in blue-chip stocks for the long term without Dollar Swapping stocks and apartments is doomed.

Therefore, non-Americans should never invest in stocks or apartments for more than three years, and they should follow the third step of the Pentagon Investing Method, which is to swap stocks and apartments for dollars at least once every 10 years.This is the only way to succeed in investing in stocks and apartments. After that, your investments should go through a deposits.

After that, it is usually necessary to go through another round of Dollar Swapping with government bonds before you can start investing in stocks again.
This is why the Dollar Swapping process is so important. After all, as a non-resident of the United States, it's all about the dollar. This is because it will directly affect your

returns at least 800% over the course of the investment process.

The sequence of past cyclical investment patterns is not reversed until eight years later

And let's not forget that the length of time that an investor will have to start the rotation process again with stocks or apartments, dollars, deposits, and treasuries that have already gone through the rotation process is roughly 8 years after the last rotation, before it's time for the next rotation!

This is because one business cycle is usually 10 years and there are five asset markets to cycle through: stocks, apartments, dollars, savings, and government bonds.

Only institutional investors are willing to wait this long. And even if you make it through this eight year period, by then, the stocks that were the leaders eight years ago will have completely collapsed, down 50~90% on average, and a new industry will be in its infancy. It's never a good idea to invest in a leading industry stock that has already passed.

There's only a 12.5% probability that a leading stock will come back to the market once it's gone, based on a 55 year analysis of the U.S leading sectors.
There's always a chance that a once-dominant

apartment complex will never be dominant again as new neighborhoods emerge, too.

However, it's true that more often than not, the dominant apartment complexes in formerly dominant areas won't change because they're primarily due to geography, school districts, transportation, air, views, new apartments, etc.

The old adage of new booze in new bottles equals to apartments, too.

This is where the stock market adage "new booze in new bottles" comes from. the author know that since the glory days of the stock market in the 1980s, stocks have never been the leading stocks.

There were only a few times when construction, shipbuilding, and steel stocks, which were once the leading stocks, became the leading stocks again. Since China's entry into the WTO in 2001, there has been only one reincarnation of a passing stock as a leading stock in about five years between 2003 and 2007, but that is not the normal course of events. The market always wants new industries and new growth stocks.

So if your stock is past the rotation, it's probably have no chance of becoming a leading stock already.
It may go up more bit, but you shouldn't expect passed stocks and apartments that they will reach the top of the

market.

In the end, the way for an individual investor to beat institutional investors, financial companies, and professional investors is to accurately predict when to buy and sell, and never hold on to a stock for the long term.

If you're buying stocks, you're going to want to focus on leading stocks, and once you buy them, you're going to want to hold them for three or four years, and you're going to want to make 4~20x gains, or if you're not, you're going to want to invest in a thematic ETF with leading stocks, and then one day the dollar starts to go up, and you're going to have to sell your stocks or your thematic ETF, and you're going to have to do Dollar Swapping, and you're going to have to sell all your stocks and buy back your assets in dollars.

Since apartments always move six months later than stocks, you can buy apts after you sell your stocks.
Short term investors will be happy to hear that anyone who invests in stocks or apartments for a long time is doomed, but it's also important to note that short term investors will fail faster and harder than long term investors.
Now, if you are not an American, you should follow the author's un-American investment method, the four-step Pentagon Investing Method.

Outside the U.S, there are powerful cycle buy & sell transaction in the five major financial asset markets: stocks, apartments, dollars, deposits, and government bonds.

Every time there's a major downturn, every time there's a crisis, the dollar always soars 50~90%. Correspondingly, stocks and apartments drop by 50~90% of their value just by holding them.

Therefore, if you simply invest long term in stocks, themed ETFs, or real estate, you must lose money. The only way to invest in stocks or apartments for the long term and not get screwed is to follow the pentagon investing method, which is the four-step method for Americans and the five-step method for non-Americans.

There is also a long term investment method based on the dollar average method, which is not even comparable to Dollar Swapping in terms of returns, but is introduced in detail in [Chapter 26].

By the way, Mr.Big Investor's long term investment method of investing in necessities is not a good investment method because it does not swap into government bonds, so it has a worse return than the dollar average method. When the stock market crashes in the US, 50~90% of stocks fall, just like in Korea.

Once again, it's important to remember that anyone who invests long term in a stock that was a leader, or in a thematic ETF that is a leader, or in an apartment in a popular dominant location, is doomed.

Institutions and individuals alike usually hold on and hold on until the very end of a recession and then need the money, so they sell their stocks at about the same time after the bottom falls out. This is why there are far more failures in long term investors.

If you're investing for the long term using a non-dollar-average method, you're usually going to end up completely screwed at the end of a recession because everyone is selling at the perfect bottom at the same time. When a crisis hits, everyone needs money. As a result, institutions and individuals alike often sell stocks at the cheapest prices.

Especially In many cases, the true bottom is created by ants investors, as institutional loss cuts scare retail investors into selling.

Furthermore, investors who have had a few small successes in a boom usually get caught in a bust after having made a full bet by buying on credit, or leveraging, during the peak of the boom.

Then, at the end of the downturn, when they are forced to sell back due to lack of collateral, almost all of them end up in a tin can account, which means that they are completely wiped out at the end of the downturn.

Keep in mind that if you persist in long term investing without swapping stocks and apartments for dollars when the time is appropriate, you will eventually come to the conclusion that, as another subtitle of this book says, "everyone who invests in stocks and apartments for the long term is doomed in the end?

In conclusion, all U.S residents should always follow the Pentagon's four-step rule when investing. Non-US residents should also follow the five-step Pentagon investing method.

Chapter 2) An American: September 22, 1985. I woke up in the morning and I was broke. I hadn't invested in anything.

These were the words of the average American who woke up on the morning of September 22, 1985. The day before, the dollar's value against the yen had plummeted by about 46% overnight due to the Plaza Accord between the United States and Japan. In contrast, the yen had surged 46%.

[Figure 26] is a graph that plots the yen-dollar exchange rate, the Nikkei index, and the start date of the Japanese housing index against the yen-dollar exchange rate over a 48 year period. The vertical dotted line ① in [Figure 26] is February 1985, when the yen-dollar exchange rate was 262.80.

The Plaza Accord was actually signed on September 22, 1985. but the yen-dollar exchange rate was already weak beforehand due to rumours, so it is obvious that the yen-dollar would have actually depreciated by more than 46%.

In any case, Japanese assets became 46% more expensive in one day for Americans, and American assets became 46% cheaper for Japanese. The American must exchange yen, which doubled in price overnight, to buy Japanese assets. Meanwhile, the Japanese buy U.S assets by buying dollars that have fallen.

The price of property in the United States remained the same, but the price of property in Japan was halved in one day. This is because Japanese people can buy dollars in Japan for half the price overnight.

On the other hand, to the Japanese, it is as if all the properties in America are actually the same, but their prices have been halved. This eventually led to an article titled "Japan Money buys 'New York symbol'".

On the other hand, from an American perspective, Watanabe's house actually remained the same price, but the yen had appreciated by 46%, so from an American perspective, the price of a Japanese house had nearly doubled in one day.

In this way, fluctuations in the price of the dollar, or the exchange rate, indiscriminately and forcibly change the value of assets in every country. The fluctuations in the value of the dollar indiscriminately change the value of assets in each country, and the dollar is forced to move accordingly in pursuit of profit.

U.S dollar funds are always channelled into countries

where profits are highest. This is not relevant to Americans who invest only in the US, but U.S funds, pensions, and endowments that invest abroad will always look for countries where the dollar is rising or falling, so that investment opportunities are always open to the world.

European investment money is also almost entirely in U.S dollars. They have to get their dollars from the United States. The valuation of each country's national wealth and assets is compared in dollars. This is why a crisis in the pound or euro is ultimately a crisis in the dollar.

Therefore, domestic investors should develop the habit of evaluating and investing in assets around the world from an American perspective. They should also get into the habit of always evaluating their domestic asset markets in dollars.

We are always at risk of a second Plaza Accord due to accumulating trade surpluses or a much simpler currency manipulator designation. We are off monitoring list in 2023, but I think it will be temporary.

If this happens, the opposite of what happened in the IMF case will happen: the won will surge and the dollar will plummet in a day. This would be the same situation as the Japan Plaza Accord in 1985. Therefore, it is necessary to study and organise your thoughts in advance.

If Korea is designated as a currency manipulator and is forced to adjust its exchange rate, it will be in the same situation as the Japanese Plaza Accord. Instead of what most people think, which is a massive crash in stocks and apartments, the Korean asset market will surge. American money should rush into the Korean asset market, just like it did in Japan after the Plaza Accord….

According to the principle of the diamond dollar investing method, the price of the domestic asset will rise in time with the collapse of the dollar.

The situation in Japan before lines (B)②(C') in [Figure 26] is the normal state of the economy, i.e., the period when the Diamond Dollar Investing Method is still applicable. Consider this period(1971.1.4.~1988.12.1.).

As the yen-dollar exchange rate has been falling continuously for about 18 years, the Nikkei index has been rising as much as the yen-dollar exchange rate has been falling during the same period, according to the Diamond Dollar Investment Method. It can be inferred that the housing index would have also risen sharply under the Diamond Dollar Investment Method, even though it was not published at the time.

On September 22, 1985, the Plaza Accord was signed overnight, reducing the exchange rate by 46% from 240 yen to 140 yen, but the Diamond Dollar Investment Method did not adjust the prices of all assets in Japan at once.

Therefore, the price of assets in Japan jumped 46% in response to the exchange rate drop, and while it adjusted over time, the Japanese stock and apartment markets continued to soar.
You can see the surge in the yen-dollar and stock markets under the diamond dollar investment method before the vertical dotted line in (B)②(C'). After the vertical dotted line is the long term deflationary period.

Japan became a long term deflationary country from then on, and the Abenomics policy desperately wanted to escape from long term deflation. As of Early Nov. 2023, the yen-dollar exchange rate was around 151 yen, so we can now consider it completely out of long term deflation. Since the Plaza Accord, the Japanese have been busy. Domestic stocks and apartments had to enjoy a spike in price that was compensated for by a sharp drop in the yen-dollar exchange rate.

They would also have had to acquire relatively cheap U.S real estate and businesses such as film companies. Imagine how greedy they would have been, as their assets in the U.S plummeted by 46% under the Diamond Dollar Investment Method.

On the other hand, for Americans, U.S assets plummeted in yen terms with the Plaza settlement.
Americans would have had a golden opportunity to sell their unsold properties and businesses to the Japanese for a reasonable price at that time.

This is how the yen-dollar exchange rate adjustment in the Plaza Accord caused the dollar to adjust property prices in the United States and Japan. This is a concrete example of exchange rate fluctuations and changes in asset values. There are numerous examples of Japanese money buying up high-profile American companies after the Plaza Accord.

In November 1989, Japan's Mitsubishi Estate bought Rockefeller Centre in the heart of Manhattan for a total of $2 billion, including other costs. At the time, the deal was hailed as a "second Pearl Harbor" of the Japanese yen. Mitsui Real Estate had been competing with each other for the property.

However, in 1995, Mitsubishi Real Estate was forced to give Rockefeller Centre back to its creditors for almost nothing as a condition of taking over the debt. It had lost almost all of its investment.

The exchange loss alone was 41% of the purchase price, as the yen-dollar price of 143 yen when he bought in

November 1989 dropped to 84 yen when he sold in 1995. That's a huge loss.

With such a low level of fintech knowledge, it only takes one mistake to ruin a company. This is where FinTech(financial technology) is so important.

They didn't know that domestic asset prices continue to fall during a long term deflation, and of course, they enough to not know fintech that if domestic asset prices continue to fall in Japan, exporting large companies will suffer more than medium-sized companies. They had no idea of the effects of the so-called low exchange rate.

This whole sequence of events was probably planned by the Jews, or they had already foreseen this outcome.

Our own government, namely South Korea, has experienced similar financial investment failures. It is no secret that the South Korean government lost a lot of money when it sold its foreign exchange bank(KEB). On 23 August 2001, Korea's IMF debacle came to an end.

The IMF crisis sent South Korea's big assets plummeting. On August 27, 2003., before the market recovered from the fall in the dollar price, the government sold KEB to Lone Star for 1.383 trillion won(exchange rate at the time of the sale: 1,175 won).

Lone Star then sold the bank to Hana Financial Holdings on February 9, 2006. for 4.66 trillion won(exchange rate at the time of the buyback: 970 won) and left South Korea. The sale proceeds alone were 3.280 trillion won, or 2.37 times the purchase price. The exchange gain alone(1,175 won-970 won=205 won) is 241.3 billion won, or 17.4% of the investment.

The total return from the exchange rate + sale profit is a whopping 254.6%. That's a return in just two years and five months. More on this later.

If some Americans with great FinTech skills had brought their dollars into Japan immediately after the Plaza Accord and started buying Japanese stocks or apartments, they could have enjoyed an appreciation of around 250% or more.
If they had sold all their Japanese stocks in December 1989, when the long term deflation was in effect, deposited the money in a bank, and then returned to the U.S to buy U.S dollars at 76.34 yen(January 2012), when domestic assets were at their cheapest, they would have made a fortune.
You might say that this is hindsight, and how could anyone have known this would happen, but if you know the theory of long term deflation, these winning trades are already answered.

Any banker or investor who reads this book should not

miss these great opportunities that come with every long term deflation. This is why fluctuations in the price of the dollar are so scary. This is how you can make a lot of money in fintech and foreign exchange technology.

Another reason why South Koreans should pay more attention to changes in the price of the dollar, unlike other countries, is that there is always a risk of war in South Korea. If there is a war, the price of the dollar on the Korean Peninsula will skyrocket.

The Plaza Accord of September 1985 gave the United States a temporary boost in exports, but it also had a positive effect on foreign investment in the United States, as the Japanese were able to buy American assets at almost half the price. The Japanese were able to acquire U.S assets at a 46 per cent drop in value.

In this case, the Japanese would be fools not to acquire the assets that the U.S is selling at a 46% discount. This would cause a sharp movement of dollars from countries with an appreciating exchange rate to countries with a depreciating exchange rate.

Meanwhile, Japan has been exporting less and growing less in the long run as the yen has appreciated. The appreciation of the yen as a result of the Plaza Accord also led Japan to shift from an export-oriented economy to a domestic demand-oriented economy.

The most important change was that the 46% appreciation of the yen unconditionally depressed import prices, creating a long term deflationary situation.

By devaluing the yen by 46% overnight, the import price of everything in Japan immediately drops by 46%. This drop in import prices was reflected in prices either immediately or slowly over time, depending on the item.

As a result, Japan has officially entered long term deflation, an endless decline in prices. The result was a rise in the price of the yen, which is the most fundamental condition for long term deflation.
The decline in import prices is slowly and steadily reflected in everything over time, and the long term deflation continues.

A fall in the exchange rate lowers the price of all imports. A rise in the exchange rate causes all import prices to spike. This is why the principles of the Diamond Dollar investment technique, which will be explained later, are so important.
The author believes that the rate hike, which began with the U.S raising its standard interest rate, still has more to go, contrary to market expectations. He believes that Powell will make a "Powell mistake" just like Paul Volcker

did.

We believe he will cut rates too soon after the rate hike phase, around May 2024, when the rate plateau, which lasts about a year or more, will be reached, and soaring inflation will force another sharp rate hike, and the financial crisis will be in full swing. At that time, the dollar exchange rate will soar again, and 1,500 to 1,600 won is considered to be the top of the won-dollar exchange rate.

In this case, domestic assets will plummet according to the principle of the diamond dollar investment method. The price of the dollar will be around the peak price of the first subprime financial crisis. After that, it will enter a long term deflation, so I think the dollar will continue to plummet in Korea like Japan. I think 600 won is possible.

Marc Faber's research has proven that stocks rise faster and more strongly than real estate when an appreciating currency plummets. This is clearly a time lag of 5 months in Japan and 6 months in Korea.

[Figure 13] is a graph that combines the relationship between the price of the dollar, the KOSPI stock index, and the Korean housing index in South Korea before and after the IMF. I'll explain in more detail below.

Using this graphs, we can see the relationship between

the three graphs during the IMF period in Korea, which further validates the usefulness of the author's continuous diamond-shaped dollar investment method.

Not surprisingly, a professor' findings are confirmed. A professor' research can be taken a step further.
It's also worth noting that real estate, such as apartments, moves six months later than stocks.

[Figure 13] is a graph of Korea before and after the IMF on December 3, 1997. Since the Korean won-dollar exchange rate and the KOSPI index react immediately to each other, we use 1982.1.1 as the starting date, and the housing index graph at the bottom is adjusted to start on 1981.7.1.

In the case of Korea, the housing index lags the KRW-dollar exchange rate by six months, so it is easier to compare the three at a glance. Therefore, it is convenient to draw an arbitrary vertical dotted line and compare the KRW-dollar exchange rate, stock index, and housing index on the same day.

Using this, you can compare the fluctuations in the exchange rate and the corresponding fluctuations in stock prices and housing prices such as apartments at a glance.

So, by comparing the three figures at the same time, you

can see how stock prices and housing prices have changed in response to the movement of the dollar before and after the IMF crisis in South Korea.

This graph can be used to indirectly predict the relationship between exchange rates, stock prices, and real estate prices in any country in crisis.

In other words, you can see what happens when the dollar changes, which can be useful for identifying when to buy and sell stocks and houses to take advantage of these crises.

If you look at [Figure 13] between the vertical dotted line ⑤ and the vertical dotted line ③ during the subprime period, the KRW-dollar exchange rate is rising sharply and stocks are falling sharply.

The housing index graph at the bottom shows that even if you sell your stocks at the peak of ⑤ and move to an apartment(house), there are still investment opportunities. In other words, when a crisis occurs, stocks immediately plummet in line with the exchange rate spike. Apartments rise for six months, even as stocks crash due to the exchange rate spike.

So even if you sell your stock and buy an apartment, you can still earn the appreciation in the price of the apartment if you don't pay taxes and other expenses for six months.

Selling stocks and replacing them with apartments is a possible way to invest in a short term deflationary or inflationary economy.
However, it is much more profitable to sell stocks and buy dollars in ⑤. Notice that the price of the dollar is rising sharply between the vertical dotted lines ⑤ and ③. On the other hand, the price of stocks is plummeting during the same period.

However, these are investments that shouldn't be made right now in Korea and around the world as we are in the midst of a long term deflationary economy.

This is where readers may misunderstand the author's judgement, arguing that if stocks and property are doing well now, why are we in a deflationary event.

However, the author's view is that the world economy has been in deflation since 2016, with a brief period of inflation in the middle of the deflationary period of three to four years due to the massive amounts of money released by the subprime crisis and the coronavirus crisis.

Another thing to consider is that the housing index graph at the bottom is for all residential properties. If we were to recreate a property index that included commercial and leasehold buildings, it would actually be quite a bit later than the downturn in the graph.

This shows that it is possible to switch between apartments(houses) and stocks, which have a sharper downturn and a slower recovery, albeit for a shorter period of time.
In this cycle, which began in May 2017, the stock market began a major decline in June 2021 and the apartment market began a major decline six months later in December 2021.

The dollar peaked on September 20, four months after the stock market crash. As expected, apartment prices surged for six months and then began to crash.

That is, you sell a stock, buy an apartment, and then sell the apartment. Then you use the money to buy dollars and sell them again. By doing so, you're selling dollars past the peak price of the dollar.

Since you have to sell the apartment before the two year capital gains tax exemption expires, you'll have to pay capital gains tax, and it's not easy to time the sale, so it's better to do a two-track investment, splitting your money between stocks and apartments.

This phenomenon is common in all capitalist countries

that do not use the dollar as their daily currency, so the approximately 7.5 million Korean expatriates and long term residents living abroad can easily multiply their wealth by 10 times using this technique.

I'm sure I'm not the only one who feels proud and sometimes pity for Koreans who are working hard on the front lines of life in other countries. If you read this book, you will find that you can actually make more money during the crisis that comes every ten years, even in your country of immigration or residence.

Pentagon investing method is a generic Dollar Swapping investment technique that can be applied in any capitalist country, except the United States, at any time and during any crisis. You should always be aware that fluctuations in the price of the dollar will indiscriminately change the value of your assets.

I don't have any assets invested overseas, but the fluctuations in the price of the dollar have halved or doubled my wealth, which is also a reason to change my portfolio of investments.

[Figure 13] shows the timing of the IMF bounce.
The short term bounce in stocks lasted one year and five months, from August 1998 to December 1999, while housing lasted two years and six months, from the second

quarter of 2001 to the fourth quarter of 2003.

After the bounce, stocks began to decline in earnest from December 1999 to October 2001, while housing didn't begin to rebound until April 2001.

You can see that you could have taken advantage of both short term bounces by selling the stocks that bounced sharply in the short term and buying apartments or houses that hadn't even started to bounce.

Stocks surged 38.1 per cent during the one year, five month bull run, while the housing index surged 19.34 per cent during the two year, six month bull run. This is evidenced by the fact that stocks rise more in shorter periods of time, as a professor's research shows.

However, it is my opinion that over the medium to long term, both assets will eventually rise at the same rate.
This is because this is the basic principle behind the Diamond Dollar Investing Method created by the author.

You can take advantage of the 6 month time lag between the rise of stocks and the rise of real estate such as apartments by buying and selling. Furthermore, when the stock market is already in a post-recessionary period, you can take advantage of the rise in real estate prices while stocks are falling, which is quite attractive.

However, in terms of returns, it's probably better to go for a two-track approach by splitting your money between stocks and apartments. It will be discussed again in detail in [Chapter 13].

Chapter 3) When the dollar exchange rate changes, your wealth changes.

Japan emerged from long term deflation in December 2020 after 32 years, but the rest of the world, including South Korea, has been in long term deflation since January 2016.

Therefore, wealth transfers will occur at a steep pace in the future, and social disruptions will naturally increase. Wealth transfers are mainly caused by currency evaporation, exchange rate appreciation, and exchange rate depreciation. The most severe wealth transfers occur during hyperinflation and long term deflation.

In countries that don't use the dollar as their everyday currency, the price of everything, including real estate and stocks, is determined by the price of the dollar, i.e., the exchange rate. So when the exchange rate changes, your wealth changes accordingly. Japan is a country that has failed because its exchange rate has fallen , meaning that asset prices in Japan have consistently fallen.

There is an international price and a domestic price for the dollar. The international price of the dollar is the Dollar Index(DXY) price. The DXY is a measure of the average value of six currencies against the U.S dollar.

The six currencies are 57.6% euro, 13.6% yen, 11.9% pound sterling, 9.1% Canadian dollar, 4.2% krona(Swedish), and 3.6% franc(Swiss).

Since the dollar exchange rate varies from country to country, it is more accurate to use the dollar index to determine whether the dollar has risen or fallen in absolute terms. The dollar index price is compiled and published by the FRB with March 1973 as the reference point(100).

Therefore, the international price of the dollar is not 100% related to the Korean domestic price, and the Japanese yen's share of the dollar index is 13.6%, so the yen price is also not 100% related to the international dollar price.

[Figure 1] International price of the dollar: dollar index(2006.1.1.~2023.1.2.1)

The euro has the largest impact on the dollar index, as it accounts for more than half of the index. The Korean won is not included in the six currencies, so its relationship with the dollar index is insignificant.
Let's look at the international and domestic prices of the dollar through [Figure 1] and [Figure 2].

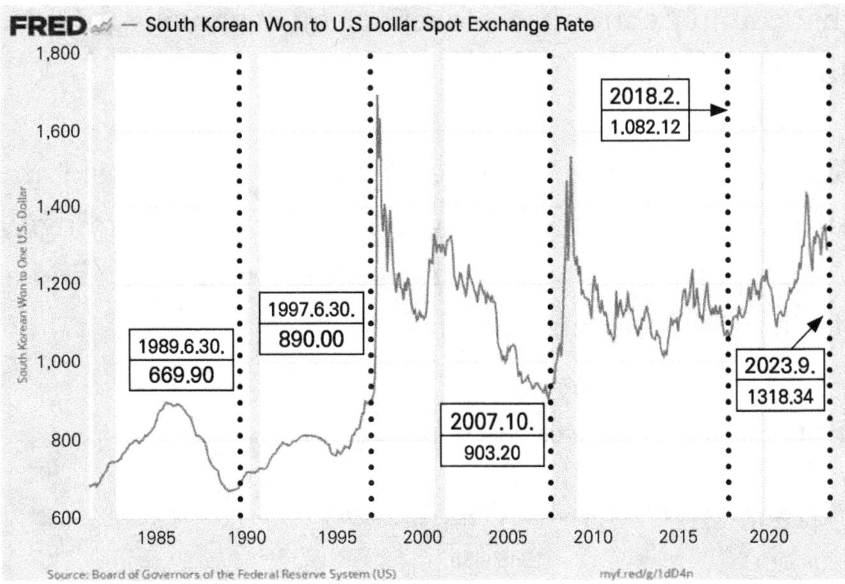

[Figure 2] Price of the dollar in South Korea(1981.4.13.~2023.12.29.)

Predicting the exchange rate is not easy. Looking at [Figure 1], the dollar index seems to have risen steadily. However, the best way to judge how the international price of the dollar will change in the future is to look at the long term graph of the dollar index in [Figure 4].

It can be seen that the international price of the dollar has been falling almost continuously. This suggests that the dollar will continue to trend downward in the long term.

The writer's rule of thumb is to use large fluctuations of 1.5% per day as an inflection point in the direction of the exchange rate trend. We know from Japan that during a long term deflation(deflation lasting more than three years, but less than 30 years), the price of the dollar in that country continues to decline and eventually forms a significant depreciation.

Since January 2016, Korea and the rest of the world are already in the midst of a long term deflation. Accordingly, the author expects a sharp rise in the Korean won and a decline in the domestic dollar.

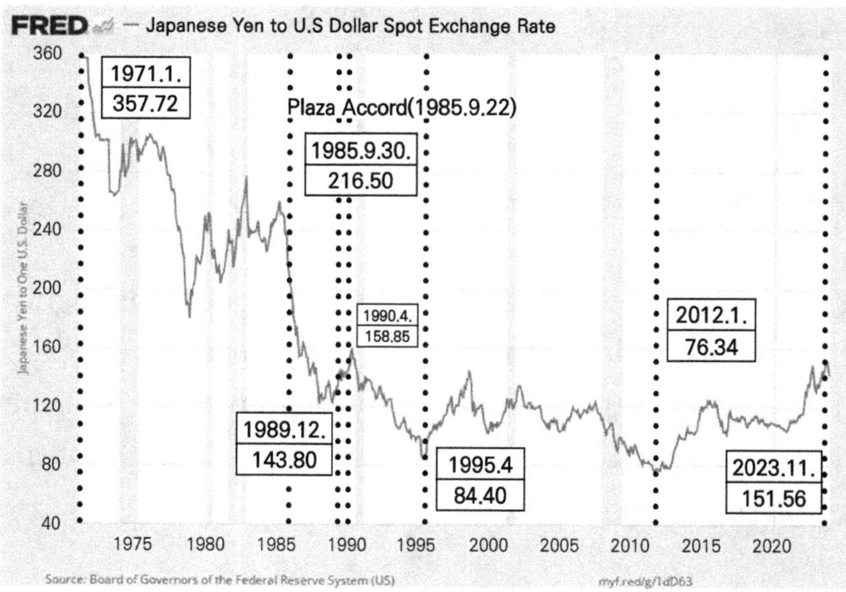

[Figure 3] yen-dollar for 53 years(1971.1.4.~2023.12.29.)

Let's take a look at the yen-dollar exchange rate in [Figure 3] for about 53 years(1971.1.4.~2023.4.28.). In 1971, it was 357.56 yen, or almost 360 yen. The price of this expensive domestic asset fell almost continuously every year until it hit 76.34 yen in January 2012.

In particular, during the Plaza Accord on September 22, 1985, the domestic U.S dollar plummeted from 260 yen to 140 yen overnight. It was a long time before the Plaza Accord, so the price of the dollar had been slowly falling from around 360 yen in the 1970s.

Since then, Abe's Abenomics, which took office in December 2012, has seen Japan's yen to dollar exchange rate hit the 150 yen mark in early November 2023. Abenomics has been successful and may be on its way to a normalized economy, but we'll have to wait and see.

From a long term deflationary economy that lasted for more than 30 years, Japan has now transformed into a normal economy. The world would benefit from knowing how the yen-dollar exchange rate and the prices of stocks, apartments, government bonds, etc. in Japan, as well as the prices of crude oil, gold, silver, copper, etc. in Japan, changed during these 32 years(Dec.1989-Dec.2020).

Because, since January 2016, the world, including Korea, is already in the midst of a long term deflation. The world now knows that it is possible to escape long term deflation based on Japan's methods and results in fighting long term deflation. The U.S accounts for about 25% of the global economy. The U.S dollar is likely to become even weaker than before. According to media reports, there are many articles predicting a decline in the price of the dollar.

1) An article titled "Dollar's 'privileged era' is over" in 『BUSINESS plus』 on June 19,2020 suggests that a 35% drop in the dollar is inevitable.

2) According to an article titled "Crashing U.S dollar… Observations of '40% more to come'" published on 2 September 2020 in 『Korea Economy』, the dollar is expected to fall by 40% against the euro by 2024.

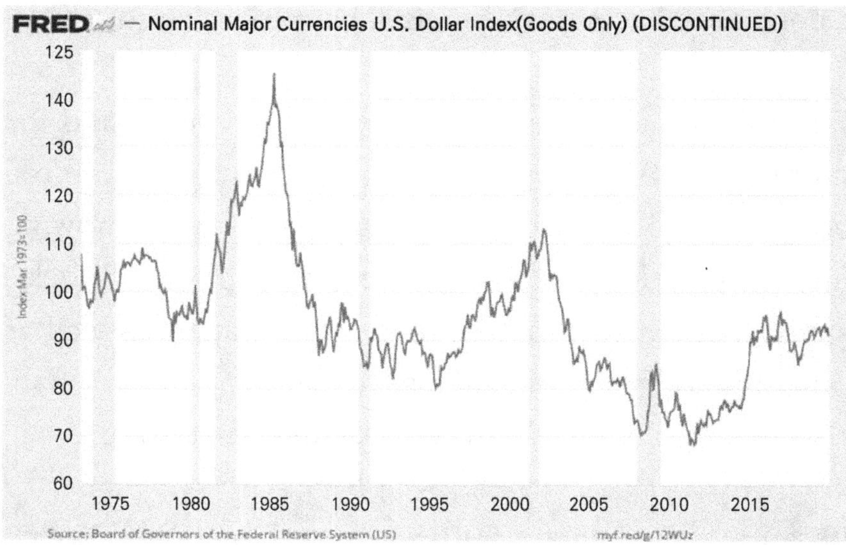

[Figure 4] Long term dollar index(1981.4.13.~2019.3.12)

3) According to an article titled "Dollar value falls 10%, gold price jumps 35%" in the 『Chosun Ilbo』 on August 20, 2020, the dollar's hegemony is shaken as the value of the dollar falls due to the subprime crisis.

As such, many experts are predicting a decline in the dollar's price. In fact, if you look at the dollar index graph [Figure 4] in isolation, it is clear that the dollar is in a long term downward trend. A declining dollar means that the value of each country's currency is increasing.

In addition, British Petroleum(BP), a British oil company, delivered 3 million barrels of Iraqi crude oil to China in early July 2020 and was paid in the Chinese currency, the yuan. This was the first time a major oil company in the world traded crude oil in yuan rather than dollars.

According to December 26, 2020 『News1』 article titled "China to overtake U.S as world's largest economy five years sooner than expected", the U.K think tank Centre for Economics and Business Research(CEBR) said in its annual outlook report that China will overtake the U.S as the world's largest economy in 2028, five years sooner than expected.

And according to the IMF, the yuan's share of central banks' foreign exchange reserves rose to 2.9 per cent in 2022. The dollar accounted for 58 per cent, the euro 20.0

per cent, the yen 5.1 per cent and the pound 4.4 per cent

Meanwhile, China's central bank, the People's Bank of China, has issued the world's first "digital currency. The digital yuan is seen as China's challenge to U.S dollar hegemony. However, it is currently inconvenient to conduct financial transactions using the dollar outside of the U.S financial system.

In response to the U.S SWITF CODE remittance system, China's CHIPS includes Russia, Saudi Arabia, and Brazil, but not yet. There are some cracks, but few countries can shake the dollar system.

In short, China's challenge is not yet.
However, in the long run, if China's digital currency technology spreads, countries and companies that trade with China will not have to use the U.S financial system, which will weaken the dollar system, so the U.S will have to issue a digital currency, or digital dollar, at some point.

In the United States, the dollar is free to trade and exchange, and we never manipulate exchange rates and interest rates or regulate the disposition of the dollar. That's why the world trusts and invests in the dollar.

The Chinese yuan, on the other hand, is an unwelcome investment, let alone a reserve currency, even though

China is a G2 country. This is because your hard-earned wealth could be wiped out overnight due to unpredictable regulations by the Chinese government.

Few experts on Wall Street disagree that the dollar will fall further than it has. [Figure 5] shows the international gold price with a five month lag to the international dollar price. This graph suggests that the price of gold will fall further in the future.

The reason this graph [Figure 5] is so important that I figured it out and put it together myself is because, while it's not patentable, it's the key and only way to determine if we're entering or exiting a global, long term deflation.

The Ⓐ line in the graph above, which represents the international dollar price, or dollar index, is the starting period for the international dollar price graph, January 2016. Before January 2016, the dollar and gold prices moved in opposite directions, as usual, and then the relationship between the dollar and gold began to change to a direct proportion.

Let's take a look at the two graphs.
According to the Diamond Dollar Investing Method, the international dollar price and the international gold price are inversely related. When they change from a direct relationship to an inverse relationship, it signals a

transition to long term deflation.

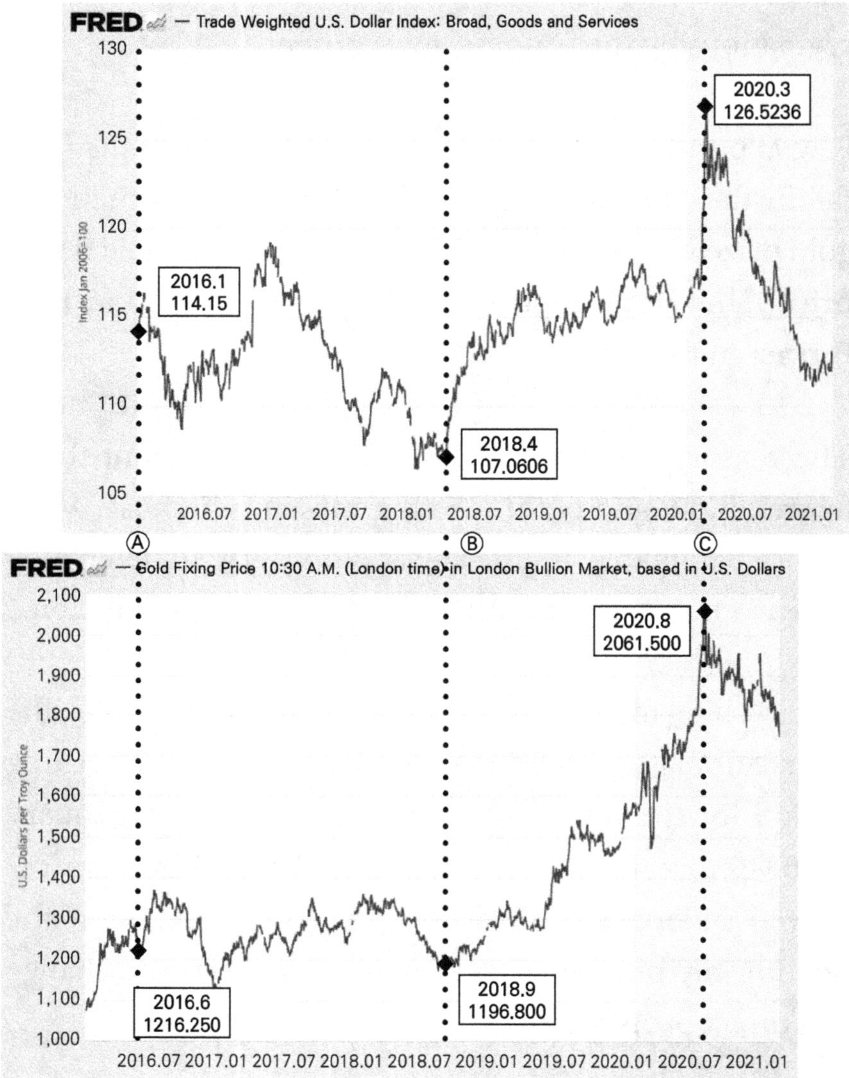

[Figure 5] International gold price with a 5 month lag on the international dollar price

The vertical dotted line Ⓐ through the graph below represents the international gold price in June 2016, five months later than the corresponding dollar international price on the same date.

The graph of the international gold price below has a start date of June 2016, which is five months earlier than the start date of the international dollar price.

In other words, it shows the international gold price with a five month lag to the international dollar price. With a lag of about five months, gold follows the same trajectory as the dollar graph. You can see that since September 2018, the two graphs are almost identical.

This proportional or inverse relationship between the international dollar and the international gold price can be used to determine whether the world is entering or exiting a long term deflation.

This is the only original indicator that the author has found that can determine whether an international long term deflation is entering or exiting. When the trajectories of the graphs of the international dollar price and the international gold price start to diverge, it means that the international long term deflation has returned to a normal economy.

Based on the behaviour of this graph, we can summarise here how to invest in gold when a long term deflation is underway. It is an application of the fact that the international dollar price, or dollar index price, follows a very similar trajectory five months after the international gold price. The synchronisation rate seems to be almost 90% or more.

The key question, therefore, is how much further the dollar price will fall. Knowing this, the future decline in the international gold price is self-explanatory. Furthermore, the price of the dollar five months ago is already known, so investing in international gold is a no-brainer.

Contrary to the predictions of the British think tank, the Center for Economics and Business Research(CEBR), no country will be able to compete with the United States within 100 years. In other words, the dollar is forever.
There is no currency substitute for the dollar. China wouldn't last more than a few years if it completely cut off trade with the U.S, as its economy and financial system would collapse into chaos.

The United States produces 25 per cent of the world's wealth, has an official population of 3.4 billion, and dominates the Pacific and Atlantic oceans. The United States is also so powerful that it has troops in more than 150 countries. The dollar is almost the only international currency.

By comparing the price of the dollar to the price of other

commodities such as stocks, apartments, and gold, the author can predict whether the economy will experience short or long term deflation.

The international long term deflationary trend is simply and accurately determined by the proportional, inverse relationship between the international dollar and the international gold price, and the long term deflationary trend in a country is simply and accurately determined by the proportional, inverse relationship between the domestic dollar exchange rate and the domestic stock index.

We are confident of a hit rate of over 95 per cent because we use 30 years of data for Japan. According to the Diamond Dollar Investing Method, the price of the dollar determines the price of everything.

The U.S dollar is always cash within the U.S, but outside of the U.S, it's a different story, meaning that outside of the U.S, it's cash in normal times, but if there's a crisis in that country, the dollar suddenly becomes more of a property.

The dollar is a speculative asset whose price can skyrocket or plummet. Almost all international trade is transacted in dollars, which means it's all about the U.S dollar. If you know the dollar, you'll be successful, whether you're making money or running a country.

One place where the dollar is truly everything is Argentina. When Argentines buy and sell domestic property, they do so only in dollars, not in pesos, their currency.

They are now only trading in dollars to ensure that the price of their property is only reflected in the price of the property due to purely supply and demand, as price fluctuations due to exchange rate changes have a greater impact on the price of the property. That's how smart Argentines have become.

Their fellow South American country, Venezuela, has begun to trade all of its goods in dollars only. The same principle of excluding fluctuations in the price of the dollar applies to property transactions in Argentina.

Countries that have experienced extreme fluctuations in the price of the dollar have simply begun to trade goods based on supply and demand, ignoring the fluctuations in the price of properties as the dollar falls and rises.
The public is smart.

They are right.
They've learnt from experience, not from the government.
In a long term deflation, it's especially easy to be wrong, i.e., to invest in the opposite direction. The fact that in normal times, i.e., under short term deflation and inflation, everything that has a property value is priced

in the opposite direction of the dollar should never be applied to long term deflation.

The author argued that in a short term deflation, all investments should be made against the direction of the dollar. This is what we call the Diamond Dollar Investing Method. Stocks, apartments, dollars, government bonds, everything.

The same goes for gold, silver, and crude oil.
However, in a long term deflation, the rules are reversed, meaning that in a long term deflation, you need to invest in the same direction as the dollar to survive. In other words, you should invest the opposite of the traditional diamond-dollar investing method.

This is a phenomenon that economic experts didn't know about and the Japanese didn't know about for 30 years. So they had 30 years of wealth destruction. But now Abe seems to have saved Japan with his Abenomics economic policies.

This is the conclusion that I reached by tracking the relationship between domestic wealth and other wealth in Japan for about 30 years after 1990. You should always keep in mind that investment assets fluctuate significantly according to the dollar exchange rate. In other words, a change in the exchange rate can secretly transfer wealth from me to others. In normal times, when the dollar goes up, all the stocks, apartments, gold, oil, etc. in the world go down proportionally, and when the dollar goes down, all the stocks, apartments, gold, oil, etc. in the world go up proportionally.

Here's a quick explanation of why.
Imagine an American who wants to buy shares of Samsung Electronics. Let's assume that the local price of Samsung Electronics stock hasn't changed.

1 share of Samsung Electronics is 59,000 won··· Exchange rate is 1,100 won··· Foreigners, including Americans, can buy a share for 53.6$.

1 share of Samsung Electronics at 59,000 won··· Exchange rate 800 won··· Foreigners, including Americans, would have to pay 73.75$ to buy a share.

If the exchange rate drops, foreigners, including Americans, will have to pay 73.75-53.60=20.15$ more to buy the same one share of Samsung stock because the domestic price of Samsung remains unchanged.

Remember that we have assumed that the dollar exchange rate fluctuates, but the price of Samsung neither increases nor decreases in Korea.
Now, if you buy when the exchange rate goes the other way, i.e. when the domestic dollar is more expensive, you

will pay 20.15$ less for a share of Samsung.

If the exchange rate goes down, the price of Samsung stock in South Korea would have to go up to 20.15$ to get the full value. Therefore, the price of Samsung Electronics in Korea will increase by 1100/800×100%=37.5%.

Why would a foreigner buy Samsung Electronics for 37.5 percent more just because the exchange rate has plummeted, when the company hasn't changed at all?

In the end, a stronger won increases the value of Korean assets and provides foreign investors with an exchange rate advantage. If the strengthening of the won is a trend, foreigners will not be able to resist buying Korean stocks, even if it is only because of the attractiveness of the exchange rate.

This is what happened after the Plaza Accord in 1985, when a flood of dollar funds entered the Japanese asset market. It was a rush of dollars to buy assets in Japan that were not fairly priced due to the plummeting exchange rate.

While it is commonly said that a stronger won is negative for exports because it reduces international competitiveness, South Korea is no longer the same country. Korea is now the de facto number one in international competitiveness in manufacturing. In terms

of quality competitiveness, we are either number one or number two in the world.
Therefore, there is no reason to worry about the exchange rate appreciation. Our quality competitiveness has made it possible for us to pass on the cost of goods as the exchange rate falls. It goes without saying that the dollar has an absolute advantage in inflation or hyperinflation. Even in short term deflation, the dollar is the best.

But in a long term deflation, it's not the dollar. Not gold. Not silver. Not even grains. We can see this by analysing Japan's long term deflation. [Figure 26] is self-explanatory. In countries with long term deflation, the domestic dollar plummets like Japan's. Long term deflation has already arrived in Korea in January 2016. This is the main reason for the strengthening of the won and the weakening of the dollar, just like in Japan in December 1989.

Its intensity can be seen in the long term graph of the Japanese yen in [Figure 3]. [Figure 3] shows the evolution of domestic asset prices in Japan, a country that has been experiencing long term deflation.

In December 1989, it cost 143.80 yen to buy a dollar.
In April 1990, it cost 158.85 yen to buy a dollar.
In April 1995, a dollar cost 84.40 yen.
In January 2012, you could buy a dollar for 76.34 yen.
In September 2023, it cost 146.20 yen to buy a dollar.

By January 2012, 24 years after the Great Depression, the Japanese domestic dollar had plummeted 46.9%. Thanks to the success of Abenomics, it hit 151 yen in early November 2023. It's safe to say that Japan is no longer the only country in long term deflation and has been back to normal since the fourth quarter of 2022.

After the vertical dotted line ④ in [Figure 27], the yen-dollar exchange rate is rising and the Nikkei index is falling. This is short term deflation, and the vertical dotted line ④ is the date when it switched from long term deflation to short term deflation. This is December 2020.

Until the second of these graphs, the start date is January 1, 1988. On the other hand, the graph of Japan's housing index at the bottom has a start date of June 1, 1988. Japan has a five month time lag, so if you look at vertical dotted line ④, you can see the yen-dollar exchange rate and the Nikkei index on the same day and the Japanese housing index five months later.

The author has lagged the bottom graph of the housing index by 5 months because the Japanese housing index follows the same trajectory as the Yen-Dollar index 5 months ago. You can see that the bottom graph, the Japanese housing index, has not yet fallen.

In other words, if the yen-dollar exchange rate and the

Nikkei index are inversely correlated on the same day, it is considered to be short term deflation. In other words, even if the housing index is not inversely correlated with the yen-dollar exchange rate and the stock index, it is considered to be short term deflation.

Using the Diamond Dollar investing method, Japan is still technically in the midst of a long term deflation. However, we believe that Japan will soon return to a fully normal economy.

In a long term deflation, the dollar and all assets — stocks, apartments, gold, crude oil, etc. This is what we saw in the U.S in 1929 and Japan in 1989 for 20~30 years. That's why Japanese people who have experienced this for a long time have stopped buying apartments and are almost all renting.

They knew from their parents' and their own experiences that it would be foolish to buy a house when the price of an apartment would fall relentlessly for 30 years or more in a long term deflation.

It was also unthinkable for them to invest in profitable real estate, which had recently become popular in Korea, i.e. to buy a house as a profit property and rent it out.
However, from now on, the Japanese have reached a point where they need to change their mindset to get rich. It's time to start investing in apartments and income

properties.

Looking at Japan's housing index, the bottom graph in [Figure 27], it seems that the country has not yet fully escaped the long term deflation, but given the relationship between the yen-dollar exchange rate and the Nikkei index after the vertical dotted line 4 in [Figure 27], it is likely that the housing index will also escape in the near future.

To determine whether a country is currently in a state of long term deflation or not, only the inverse relationship between the yen-dollar exchange rate and the Nikkei, or stock index, is required according to the author's Diamond Dollar Investing Method. It is important to note that this criterion does not include the real estate index, i.e. the apartment index.

The Japanese housing index follows the same trajectory as the Nikkei for five months. In Korea, the housing index follows the trajectory of the KOSPI six months later.

These relationships are illustrated in [Figures 26] and [Figure 27]. Japan's long term deflation, which began in December 1989 at the vertical dotted lines (B)②(C'), ended 10 years after the start of Abenomics on 16 December 2012 at the vertical dotted line (A), around December 2020 at the vertical dotted line ④ in [Figure 27], under normal economic conditions, i.e., under the diamond dollar investing method, the yen-dollar exchange rate and all domestic assets began to behave in an inverse relationship. This is the strongest and only sign of the success of Abenomics. There is no other indicator than the inverse relationship between the yen-dollar exchange rate and the Nikkei.

Looking at Japan's Lost 30 Years [Figure 26], we can see that domestic asset prices in a country with long term deflation are destined for a prolonged decline, just like the decline in Japan's dollar price after April 1990.

Therefore, after the exchange rate depreciates in the long run, your wealth continues to depreciate in dollar terms, so it is quite natural that investing in domestic assets such as domestic stocks and real estate will crash in the long run.

The main phenomenon of long term deflation is the collapse of domestic assets in the affected country, and the collapse of stock prices, apartments, and prices.

It is important to note that Korea and the rest of the world have already been experiencing a long term deflation since January 2016, and it has only just begun. Therefore, you should make appropriate investments such as restructur ing your property portfolio.

In a long term deflationary country, all asset prices fall in the long run, so you should stay invested in cash or cash equivalents, i.e. government bonds, and only start moving when the country is out of deflation, like Japan. If you enter the stock market after the annual balance of payments turns surplus, you can invest again at the right time.

This is the same for any country in the world, as it is an open economy and free trade era. It's just that the timing of new stock investments is slightly different depending on the country's dependence on trade.

Chapter 4) How to make money when Exchange rate manipulator designation

The U.S Treasury Department has been investigating countries around the world for currency manipulation since 1988, and releases two exchange rate reports each year in April and October.

If a country is designated as a currency manipulator, it means that the value of its currency will skyrocket.

Readers of this book should notice that when a country is designated as a currency manipulator, it creates a perfect opportunity for the asset markets, such as stocks and apartments.

This means that a forced correction in the dollar's exchange rate, such as the Japan Plaza Accord of 1985, is imminent. Don't make the mistake of dumping stocks, apartments, etc. in a panic.

To do so, you need to arm yourself with the theory and study the behavior of the asset market when the exchange rate rises and the behavior of the asset market such as stocks, real estate, and apartments when the exchange rate falls.

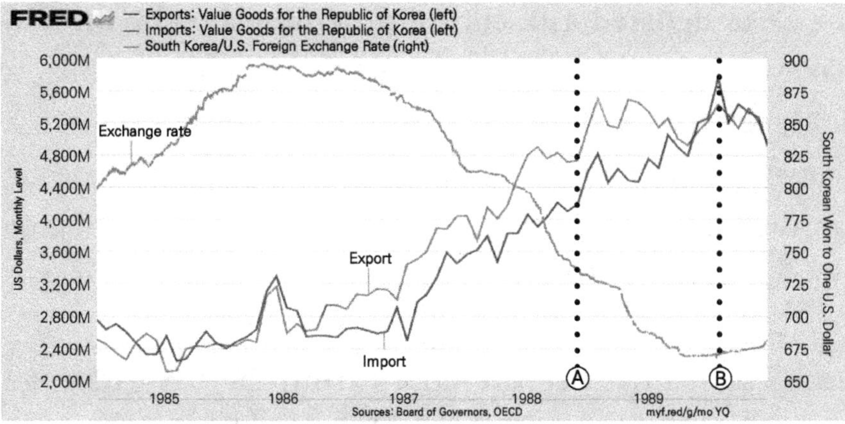

[Figure 6] South Korea Import and Export Graph

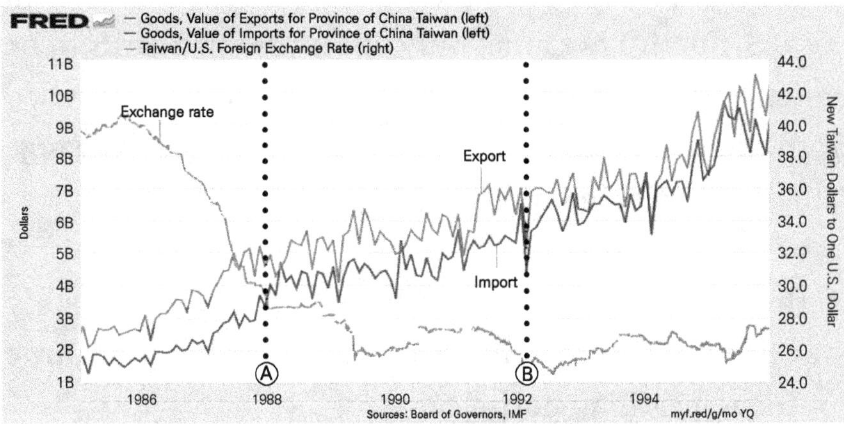

[Figure 7] Taiwan Import and Export Graph

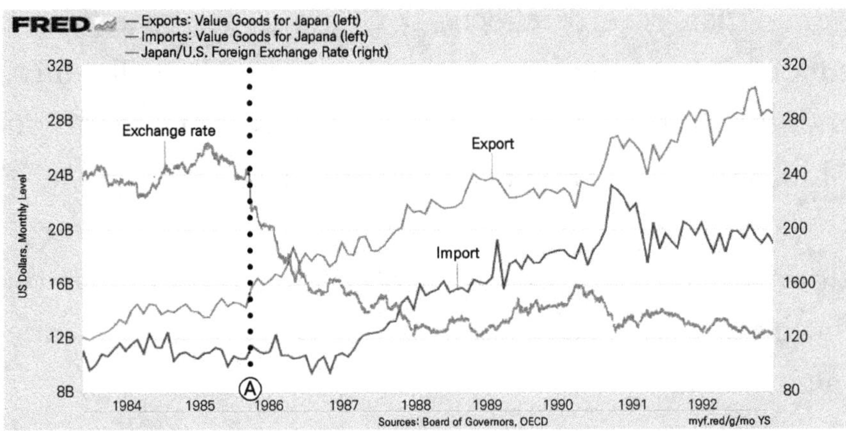

[Figure 8] Japan Import and Export Graph

To be designated as a currency manipulator by the U.S Treasury, a country must meet three requirements: a trade surplus with the U.S of more than $20 billion, a current account surplus of more than 3% of gross domestic product(GDP), and net purchases in the foreign exchange market of more than 2% of GDP.

South Korea has been removed from the U.S exchange rate watch list for the first time in more than seven years since April 2016. With a trade surplus of $38 billion with the U.S, South Korea met only one of the standards to be designated as a currency manipulator and was removed from the exchange rate observation list in the exchange rate report released on November 7, 2023.

If the U.S designates China as the sole currency manipulator, it will have more negative economic consequences than positive.

rather than reverse effects. If China is designated as a currency manipulator, its exports to the U.S will suffer, and the Korean won, which is highly dependent on China's economy, is expected to appreciate.

However, the graphs show that the short term impact on the international payments is not as significant as one might think.

Moreover, Korean products are now more competitive in quality than in price, so there is not much difference from the time when Korea was designated as a currency manipulator in 1988. Also, if we compare the situation after the Plaza Accord with Japan, we can see that economic fluctuations in the medium to long term are more important.

This is a graph of Korea, Taiwan, and Japan's exports and imports, change of the international payments, and exchange rate fluctuations at that time. This graph shows the exchange rate and import/export fluctuations of Korea, Taiwan, and Japan, respectively, in one graph for each country. The top graph on the left vertical line(Y-axis) shows the exchange rate of Korea, Taiwan, and Japan, respectively.

If you look at the first part of the graph of Korea's KRW-dollar exchange rate and imports and exports in [Figure 6], you can see that, contrary to common sense, exports decreased sharply as the KRW-dollar exchange rate increased, and then increased sharply as the KRW-dollar exchange rate decreased.

Taiwan and Japan also show a sharp increase in exports when the exchange rate decreases, as shown in [Figure 7] and [Figure 8], respectively. These facts prove that the opposite is true.

On September 22, 1985, during the Reaganomics era, the finance ministers of the G5 (France, Germany, Japan, the United States, and the United Kingdom) agreed at the New York Plaza Hotel in the United States to force Japan and Germany to adjust their exchange rates against the dollar.

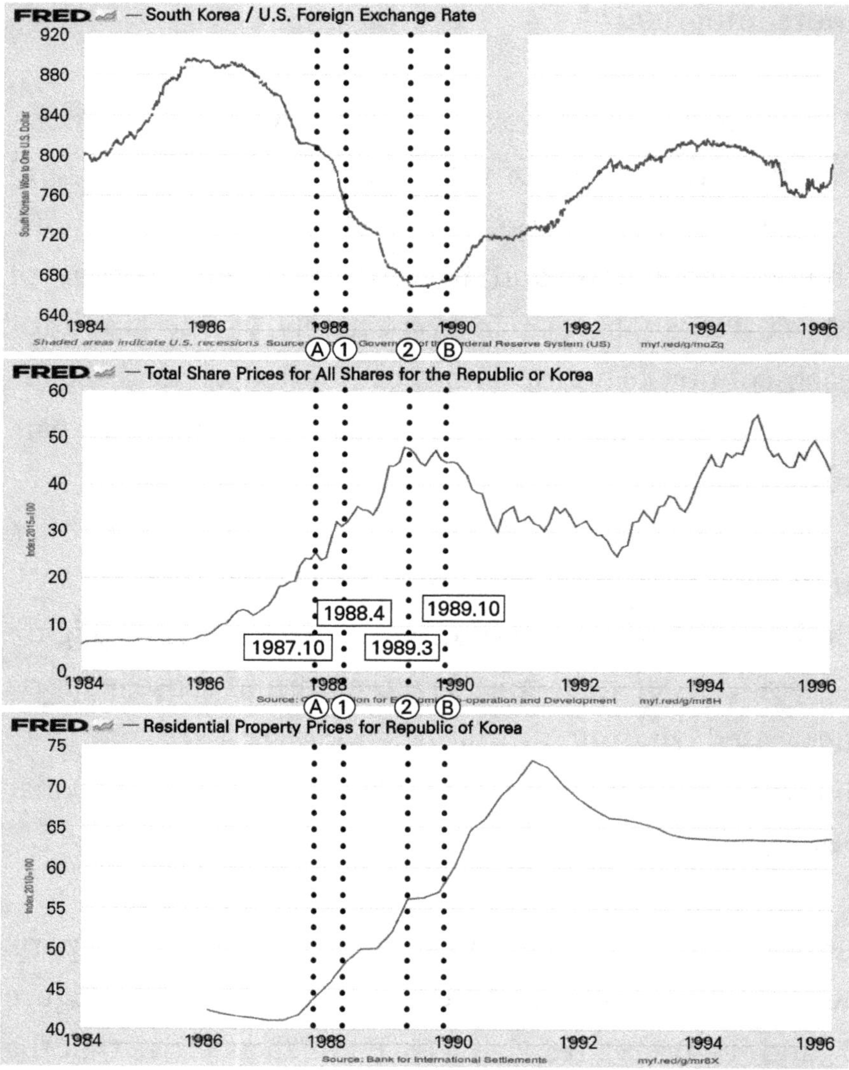

[Figure 9] KRW-dollar, KOSPI, and housing index during exchange rate manipulation(April 1988~October 1989)

As a result, it was designated as a currency manipulator. Now, it's much simpler for the U.S, as it doesn't have to go through this consensus process.

The vertical dotted line in the graph in [Figure 9] comparing the Korean won-dollar exchange rate and the KOSPI and housing indices during the period(April 1988~October 1989) when the country was designated as a currency manipulator.

The vertical dotted line ① shows that there was no significant change in the KOSPI and housing indices at the time of the currency manipulator designation in April 1988. The vertical dotted line ② is after the designation expired, and it can be seen that the KOSPI started to fall immediately afterward, but the Korean housing index started to rise sharply and then fell after a period of time.

This probably reflects the phenomenon that the housing index reacts to changes in the KRW-dollar exchange rate six months later. Although the vertical dotted line is not drawn in this graph, it can be seen that house prices peaked in the second half of 1990 and then fell.

Taiwan was also designated as a currency manipulator from 1988 to December 1992, and China in 1992 and 1994. South Korea ceased to be a currency manipulator in 1990 when it switched from a multi-currency basket PEG to a market average exchange rate system. Let's take a closer look at the U.S dollar exchange rates of South Korea, China, and Japan before and after they were designated as currency manipulators.

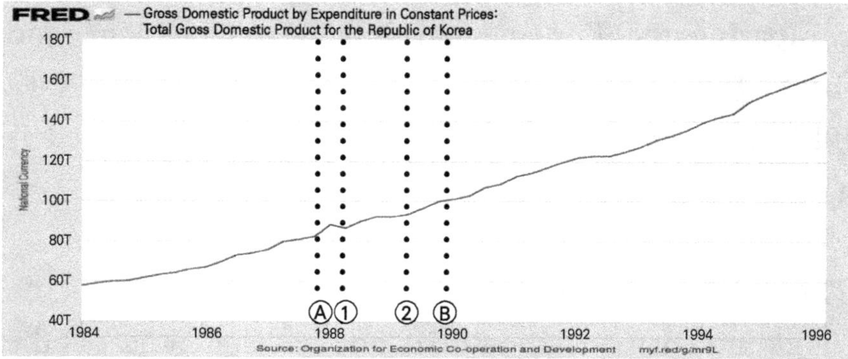

[Figure 10] South Korea's GDP during the exchange rate manipulation period(April 1988~October 1989)

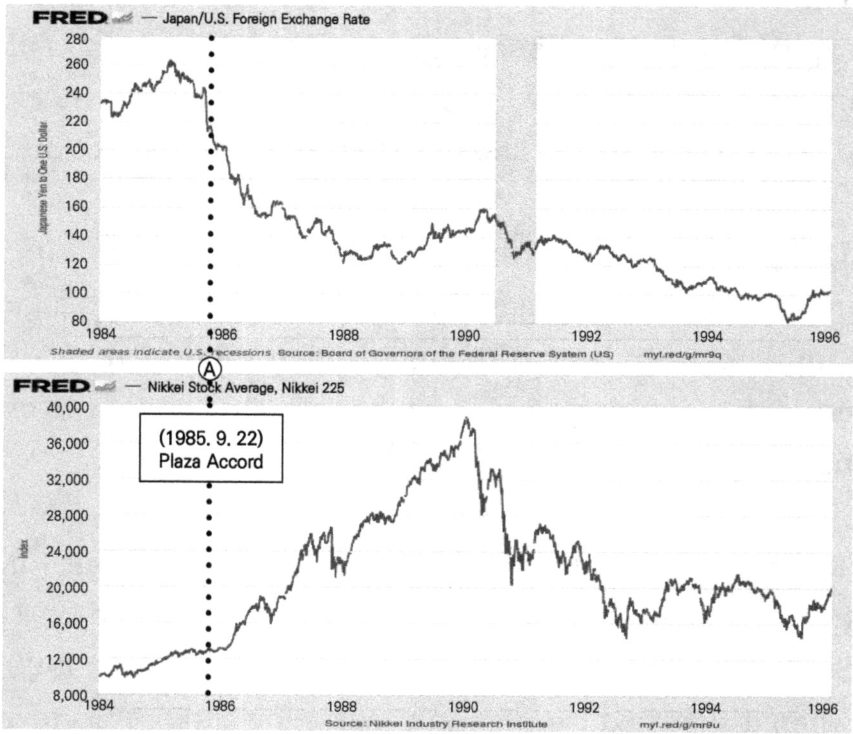

[Figure 11] Yen-Dollar, Nikkei, and Japanese Housing Index, 1984~1996

In the aftermath of the designation, the Korean won appreciated by about 24% against the dollar from its peak in 1987, Taiwan appreciated by 36%, and Japan appreciated by more than 50%, meaning the won-dollar exchange rate fell.

As shown in [Figure 10], South Korea's GDP growth took a hit at the time, with real GDP growth(GDP that strips out changes in the price level and reflects only changes in output) falling by a whopping 5.4 percentage points between 1987 and 1989.

[Figure 11] shows the evolution of Japan's exchange rate and Nikkei index since the Plaza Accord on September 22, 1985. The vertical dotted line shows the yen exchange rate and the Nikkei index on the same date, and the following graphs show the exchange rate and the Nikkei index on the same date.

The Plaza Accord was the equivalent of today's currency manipulation designation. The graph shows that Japan's Plaza Accord and South Korea's designation as a currency manipulator led to a significant spike in stocks, real estate, and other assets in each country.

[Figure 12] is a graph of the exchange rate of the Chinese yuan to the U.S dollar after reform and opening up. After the reform and opening up in 1978, China adopted a dual exchange rate system until 1993, then a managed floating exchange rate system in 1994, then a fixed exchange rate system, then a multi-currency basket managed floating exchange rate system in 2005, then a fixed exchange rate system in 2008, then a multi-currency basket managed floating exchange rate system again.

The basket of 11 currencies, including the euro, yen, Hong Kong dollar, and won, was changed back to a managed floating exchange rate system that reflects the exchange rate movements of these currencies in a weighted average manner, but the type or proportion of the 11 currencies was not disclosed.

We can see that these designations resulted in a sharp drop in the U.S dollar's exchange rate, while China's designation resulted in a different exchange rate surge.

In [Figure 12], the front vertical dotted line shows the RMB exchange rate in 1992, when China was designated as a currency manipulator, and the back vertical dotted line shows the RMB exchange rate in 1994, when China was removed from the currency manipulator designation.

In January 1992, China's exchange rate for the yuan was 5.4686 yuan, and in January 1994, the exchange rate was 8.7217 yuan. That's a 159.5% appreciation of the RMB.

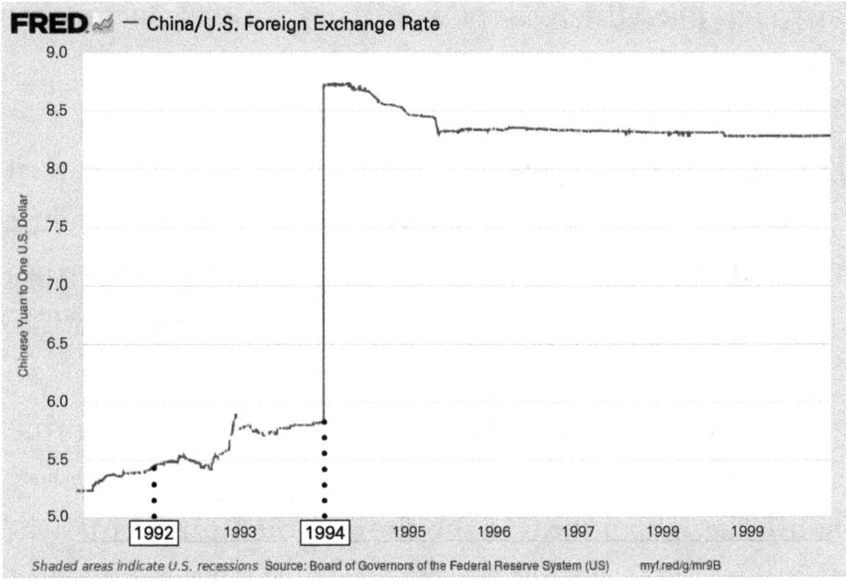

[Figure 12] 1992~1997, Chinese Yuan-Dollar exchange rate

The reason why the results are different from other countries is not clear due to the lack of data and is a subject of future research.

As long as the dollar is the key currency, the same phenomenon will continue to occur in all countries except the United States forever.

We can see from the graphs of the three countries that the designation of a currency manipulator is not a bad thing for asset markets such as stocks and apartments in the short to medium term.

However, a closer look at the Japanese economy's past shows that the decline in the price of the U.S dollar in

Japan has been the most powerful deflationary factor that has consistently depressed domestic prices.

This is a vicious cycle of falling prices. In addition, it should not be forgotten that in the long run, the decline in the dollar exchange rate due to the designation of a currency manipulator country causes long term deflation.

In other words, if you mistakenly judge something that is not a crisis, such as the designation of a currency manipulator, as a crisis in the short to medium term, such as the stock, apartment, rental market, or charter market, and participate in a response investment, i.e., selling, you will be a foolish investor. Therefore, you should

1) Acquire relevant financial knowledge in advance to seize the opportunity to utilize the crisis as an opportunity.

2) Changes in asset prices due to low and high exchange rate policies

3) The impact of exchange rate fluctuations on stocks, apartments, government bonds, etc. are sprinkled throughout the book and should be carefully memorized.

When a country devalues its currency, contrary to what you might think, its trade balance first gets worse.
After that, the country's trade balance slowly starts to

improve.

This is called the "J-curve effect". It's important to remember this phenomenon in comparison.
In both cases, because there is a time lag between the adjustment of import and export prices to exchange rate changes and the actual change in import and export volumes.

Chapter 5) Dollar Swapping is a must for assets market rotation investing fomula: when the dollar goes up, stocks and real estate go down.

I explained that when the won-dollar exchange rate rises, domestic assets such as stocks and real estate fall sharply; otherwise, it is as if domestic assets have risen by the same percentage as the dollar has risen.

In the case of the IMF crisis in Korea on December 3, 1997, those who knew this fact were the first to sell, knowing that their real estate was about to crash, and those who didn't know were forced to sell, even at bargain prices, after the crash. Because they couldn't pay the interest on their bank loans.

Those with cash, on the other hand, watched stocks and apartments drop for a while, and then snapped up the falling real estate and stocks at almost nothing. An acquaintance of mine bought a commercial building in Nonhyeon-dong, Gangnam, which was worth about 6 billion won before the IMF, for a bargain price of about 2 billion won. The building is now worth about 13 billion won.

The example in the previous chapter was Samsung

Electronics, but the inverse relationship between the dollar price and the price of any asset applies equally to stocks, apartments, etc. At the time of the IMF, soaring bank interest rates caused gap investments to be sold. If you didn't sell, you were subject to auction.

However, the soaring price of the dollar in South Korea has been roughly normalised in about a year and seven months. The dollar is essential for international transactions of all assets. Recently, Russia, China, Saudi Arabia, Brazil, and others have started using the CIPS system, which is independent of the SWIFT code system. This is a threat to the yuan's hegemony over the dollar, but the dollar is the true reserve currency.

While Saudi Arabia, Brazil, and others are showing some signs of moving away from the dollar system, they are a drop in the bucket compared to the total amount of dollar use. The world compares and invests in all assets in dollars, as well as the GDP of each country in dollars.

That's how we compare, and that's how we trade. No matter what anyone says, the world is a world that is evaluated and compared centred on the dollar. Some countries are not happy about this, They try to make SDR, EURO, Yen, and RMB the world's currencies to enjoy these benefits, but when you look at the actual usage, it's just ridiculous. If your neighbours or other people want to pay for goods in dollars, will these currencies be accepted?

The thing to remember about the IMF situation in Korea is not that the dollar surged and domestic stocks and real estate crashed, but that in just one year and seven months, the crashed stocks are almost back to where they were, and the surging dollar is back to where it was.

The fact is that those who bought dollars before the dollar went up got about 100% of their money back when the dollar went up, and those who sold those dollars and bought stocks quickly got 100% of their money back.
Real estate is literally an asset that doesn't move very well, so it's about six months behind stocks in terms of crashes and recoveries, so it's always a lagging variable compared to the leading variable, which is the dollar price or interest rates.

The fact that the exchange rate fluctuation increased his wealth by 1×200%(profit on stock investment)×200%(profit on dollar investment)=400% in one year and seven months.

This is because the author had already told the reader to start investing in stocks after the annual balance of payments was in surplus a year ago, so the reader would have already earned about 200% in stocks investments before the surge in the dollar exchange rate. And you're going to get another 200% in dollars.

However, in this case, Korean-Americans, too, living in the U.S may be able to make 2~4 times as much. You can sell your dollars that you've carried from U.S to Korea when the dollar price in Korea is at its peak, buy dollars when the dollar price in Korea is almost back to normal, and take them back to the U.S to pay back the bank.

If you're an Korean American living in the U.S, you can sell your dollars after bringing them into Korea and use the money to buy Korean stocks that have fallen as the dollar has risen.

In other words, if you buy a Korean stock when it's rising and sell it when it's falling, you can easily double your money, or even quadruple it. In this case, it's hard to time individual stock, so it's better to use ETFs as a trading target.

Also, if there is another IMF-like situation, don't return America immediately, even if you are an overseas Korean, because Korea's interest rates will continue to fall after the upcoming "Powell's mistake," and you can make a fortune by investing in long term government bonds, probably around 10 times.

In addition, since we are in the midst of a long term deflationary period, the exchange rate will continue to depreciate, so you will get a 60~70% exchange rate gain, too. If we were to have an IMF – like financial crisis in Korea again, it would be easy for U.S residents and oter countries to borrow their money for investment to relatives in Korea.

In other words, the surge in the price of the dollar is limited to countries that are experiencing foreign exchange crises, financial crises, fiscal crises, household crises, and war crises, so the price of the dollar in the country where your relatives live will remain the same price, so you can take advantage of this opportunity to make a lot of money.

You can make a lot of money by financing your relatives abroad with dollar locally, but only for about 2~3 years. Then, after the crisis passes, you can gradually buy back the dollar at its previous price and pay your relative back.

There is one more way.
There is another way to make money if both of the above opportunities are lost. You can get a dollar loan from Korean banks.

The reason why stocks, real estate, gold, crude oil, etc. plummet when the dollar rises is because all assets converge to a fair price when the exchange rate is taken into account. This pricing principle is clearly summarised in the author's diamond dollar investing method.

Dollar Swapping is a mandatory cyclical investment process that should be practiced in any country, except the United States, during any type of crisis, in every business cycle. To be more specific, Dollar Swapping is an essential cyclical investment process that involves selling stocks or apartments and replacing them with dollars.

This is because when the dollar goes up, stocks and apartments always go down. Conversely, when the dollar goes down, i.e. when the local currency gets stronger, stocks and apartments go up. At the end of every business cycle, whether it's a self-correcting bubble burst or an economic or currency crisis, stocks always fall and the dollar rises.

No one has ever realized that there is an investment technique that applies this simple and obvious fact, the diamond dollar investment method, and therefore, except for a few investors, no one has ever been able to capitalize on this great opportunity and make huge profits.

Even the people who took advantage of the opportunity to invest in real estate by chance and became very wealthy did not do so because they knew or prepared for the Dollar Swapping technique, or because they had theoretical knowledge. The IMF in Korea happened to have a lot of cash at the time, and coincidentally, stocks and real estate went from crash to crash because the dollar was soaring.

Six months after a stock crash, real estate always starts to crash, including apartments. The process of investing to capitalize on this is a cyclical investment formula that follows the market's cycles, which I will reveal exclusively in this book as the Pentagon Investing Method.

To utilize this opportunity, Americans should realize that there are always 2~4x jackpot investment opportunities in crisis countries. This is another benefit of the dollar being the reserve currency. The logic and details will be explained in more detail in [Chapter 15], [Chapter 20], and elsewhere.

Chapter 6) Is the Dollar Always Safe?

In normal times, i.e. during short term deflation, the dollar is always a safe haven. The dollar is the ultimate key currency and the safest currency in the world. Due to the fact that it has almost no inflation and is always accepted everywhere in the world, it is always the safest asset for people living in the United States.

The desirable inflation rate is usually around 2%. This is the inflation rate that politicians want to see. People's salaries rise in line with this inflation rate, and asset prices slowly increase, creating a monetary illusion and a false sense of security.

For U.S residents, the dollar is cash, a safe haven with no inflation and little price fluctuation, so they can earn a decent return on their savings according to their plans.
On the other hand, for U.S residents, the dollar is cash, and its price rarely fluctuates, so U.S residents do not have the opportunity to make 2~8 times as much money as non-US residents from Dollar Swappings as the price of the dollar fluctuates.

The U.S government, on the other hand, benefits greatly from the seigniorage effect. The actual cost of producing the money is less than 10% of the value of the currency, so there is little difference between the cost of producing a 100$ bill and a 20$ bill.

Therefore, the U.S always makes a large profit whenever it issues paper money. The difference is free money for the U.S government. The effect of the difference between a currency's manufacturing cost and its face value is called the Signorage Effect.

All key currencies, such as the euro, yen, and yuan, benefit from this effect just as much as the dollar key, as long as they are widely used both domestically and internationally. Only when the U.S imports goods from abroad with this money are dollars released abroad, i.e., only through U.S consumption are dollars supplied to the world.

Of course, Korean banknotes also enjoy the signorage effect domestically. It is different from the key reserve currency in that Korean banknotes are not accepted as money outside of Korea, except in a few countries, so the effect is only enjoyed in Korea.

However, the U.S dollar will always be a safe currency, a safe asset, anywhere in the world, and a safe asset that has benefited the United States tremendously.
It's important to remember that the dollar is the best investment in a currency crisis or short term deflationary

situation. In a financial crisis or currency crisis, the dollar can easily double or even drop by 50% in a short period of time, making it a monster asset.

On the other hand, in normal times, when the economy is doing well, the dollar is a safe-haven asset, meaning that the average person only needs to hold dollars for survival, not for investment. A safe haven asset should be one that has little price fluctuation and is accepted as valuable by everyone.

However, when a country is in a financial or currency crisis, the dollar becomes a top investment and speculative asset, meaning its value fluctuates rapidly.

The reason why the dollar is more attractive in times of crisis is that while the dollar is rising, the domestic assets of each country are falling. In other words, if you sell the dollar, which has risen to the top, and buy the domestic assets(stocks, real estate) of a country that has fallen, you will be doubly rich.

This is why the dollar is so attractive in times of crisis outside the US. Usually, foreign exchange and economic crises are resolved or calmed down in 2~3 years at the most, so the dollar soon returns to its rightful place, like a missile from the top to the bottom.
This is because the dollar is more expensive in the crisis

country than the dollar index. This indirectly proves that there is also a staggered attack by hot money in anticipation of economic improvement in the crisis country and the resolution of the crisis.

The world is now in the eighth year of a long term deflationary situation. In a long term deflation, a country's domestic asset prices fall continuously. Consider the domestic asset prices of Japan, which was in a long term deflation for 32 years(1988.12.~2020.12.), plotted against the yen-dollar exchange rate(1971.1.4.~2023.9.1.) in [Figure 3]

Since 1971, the yen-dollar exchange rate has been falling almost continuously. In April 1990, when Japan's long term deflation began in force, the yen-dollar price was 158.85 yen. Twenty-five years later, in January 2012, it dropped 64% to a low of 76.34 yen.

More specifically, Japan entered a long term deflation in December 1988 and remained in a long term deflation until December 2020, 32 years later, with the yen-dollar exchange rate dropping 64% in 25 years. This means that import prices dropped by 64%.

The world has been in long term deflation since January 2016. The author sees Japan as having exited the long term deflation after 32 years.

Based on Japan's experience, the author believes that the world's long term deflation may continue until 2048. The reason is that the world's long term deflation could last 32 years, just like Japan's. As of 2023, the world is already eight years into its long term deflation.
If the long term deflation lasts for 32 years, the same length of time as Japan's, it will end in 2016+32=2048.
That leaves 2048-2023=25 years to go.

In other words, if the whole world except Korea goes through a long term deflationary period like Japan, it is very likely that the world will be in a long term deflationary state for about 17 years from now. Korea has 7 years left.
Only in 2023, i.e., 17 years from now, I believe that the global long term deflation will end in 2048. South Korea exits long term deflation around 2029. This is a 10 year earlier exit from long term deflation than the rest of the world.

This also means that the rest of the world, with the exception of Japan, will be falling at dollar exchange rates by 2029 for Korea and 2048 for the rest of the world. Since Japan has done so….

After all, we have 25 years of low interest rates, low inflation, low exchange rates(low dollar), and low growth ahead of us. This is the long term deflation, and this is the period of time that the long term deflation will last, 25 years.

Korea has seven years left. Nobody will survive. There are no investments assets except for one or two.
So going forward, until 2029 for Korea and 2048 for the rest of the world, the price of the dollar will continue to fall in every country in the world except Japan.
If you invest in dollars, that is, you should never invest abroad.

The dollar is not a safe haven asset during the 17 years or so of long term deflation. The world is already in a long term deflation, so the dollar will always be a risky asset until 2029 in Korea and 2048 globally. You have to be very careful. risky asset. You have to be very, very careful.

Chapter 7) The dollar is both a monster asset and a jackpot asset

Every investor thinks that the dollar is always a safe haven. But the truth is, the dollar is a monster. No, it's a monster asset. In the U.S, the dollar is just cash, but outside of the U.S, the dollar is a safe haven asset in normal times, meaning that its price doesn't fluctuate much in normal times.

But when there's risk, whether it's global or local, whether it's a financial crisis or an economic crisis or just plain risk, the dollar becomes a monster. Its price skyrockets. It becomes a monster asset.

When it is in crisis, its price skyrockets.
When the risk subsides or disappears, it returns to its old price, either sharply or slowly. So the dollar is a monster.

Even for Americans who don't live in the US, the dollar is a monster. Americans living in Korea also have to exchange Korean money to live in Korea, and when they need to leave the country or travel abroad, they have to exchange Korean won for dollars.

The price of the dollar in each country rises uncontrollably when there is a financial crisis, a fiscal crisis, a currency crisis, a household crisis, etc. in his country.

When that happens, everyone in that country has to buy or sell dollars at the local exchange rate. The same goes for local Americans who don't hold their wealth in dollars. So, while the dollar is normally a safe haven asset because it has little international price fluctuation, it becomes a monster asset when the price of the dollar in a country starts to skyrocket due to a currency crisis.

Even if you're an American, you can't avoid temporary spikes and drops in your country's currency. They will have to buy and sell dollars and goods(stocks, real estate, necessities, etc.) at the same price as a local.

To avoid this, i.e. to reduce the impact of fluctuations in the price of the dollar, foreigners may choose to pay their rent in dollars.

If the rent is due to be refunded due to a shortened stay, the lease contract may stipulate that it will be refunded in dollars. This is probably wisdom from the long experience of Americans living abroad to avoid the risk of exchange rate fluctuations.

If an American living in Japan at the time of the Plaza Accord in September 1985 had held their property only in yen, their wealth would have nearly doubled overnight, i.e., by the rate of change in the yen-dollar exchange rate. In other words, if your country is experiencing an economic crisis that causes the price of the dollar to soar or plummet, Americans living in that country should keep in mind that there are opportunities to make a fortune or lose money.

The 7.5 million Koreans living abroad should also take advantage of this huge opportunity if something like this happens in their country. This is something that conventional financial theories don't cover at all. These opportunities are the same for anyone living in a crisis country, whether they are American, British, or domestic.

Also, whether it is Japan, the UK, or Singapore, when there is a crisis(such as a foreign exchange crisis), the price of the dollar in the crisis country rises sharply. And stocks, real estate, etc. in these countries plummet in proportion to the dollar's rise.

So the dollar is always cash in the U.S, but outside the U.S it goes from cash to monster asset. When the dollar turns into a like monster, it means that a crisis is already on the rise at that time. This means that the dollar functions as an asset that has more of an asset function than a cash function.

There are countless examples of the dollar turning into a monster and then returning to normal within a short period of time. The IMF in Korea, the situation just before the IMF in Japan in [Figure 19], the entry and exit of Japan's 32 year long term deflation, and the changes in the dollar price during the 2008 financial crisis are reviewed one by one. [Figure 20] shows the rise of the dollar in the U.K after the Brexit decision on June 23, 2016.

The value of the currency, or assets, of a country in crisis, such as a foreign exchange crisis or financial crisis, plummets.

In addition, no country can avoid a spike in the price of the dollar within a crisis country. At the time of Brexit, the value of the pound fell by about 4% in a single day, and the U.K FTSE 100 stock index fell by about 6%.

An example of the dollar acting as a monster asset is when the dollar surges, like it did during Brexit in the U.K or in South Korea and Japan. When that happens, the price of the dollar skyrockets

In this way, the dollar sometimes acts more as a property, with its value rising and falling vertically, than as cash, with its value remaining unchanged. This is why the dollar is sometimes cash, sometimes safe haven, and sometimes a monster in times of crisis.

The dollar itself is a monster asset, but when the dollar goes up, stocks, apartments, and everything else goes down, and when the dollar goes down, everything goes up. When the crisis passes and the dollar starts to fall, stocks and apartments continue to rise. In other words, the dollar becomes a great asset.

I can assure you that this book is the only book in the world that explains this phenomenon of the dollar and all other assets moving in opposite directions, and how to take advantage of the monstrous behaviour of the dollar itself to multiply your wealth by 2~8 times in a short period of time. It's an investment technique that no one else knows about.

And you should be aware of the type of crisis and the dollar's reactivity and resilience in advance. In the following sections, we'll take a closer look at an investment technique that can help you multiply your wealth by up to eight times in a short period of time.

This feature of the dollar can be used to multiply your wealth eightfold in a short period of time, and it can also be used as a technique to protect your wealth forever by applying the principles of the diamond dollar investing method.

By applying this principle, the author was able to create a

wealth preservation dichotomy consisting of two things: dollars and property, instead of the traditional wealth preservation three principles.

Chapter 8) Capture the moment the dollar turns into a monster!

Catching the moment when the dollar turns into a monster is the most important because it is the moment when you need to swap stocks or apartments for dollars, i.e., the Dollar Swapping point.

The reason the dollar suddenly turns from a safe haven to a monster is because
1) at the end of every business cycle, bubbles burst and naturally rebound with falling stock prices,
2) an economic crisis or a foreign exchange crisis, there is always a mass decline in real estate, such as stocks and apartments, while the dollar soars.
3) South Korea is a so-called dollar ATM country, which means that in the event of an economic crisis in another country, it could be the first country to see an outflow of dollars. This could lead to an unfair collapse of the domestic asset market.

Even if you don't normally buy stocks, you should at least know how to take advantage of this opportunity, the moment when the dollar goes from safe dollar to monster dollar and from monster dollar to jackpot dollar. At the end of the day, you need to be able to use the dollar to your advantage to take advantage of the big opportunities.

A big paycheck doesn't make you rich. A very large paycheck can make you live comfortably, but it doesn't make you rich. Economists have theories, such as the lifetime income hypothesis and the always-on income hypothesis, that explain why people don't get rich even if they earn a lot of money.

That's why we all need to make a splurge once in a while to get to the starting line of riches when the opportunity presents itself. Even if you don't normally invest in stocks or aren't very good at it, this technique can help you utilize opportunities.

This Dollar Swapping technique is so important and so simple. Even if you don't have a basic knowledge of stock investing, you can easily multiply your wealth by 2 to 8 times in a short period of time through Dollar Swapping. Every country goes through a boom and bust cycle roughly once every 10 years, which means there are usually 5 years of boom and 5 years of bust, and the cycle spins like a water wheel.

It is common to see five years of economic growth followed by five years of recession, and governments try to eliminate or weaken this distinction. However, there are few cases of success, and there is a feeling that the cycle is accelerating, with 2.5 years of good times followed by 2.5 years of bad times. In other words, In other words, it's not a change every 10 years, it's a change every 5 years.

Why are economies cyclical?
Scholars have studied sunspot theory, entrepreneurial innovation theory, Zugla wave, Kontradieff wave, and many other things, but in my experience, economic fluctuations are caused by human greed, too. Human greed hasn't changed in the past, present, or future. Therefore, there will always be boom and bust cycles.

Since this is an automatic cycle, governments try to shorten or eliminate it, but it is impossible to eliminate recessions because human greed is endless. It can only be shortened or slightly mitigated.

Recessions are caused by the overproduction of goods due to human greed: people think that the good times will last forever and their products will sell well, so they mass-produce them, and when the good times end, they have tons of inventory. This is the beginning of a recession.

If you want to multiply your wealth by 2~8 times in about 5 years using the Dollar Swapping technique in this book, which really shines when a recession starts, you need to follow these rules.

Whether you invest for a living or decide to invest full-time, the outcome is the same.: the best opportunities come at the end of a natural economic cycle or during a crisis, and they don't come often. More precisely, they occur in 3~5 years out of a 10 year period.

During the first two and a half years of a full-blown boom and the second two and a half years of a full-blown bust, these dollar price spikes are rare. This is when we see more moderate fluctuations. The spike in the dollar price occurs mainly in the 2.5 years after the end of the boom, plus about 2.5 years after the start of the recession, for a total of 3~5 years.

1) Dollar surge

In a good economy, the dollar trends downward as stocks and apartments rise, but the moment the economy goes from good to bad, i.e. the bubble bursts, the dollar starts to surge. This is the buying point for the dollar. From here, you're on the circuitous highway to 8x your investment.

Since the main bull market in the Korean stock market started in May 2017 and the main bear market started in June 2021, this is around the vertical dotted line ⑦ in [Figure 18]. This is a great buying opportunity for the dollar.

First things

When the stock market starts to drop dramatically, and news reports are popping up all over the place that the bubble has burst, it's time to sell your stocks and buy dollars. In particular, if you hear about a currency spike on the KBS 9 o'clock news, which is South Korea's leading media organization, you should be ready to act.

I say this not because I'm from KBS, but because KBS News is the most cautious, conservative, and reliable of all Korean media organizations, including public television. In each country, there are media organizations that represent the country.

Also, if it's a top story in the Chosun Ilbo or on the front page, you can assume that the bubble is bursting and the dollar is about to start a major rally.

If you see a story like this, it's most likely the reversal day, so check to see how much the dollar has risen in the meantime. The day of a reversal day is when the dollar price surges by around 1.5% in a single day. Volume should also increase significantly. The higher the volume, the higher the confidence.

If we assume a base of 1,200 won, 1,200 won×1.5%=about 18 won. In other words, if there is a day when the fluctuation tip rises and falls by about 15 to 18 won, reversal day. Of course, it's more certain to check reversal day and then check the three line break again to see if the dollar price has reversed certainly.

After confirming the reversal day with three line break, you can follow and trade. It is too burdensome to predict the dollar's surge and the drop of stocks or apartments in advance.

When the dollar surges because bear market , you sell the stocks and buy KOSEF U.S dollar futures or KOSEF dollar futures leverage(synthetic) within 1~3 days. Naturally, dollar cash is also a buy, including dollar deposits.

You are now in the same yield game as someone who sold stocks and bought the dollar at the bottom, or someone who has a dollar loan now, or an investor who has financing from relatives abroad.

At the top of the dollar price, when the dollar drops sharply, presumably on the reversal day, it's time to sell the dollar and buy the stock.

That the price of the dollar usually doubles from its lowest price can be seen by looking at the price difference between the vertical dotted lines ② and ⑩ in [Figure 18] and the price difference between the front vertical dotted line and the back vertical dotted line in the graph of the dollar and the Japanese Nikkei for about two years(June

1996 to June 1998) in [Figure 19].

Stocks and real estate are inversely correlated to the dollar, which means that they will always track the dollar's price, both up and down.

The holding period for the dollar during a spike, i.e., when stocks are falling, is usually about one to two years. During this time, stock prices drop and the dollar soars. The idea is to take advantage of this and swap stocks for dollars. During the IMF, the dollar surged for about a year and a month, and during the subprime crisis, the dollar surged for a year and four months.

After peaking, stock prices continue to fall, and the dollar continues to rise proportionally. Roughly speaking, the same situation as in the example above will continue for a period of 1 year and 1 month to 1 year and 4 months. We will discuss this in more detail later.

After that, the stock price drops and rebounds once or twice, but the dollar continues to rise, so long term investors are better off sitting on the sidelines. Investors who have enjoyed the ups and downs of the stock market will breathe a sigh of relief when they look at the stocks they sold. However, as soon as you sell your stocks, you need to buy dollars.

If you then sell the dollar in a short period of time, your

investment will have nearly doubled.
The dollar will continue to rise every day, even if only slightly, and the stock price will continue to fall every day. If you notice that the dollar's surge is slowing down and the dollar trading volume is decreasing significantly, it's a sign that the crisis has calmed down and the dollar price has reached its peak.

2) Short term drop in the dollar

The dollar rises sharply in the first surge, followed by a short term decline. Afterward, the dollar surges again and the stock price falls again. It takes almost a year for the dollar to make its first rebound. Those who missed out on selling stocks in the early stages of a major stock market decline can take advantage of a sharp rebound to get out.

The selling price is shoulder price, which means that the short term rebound price is quite high. We will go into more detail about the duration and rate of decline in each case later. This is the period when most people mistakenly believe that the stock market or apartment market is still in an uptrend, but it is not.
You may or may not participate in a short term sharp rebound of a falling dollar. This is because after a short term bounce, there is a secondary decline.

In the case of the IMF, the short term spike in stocks lasted about 8 months, and in the case of the financial crisis, the spike in stocks lasted about 1 year and 2 months, followed by a secondary decline in the dollar. In practice, the stocks that fell the most during the first decline will rise the most during the first rebound, but there is a high probability of getting it wrong.

Therefore, it is better to buy KODEX 200 or KODEX 200 leverage when you want to enjoy a short term stock market spike. This is an omnibus futures bucket that contains a percentage of 200 stocks. Buy a dollar-related ETF. If you buy an ETF, you'll get almost exactly the average return, and if you buy a leveraged ETF, you'll get twice as much.

3) Dollar enters a full-blown secondary surge

The dollar rises sharply in the first surge, followed by a short-lived downturn. Afterward, the dollar surges again and stocks go into another sharp decline. The dollar's rebound takes nearly a year.

In the meantime, investors who have enjoyed the bull market for 3 or 4 years have been investing mainly in leading stocks.

Maybe, you had done already more than doubled your assets, even if it's not 4~20x. Thematic ETFs were created in 2002, so they haven't been studied as much, but they're likely to perform a bit more modestly than lead stocks.

The dollar naturally reverts to its old price as the crisis subsides or is resolved. During the IMF situation in South Korea, it took nearly a decade for the dollar to return to its normal price.

However, within the same time period, it took only one year and seven months from the peak to the first decline.

This retracement period can be seen schematically in [Figure 18] by the movement of the dollar price between the vertical dotted lines ② and ⑩. We can see that the rate of decline of the dollar price decreases significantly as the period progresses, as shown at points (1) and (2) in [Figure 18].

At points (1) and (2), which are significant tipping points in the dollar's decline, it is more favorable to repay the dollar loan by buying back the dollar and repay the dollar borrowed from the overseas relatives.

This is because, although the rate of price decline is larger after points (1) and (2), it is more favorable to repay the dollar loan in the middle of points (1) and (2), compared to the duration and rate of decline.

Of course, in the vertical dotted lines ⑩ and ⑪ in [Figure 18], there is no problem to repay the dollar loan from the bank or borrowing from friends by buying dollars. The efficiency of the investment is only slightly worse, but the exchange rate gain over the same period is the largest.

It's worth noting that even if stocks rebounded sharply during a major decline and then started to decline again, real estate would still be in the midst of a boom. This is because real estate always lags stocks by 6 months.

And no matter how many months the stock market rebounds, six months after the stock market starts to rebound, apartments also start to rebound, and they rebound for the same period of time as stocks. Not surprisingly, the duration and rate of rebound are almost identical for stock indices and apartments.

Chapter 9) Don't Hold the Dollar in a Long Term Deflation: Take Advantage of the Perfect Short Selling Opportunity!

Shorting stocks can make you a lot of money over the long term. You can also make a lot of money shorting stocks in the short term. Long term short selling, especially when combined with the author's theory of long term deflation, is a great opportunity to short all stocks, grains, commodities, gold, etc. with the ability to accurately predict the extent and duration of a long term decline in advance.

Long term deflation takes a minimum of 22 years and a maximum of 30 years, as seen in the U.S in 1929 and Japan in 1990, and apartments, stocks, etc. plummet by up to 80~90% before the period begins, including the previous and subsequent declines.

Based on these two facts, short selling stocks, apartments, gold, etc. is a complete jackpot opportunity that can change your position to become an employer or remain a worker. You can short the stock directly or buy KODEX 200 Inverse or KODEX Inverse Leverage and make a lot of money safely.
You can also short apartments.

Shorting apartments may sound unfamiliar to you, but you can accurately predict the market price according to the theory of long term deflation, so you can sell your apartment when it is expensive and buy it back at the bottom, which is the same effect as shorting stocks, so remember everything, I am saying that you can short apartments.

The opportunity for wealth to fall and move, and for new wealth to be created, is open to everyone. Long term deflation is as big a money war as hyperinflation, changing the ranks and fortunes of the tycoons.

As long term deflation progresses, the price of the dollar plummets, international gold prices plummet, stock prices plummet, and apartment prices plummet. For 30 years, there's nothing left to invest in, like in Japan. So it's an economic phenomenon that no one has ever experienced before, and it can last for 22 to 30 years.

If you have a long term deflation for more than 30 years, it means that the price of the dollar and the price of gold in that country have been falling or weakening for more than 30 years.

In other words, conglomerates and exporters should know that when a long term deflation is in full swing, a big money war is just around the corner.

Export conglomerates will see their profits continue to shrink as the dollar continues to depreciate day after day. Small and mid-sized companies will see a prolonged decline in the price of their imported commodities. Therefore, their profits increase every day, so they are happy.

The Japanese conglomerates that were reaching for the sky before 1989 began to fizzle out due to the long term deflation in Japan, without them even realising it.

Sony was the world's top electronics company, and for a while, it was struggling to stay afloat. TOYOTA's foreign currency translation losses alone amounted to 13 trillion yen in sales for the year.

This shows that these Japanese conglomerates had not been able to cope with long term deflation at all. Samsung has 136$ trillion in cash on hand. Hyundai has about 50 trillion won in cash. They are already preparing for deflation, and they already know that cash is one of the best assets in a deflation.

Cash, government bonds, and the Macquarie Infrastructure Fund are cash equivalents. If we look at government bonds, short term government bonds are very similar to cash, but long term government bonds are slightly different because they are more sensitive to interest rate changes and are not as freely tradable as short term government bonds. Even Mr.Big Investor is now buying short term Treasuries, but he seems to be cautious about buying long term Treasuries.

A great opportunity to make a lot of money short selling comes from a long period of decline in the domestic dollar and gold prices. Of course, real estate prices also plummet. This is when cash and cash equivalents are king.

In a long term deflation, you shouldn't hold dollars outside of the United States. Only cash and cash equivalents should be held. In this case, the dollar becomes property, not cash, and the dollar becomes a monster.

Chapter 10) It's all about the dollar. This is because there is no substitute for the dollar.

Under the dollar key currency system, the dollar is everything. Therefore, you need to know how to handle them. By investing in the dollar, you can hedge against risk and reap huge returns. Often, people will invest in stocks or ETFs in countries like Japan, India, or China and say, "I don't have anything invested in dollars." They don't care if the dollar goes up or down.

It's easy to think that the dollar's rise and fall has nothing to do with your wealth, but if you've invested money overseas, it's all in dollars. If you invested money abroad, it's all in dollars, because you have to convert it back to local currency, invest it in stocks or real estate, and get it back.

It's easy to think that the yen is a little different, but since the yen doesn't have a foreign exchange market in Korea, the exchange rate of the yen to the dollar is determined based on the value of the dollar and the yen.

This is called the arbitrage rates. In the case of Korea's foreign exchange market, only the U.S dollar and the Chinese yuan are directly traded. Therefore, all other countries' exchange rates are using arbitrage rates.

Dollar investment technique:

Traditional investment techniques offer extremely low returns due to hefty currency exchange fees, usually 2.5% each way, and trading dollar futures is extremely risky.

In addition, the dollar is not a good investment because it rarely fluctuates in price during normal times, so it is not recommended for casual investors. Therefore, the dollar investment technique is divided into traditional investment techniques and the writer's own diamond dollar investment technique.

1) Traditional Dollar Investment Techniques

a) Dollar cash purchase

You simply exchange dollars and hold them outside the bank. This is the most classic of the Dollar Swapping financial investments. Exchange fees are expensive, so you need to take that into account, and the IRS will be notified if you exchange more than a certain amount, say 50,000$.

It's always a good idea to keep some dollar cash on hand for emergencies. However, it should be stored outside of your bank so that it is a for risk. This is because there is a good chance that your dollar withdrawals will be suspended if you genuinely need them.

b) Dollar Deposits

They are divided into foreign currency term deposits and foreign currency savings accounts, and they also offer depositor protection up to a limit of 50 million won. It is mainly aimed at exchange rate gains rather than interest.

c) Dollar Insurance

This is insurance in dollars. It is transacted in dollars even when paying premiums and maturity refunds, and also protects depositors within 50 million won, and is tax-free if you join for 10 years or more.

d) Dollar RP

This is a dollar-denominated bond with a repurchase condition. Of course, it also generates interest income of about 1%. With the recent hike in U.S Treasury rates, it's not uncommon for U.S Treasury bonds to yield 3~4%.

e) Dollar ETFs

These are ETFs that invest in the dollar, and there are also leveraged and inverse ETFs.

f) Invest in U.S stocks

This is a way to invest directly in U.S stocks.

What investors should not misunderstand is that investing overseas, whether in the US, Japan, the UK, China, or elsewhere, is the same as investing in dollars.

All overseas investments involve paying a 2.5 per cent one-way exchange fee to convert your money into dollars, then another 2.5 per cent local currency conversion fee to invest in local assets.

When you bring money back into the country, you have to go through the exact same process. This alone will cost you around 5~7% in exchange fees, and you'll have to pay for the conversion twice. In the end, every foreign investment involves buying and selling both dollars and local currency.

It's a difficult game of trying to keep up with the appreciation of the local asset while paying all of the exchange fees and exchange gains and losses. This is why I don't recommend investing abroad.

g) Other methods such as investing in dollar futures and ELS.

These methods are extremely risky and are not recommended. However, the author has compiled an original dollar investment technique and introduces it.

This is a new and original FinTech dollar investment technique that takes a macro approach to investing in the dollar and the five major assets of stocks, apartments, dollars, deposits, and government bonds in Korea instead of investing overseas.

2) New Dollar Swapping FinTech, Dollar Fintech Technique The Diamond Dollar Investing Method

The dollar investing methods discussed above are traditional. This book introduces the new Dollar Swapping and Dollar Fintech method, the Diamond Dollar Investing Method, which is unique, groundbreaking, and can generate 2~8 times the profit in a short period of time.

This book is written to explain the Diamond Dollar Investing Method, a new fintech technique created by the author, and this Dollar Swapping method is a completely proprietary dollar investing technique that is revealed in this book.

The dollar is a safe-haven currency in normal times and a monster currency in times of crisis — a speculative asset that skyrockets in price. For the first time ever, the author has compiled a list of techniques that can make you a fortune in a short period of time.

The dollar is a speculative asset that can be a safe haven in normal times and a monster in times of crisis, but its status inside the United States and outside the United States is different.

Inside the U.S, it is just cash, and outside the U.S, it is a safe haven asset with a strong cash character, and in a crisis, it has the additional function of being an important asset, or property. Therefore, anyone who wants to succeed

in financial technology needs to be able to move dollars around freely, depending on the situation.
In the past, every decade or so, the world has experienced a financial or economic crisis. At such times, out side in U.S investing in dollars can multiply your wealth by two to eight times in a short period of time.

South Korea, in particular, has become a dollar ATM country in times of crisis. South Korea has been nicknamed a dollar ATM country due to its foreign exchange liberalisation, which has allowed the country to move dollars in and out of the country.

As a result, South Korea's frequent dollar inflows and outflows have made the country's crises seem bigger than they actually are. This is due to the abundance of dollar liquidity and the liberalisation of foreign exchange, too

There is also a well-developed stock market and government bond market, so you can buy and sell large amounts of dollars at a moment's notice. Therefore, if there is an international crisis, Korea is one of the first countries to take money out of the country, even if there is no crisis in Korea.

In other words, it's great as a dollar ATM nation. It has been my experience that during short term deflation, i.e. when an economic crisis strikes even in normal times, the dollar suddenly soars in price and domestic assets plummet.

"Why would prices change so much? Isn't there a way to make a lot of money off of price fluctuations?" I asked myself.

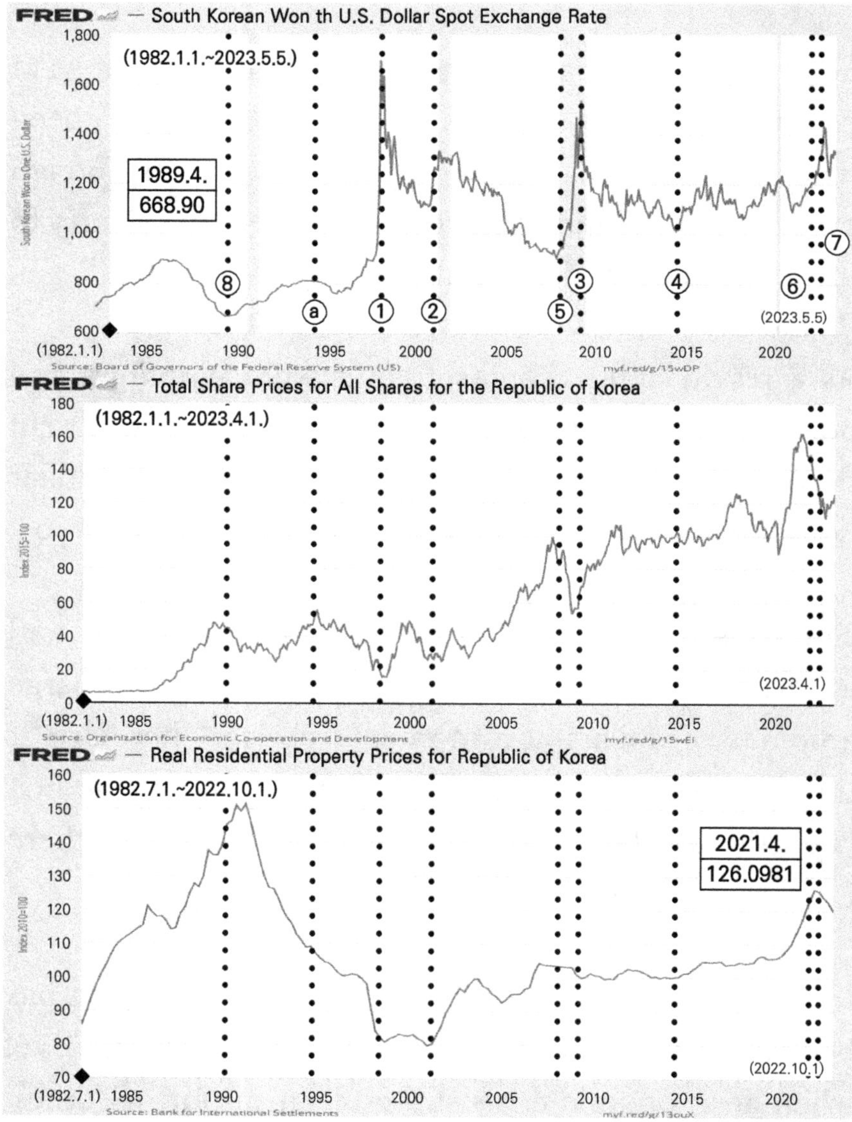

[Figure 13] South Korea's dollar, KOSPI, and real housing index over 42 years(1982~2023)

The writer has about 50 years of experience in stock, apartment, and dollar investing, and about 30 years study of theorising and writing about it about 10 years. About 10 years ago, he has been publishing books on finance technology i.e. Fintech.

We have seen that during economic and political crises in South Korea, foreigners have taken advantage of this inverse correlation between the dollar and domestic assets to make huge gains in the short term. Then, when the crisis passes, they bring the dollar back into the country and dominate the domestic asset market, enjoying the rise in asset prices.

I've always been disappointed with the reality that foreigners' money can freely move across borders for profit, and I've always wondered, "Is there a way for Koreans to utilize it?".

After analyzing a lot of experience and data, I realized that there is a way for domestic residents to get a bigger return than foreigners, and I've put it together in the form of a diamond dollar investing method.

In other words, the price of the domestic dollar is always inversely related to the price of domestic assets such as stocks and apartments. Therefore, when the domestic

KOSPI is at its highest, the domestic dollar price is at its lowest.

Specifically, if we look at the vertical dotted line ⑧ in [Figure 13], we can see that the KOSPI was just past its peak and the dollar price was at its lowest. It is easy to see that the housing index was also just below its peak by looking at the graph of the housing index at the bottom.

Next, let's look at vertical dotted line ①. This is the IMF situation in Korea, and you can see at a glance what was happening. You can see that the dollar was at an all-time high and the stock and housing indices were at a low. You can make a lot of money by taking advantage of these big and slightly long opportunities to Dollar Swapping stocks and apartments.

The writer realised that it was possible to make a fortune in a short period of time by simply using the investment techniques of foreigners and multiplying their wealth by 2~8 times or more.

This is what the writer calls the diamond dollar investment method, which is a Dollar Swapping, dollar FinTech(financial technology) technique that he discovered with a new perspective.

The Diamond Dollar Investing Method is a theory that

analyses the relationship between domestic asset prices and the stock market apartment market in the world's only country that has experienced long term deflation for more than 30 years, such as the IMF in Korea, the 2008 financial crisis, the corona crisis in Korea and Brexit in the UK, and Japan, and draws new results.

One of the surprising findings was that the U.S dollar and stock and housing prices in Japan change from an inverse relationship to a direct relationship when there is a long term deflation, as opposed to a short-run deflation.

The vertical dotted line in the middle graph shows the KOSPI rising from a high of ① to a low of ⑤ after the IMF situation was resolved.

The recovery of the housing index during the same period can also be seen in the bottom graph of the housing index. Note that the start date of the housing index at the bottom is adjusted six months later than the KRW-dollar exchange rate.

Next, if we simultaneously look at the gap between vertical dotted lines ③ and ④, which appeared when the subprime crisis subsided after the sharp drop in the stock index and housing index due to the surge in the dollar during the subprime crisis in vertical dotted line ③, we can see that the price of the dollar fell sharply and the stock index and housing index rose sharply during the same period through the KOSPI index and the housing index.

These facts are the basis of the theory behind the Diamond Dollar Investing Method, and they are also the basis for determining when long term deflation will occur and when it will escape.

As shown in [Figure 25], these phenomena of long term deflation were first identified by the writer by analysing the relationship between the Japanese domestic dollar and asset markets such as stocks and apartments over a 48 year period.

For more than 30 years, the Japanese have shed tears of blood by investing domestically and internationally. However, Japan has now escaped the long term deflation in December 2020.

It took exactly 32 years. This is the success of Abenomics. More on this in [Chapter 27].
The era of "Japan's Long term Deflation" is over!
On the other hand, since January 2016, the "tears of the world" have begun, except for Japan.

The majority of Japanese people still don't know why they got screwed on everything they invested in, because they didn't know diamond dollars investing theory and just went for it.

Since the dollar had fallen by up to 78.6 per cent, their overseas investments had already fallen beyond the level of collapse due to the fall in the dollar price alone, regardless of the success of their overseas investments.
No wonder their wealth had been at crash levels for more than 30 years. This was due to the continued weakness of domestic Japanese asset prices, too

They didn't know that Japan had been in a long term deflation for more than 30 years, and they didn't know that a collapse in all asset prices is a necessary economic phenomenon in a long term deflation.

However, by analysing Japan's lost 30 years, the authors were able to analyse the relationship between various economic indicators. He concludes that the collapse of the dollar and asset markets such as stocks and apartments was expected.
Therefore, analysing Japan in the midst of a prolonged deflationary period can give us a preview of what is to come for the rest of the world.
Now that the world is fighting inflation with the money created by the 2008 financial crisis and the 2020 coronavirus outbreak, many people may wonder, "Why are we talking about deflation?".

However, with rising interest rates and credit contraction from QT(quantitative tightening) and the repayment of excess debt, the world is likely to see a short period of high interest rates and high inflation rates once inflation is taken care of. Then, more likely, we will see a long term deflationary period. As we will explain in more detail later, South Korea will not return to a normal economy like Japan's until 2029.

Therefore, by applying the basic principles of the Diamond Dollar Investing Method and the results and experience of Japan's 30 years of long term deflation, we can derive an investment method that can increase your wealth by 2~8 times or more by investing in dollars for a short period of time.

Investing during a long term deflation is completely different from investing during a normal recession. Japan has been going through their own long term deflation for more than 30 years, 32 years to be exact, and it's left a scarred record of results.

For a variety of reasons, the world, including South Korea, has already been in a long term deflation since January 2016. The author has analysed Japan's 32 years of long term deflation in detail.

By applying the data and experience of Japan for more

than 30 years to each country, investors can know the future of various assets in advance and gain great wealth in the era of long term deflation that has hit the world.
In short, you shouldn't invest in anything during a prolonged deflation. It's time to get out of what you've already invested in and go long in cash and cash equivalents.

However, in a short term deflationary environment, i.e. during normal times, anyone can increase their wealth by 2~8 times or more in a short period of time by using just one investment technique using the dollar. This is the Dollar Swapping technique, which we have analysed and broken down to a new level.

It is an investment technique that works in any country in any era in normal economic times, and the only difference is that you need to Dollar Swapping stocks or apartments to be successful.

Therefore, the phenomenon described in [Figure 13], i.e., the reverse movement of the dollar and real estate such as stocks and apartments, means that under the dollar-based currency system, citizens of any country, even the 7.5 million overseas residents, can make a lot of money by swapping dollars, stocks, and apartments in the country where they live. However, this diamond dollar investing technique cannot be used if the country is in a long term deflationary state.

It is also important to note that this alternative investment technique is not available in the United States. Because the dollar is always an absolute safe haven in cash in the US.

However, dollar is important to remember that outside the US, the dollar is a safe haven asset that is more cash-like in nature during normal times, and a speculative monster asset that skyrockets in price during times of crisis. Therefore, you need to study the dollar separately from studying the diamond dollar investment technique.

To this end, the book "Assets Market Rotation Investing Formula, The Pentagon Investing Method, and Only Dollar Swapping alone makes 800% profit!"

The subtitle is Tears of Japan 'Why everyone who invests in stocks or apartments for the long term is doomed in the end? i.e. Long term investment in stocks and apartments ruins everyone.

In fact, the dollar is not even an investment in normal times. It's almost a cash asset in normal times, as its price rarely fluctuates.

In this book, you'll learn how to make the most of the fact that the dollar has turned from a safe and secure currency to a monster currency, a speculative currency, and back safe currency, so that you can make huge returns on your investment in a short period of time by switching between dollars and stocks.

This diamond dollar investing method is basically a dollar investing method that requires about one to two years to invest in the dollar in this book, and it is not a method that can be completed within a few months or days like other dollar investing methods. To explain this investment technique, let's take a look at everything you need to know about the dollar.

The dollar is both a safe haven and a monster asset, but in a dollar-based currency system, it's always all about the dollar. It matters. When the dollar moves, that is, when the exchange rate changes, your wealth changes with it.

Chapter 11) Assets Market rotation investing formula. A theorization of the Pentagon investing method.

There are many assets in the asset market that people can invest in to make a fortune. There are spot assets such as gold, silver, crude oil, copper, and paintings, and there are investment assets such as stocks, apartments, dollars, and government bonds. By buying and selling these assets in the asset market, people make money. This is the asset market, and there are dozens of different assets to invest in.

In such a large asset market, there are only five investment assets that we can choose to invest in: stocks, apartment dollars, deposits, and government bonds, which are the five representative investment assets, and in fact, we should only invest in these five assets.

Outside of these five representative investments, other investments have too low a rate of price change to be considered worthy of investment because they offer too little return, are too risky, or are not fairly priced.

The challenge is to find the right investment order and way your money among these many assets. The goal of this book is to analyze and explain the reasons and rationale. The modern era is an open economy. In an open economy, trade is the first and most important factor that affects a country's economy. Therefore, economic circulation fluctuations are triggered by increases and decreases in trade volumes. A simple way to compare the economic impact of trade for any country is its trade dependence, i.e.,

Trade dependence is a measure of how dependent a country's economy is on trade, expressed as a ratio of total exports and imports to GNP. Export dependence and import dependence are sometimes calculated separately.

As of 2020~2021, the trade dependency ratio(%) of major countries is as follows.

KOR	70	UK	37	DNK	62
FRA	44	ITA	55	NLD	108
POL	87	SWE	59	JPN	20
CAN	51	AUS	39	IND	31
CHN	34	DEU	72	USA	20
BEL	176	SGP	217	HKG	375

[Table 1] Trade dependency ratio of major countries(%)

A high dependence on trade means that a country's national economy is more likely to be unstable to fluctuations in the global economy. It goes without saying that changes in a country's international payments will have a significant impact on its economy.

Therefore, by tracking the increase and decrease of the balance of payments, the flow of the domestic economy can be predicted, and in the case of Korea, after analyzing 33 years, we concluded that if Korea's annual international payments turns into a surplus or deficit a year ago, the domestic stock market starts to improve or decline.

Similarly, if the U.S annual current account deficit increases or decreases, not only the domestic economy but also the global economy gradually begins to improve or decline.

And the fact is that all of Korea's economic crises have occurred when the balance of payments turned into a deficit. The effect of the money released by the increase and decrease of the balance of payments on the increase and decrease of the currency through the credit creation function of the bank is enormous. It has the effect of increasing or decreasing the volume of money nine times.

Korea's dependence on trade for one year's GDP is about 70%, which means that trade has a 70% impact on the domestic economy. Today, there are very few products that South Korea does not produce, and there are no products that it cannot produce, meaning that South Korea is a manufacturing-based, export-driven country that ranks eighth or ninth in the world's trade rankings, with a trade dependency of 70 per cent.

The Korean government releases the last month's import and export statistics at 11:00 on the 1st of the following month. It's no wonder that the world's fastest and most accurate export and import statistics by industry are used by famous international banks and analysts to predict the global economy.

This means that Korea's monthly trade trend statistics can be used as data to make accurate predictions of economic flows by industry around the world. Usually, trade dependency statistics, i.e. A country's import and export statistics are not released until several months after the end of the year.

Therefore, except for Korea, late export and import statistics, or trade dependency statistics, are too late to be used by economic actors for current policy decisions, and their value is greatly compromised.
However, South Korea's import and export statistics are released to the world the very next day after the month of the year.

These fast and accurate import and export statistics mean that economic organizations can understand the current economic trends of all industries around the world at almost the same time. This is why Korea's administrative network computerized statistical system is one of the best in the world.

If we expand on this, we can infer that every country in the world is affected by the fluctuations in the balance of payments, and the more trade-dependent a country is, the more it is reflected in its domestic economy.

Depending on the stage of economic development of each country, it is natural that the period of time reflected in the economy and financial assets such as stock prices and apartments will also vary.

The authors have already demonstrated that investors can use the 33 year(1981~2013) period of South Korea's trade dependence and stock market flows as a starting point for investing.

Without them, this book would not have been written. By collecting and summarizing their research and combining it with my own research and thoughts, the first PinTech cyclical investment pattern and market cycle

cyclical investment formula, the Pentagon Investing Method, were born.

In addition, the contents of financial investments such as stocks and apartments do not change much over the years, i.e., only books that repeat themselves are always produced, and completely new books cannot be born.

Sailer analyzed the relationship between the balance of payments, apartment prices, and stock prices in Korea over a 33 year period(1981~2013) and published his conclusions in 2013 in his book The Economics of Illusion. To summarize his results,

"In South Korea, if the annual balance of payments is in surplus the year before, the KOSPI rises in proportion to the size of the surplus the following year. Seven months after the KOSPI rises, apartment prices in South Korea begin to rise."

The author will indirectly verify Sailer's findings through related data from Japan and Korea and cite them where necessary. First, the relationship between the Nikkei index and the Japanese housing index according to the change in the yen-dollar price over a 48 year period is shown in [Figure 26] after using the according data from FRED.

The results show that the yen-dollar exchange rate and the Nikkei have an immediate impact. We find that the yen-dollar exchange rate and house prices follow each other with a lag of five months.

Similarly, the Korean won-dollar exchange rate, the KOSPI index, and the housing index over a 43 year period(1981~2023) were taken from FRED data and plotted in a single graph for direct comparison and examination.

[In Figure 13], we can see that in Korea, the change in the KOSPI index for the same date in the 42 year period of FRED(1982~2023) is immediate. The Korean housing index, on the other hand, follows the same trajectory, lagging the KOSPI by six months. By comparing the relationship between the Korean apartment index and the balance of payments, Sailer concludes that there is a lag of one year and seven months between the two indicators.

However, if we compare the Korean won-dollar exchange rate with the housing index, the apartment index, we can see that the apartment index lags the won-dollar exchange rate by six months.

If we move the start date of the apartment graph forward by six months as shown in [Figure 13] and draw a vertical dotted line, we can compare and examine the KOSPI index and the KRW-dollar exchange rate on the same date.

If you check the start date of the housing index graph at the bottom and the start date of the two graphs above, you can see that they started with a six month time difference.

If the annual international payments was in surplus a year ago, the stock price will rise from a year later. The KOSPI immediately moves in the opposite direction according to the diamond dollar investment method based on the daily Korean won-dollar exchange rate.

Through this process, an invisible hand adjusts the daily exchange rate and the KOSPI to match the international payments results of a year ago to the current year's composite stock index.

Therefore, if you invest in stocks according to the daily exchange rate, the result will be the same as investing according to the annual change in the international payments last year. In other words, there is no difference if you replace the change in the balance of payments a year ago with the change in the exchange rate every day.

In addition, it is concluded that six months after stock prices start to change in Korea, apartment prices also start to change in the direction of the stock price movements. This book allows readers to solve the following questions at once.

The timing of investments around the world may be slightly different due to differences in trade dependence. However, the behaviour is the same in any country in any time period, so we can learn more about the following points

1) Changes in exchange rates, stocks, and apartment prices in response to the balance of payments
2) Reaction order and time difference of stocks and apartments
3) How to decide when to invest in stocks and apartments

and review the appropriateness of the investment timing
4) Why stocks always come first when investing?

Sailor compared last year's balance of payments to this year's stock price and the change in apartment prices seven months later. In conclusion, we can see that Sailer's and the author's housing indexes have a time lag of one month.

The outcome was by Sailor compared last year's balance of payments with this year's stock market and the change in apartment prices after seven months. The results show that Sailor and the author have a one month time lag in their responses to the housing index.

Sailer concludes that apartments start to rise seven months after stocks start to rise, while the author concludes that apartments start to rise six months later.
A one month lag is virtually negligible. However, the author's 6 month lag was verified with an actual graph from FRED, while Sailer's 7 month lag was a data from the Bank of Korea.

In other words, the author believes that FRED's data is a more objective source of evidence than the Bank of Korea's data, so the author's analysis of the six month time lag is adopted in this book.

Now, if you know the change in the Nikkei index five months after the change in Japan, or the change in the Korean won-dollar exchange rate and the change in the KOSPI index in Korea, you can predict the amount and direction of change in Korean apartment prices six months in advance.

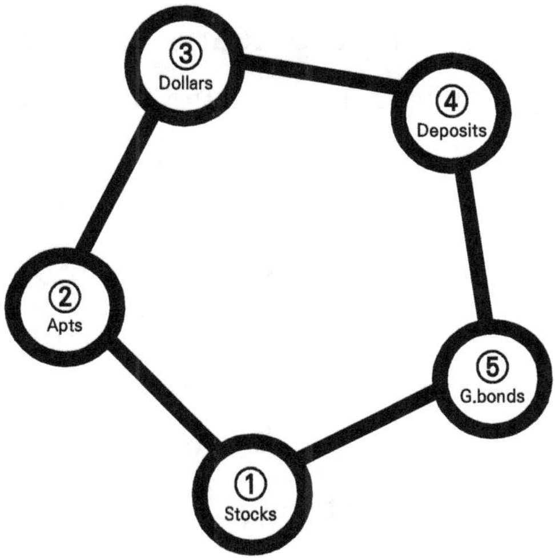

[Figure 14] Investment cycle diagram of the Pentagon's five wealth patterns.

[Figure 14] is an investment cycle diagram of the cyclical investment cycle pattern resembling a pentagon, which was created by the author to explain why and in what order the five major assets of fintech, stocks, apartments, dollars, deposits, and government bonds, should be invested in a cyclical manner.

In other words, [Figure 14] reveals for the first time in the world that there is a certain flow and regularity of money in the financial market, i.e., a circular investment cycle pattern, and depicts it in a simple way to understand it. You can use it to see how money flows through the financial markets and invest accordingly. The author has created a five-step cycle that resembles a pentagon, so investing can be fun and enjoyable.

Investors used to drive the opposite way, i.e., run and invest, losing money and sometimes making little profit, but now they have to follow the five-step investment technique of the Pentagon investing method.

Let's recap the key points of fintech fundamentals that led to the creation of the pentagon investment model.
1) Why do we always start with stocks?
2) Why should apartments always be invested after six months after stocks investment ?

This is the key point of the Pentagon investing method, and the Pentagon investing method has been completed as the world's first market-cycle investing formula. Among them, the Dollar Swapping investment technique is the key point.

Since one business cycle is basically 10 years, and there are only five assets to invest in, you need to invest in one asset for about two years, and if it is a little longer than other assets such as stocks or apartments, you only need to stay in the lead for three to four years. Not to mention that government bonds can also be invested for more than two years, depending on whether they are short or long term deflationary.

In other words, once you invest in a stock or apartment, you won't be able to buy or sell it for two to three years or three to four years, so you need to choose a stock well by referring to what is the main stream stocks in the United States at the time of purchase, and even if you buy a main stream stock and work hard to get a living, the profit will be the same.

The Pentagon's five-step approach to investing(or the Pentagon's four-step approach in the U.S) can be applied to any country in the world, except the U.S, and has a hit rate of more than 95 percent.

It goes without saying that the more trade-dependent a country is, and the more it produces and sells everything in every industry, the more sensitive its stock prices and apartment prices will be to the economy. Moreover, just last month statistics from the last month would be more valuable.

Trade dependency varies by country, so it's important for U.S residents, non-residents, and the nearly 7.5 million overseas Koreans to be aware of their country's trade dependency.

That way, you'll know when it's time to sell bonds and swap to stocks, which is the last rotation asset in the Pentagon's five-step investment method.

In other words, you'll be able to determine when to start investing in stocks, which is your first financial start of the new decade.

It's important to emphasize once again that, if you want to succeed in investing in stocks and apartments, despite popular belief, you should never invest for the long term. Everyone gets screwed in the long run.

Money "goes around in 5 step circles" and you need to rotate through the five main asset classes: stocks, apartments, dollars, savings, and government bonds.

Now, let's take a look at the process of investing in each of the five assets according to the Pentagon Investing Method [Figure 14]. Number ① is the time to invest in stocks. After the annual balance of payments showed a surplus a year ago, the stock market suddenly became to rise.

If this is a short term deflation and not a long term deflation, that is, a normal business cycle, the KRW-dollar exchange rate would have fallen and the annual balance of payments would have been in surplus a year ago.

Contrary to common knowledge, it is only when the KRW falls sharply that exports surge. This fact, as well as the trend of trade before and after a country is designated as a currency manipulator, is the reason and logical basis for the Diamond Dollar Investment Method in [Chapter 17].

In other words, when the exchange rate increases, exports decrease significantly for a long period of time, as evidenced by the J-Curve effect.

Also, when the exchange rate decreases due to the designation of a currency manipulator, exports increase for a considerable period of time. This is evidenced by the graphs in [Figure 6], [Figure 7], and [Figure 8] when Korea, China, and Japan were designated as currency manipulators.

In any case, when the stock market suddenly becomes active, I immediately check whether it is a reversal day or not and look into the trend for 4~5 days. If there's positive conversion of the three line break is confirmed, you should be bold and sell the government bonds you bought at the end of the recession.

With these funds, you should start a new fintech. You will be at the starting line of a long fintech that will take about 10 years.

Money goes round and round in 5 step circles chasing profits, so this is an almost automatic sequence of movements. Mr.Cyclic, the American master of market cycles, has been trying to find a market cycle pattern in the U.S stock market for a long time, but he hasn't found one, and he's still trying.
However, the author first broadened my horizons and found a cyclical investment cycle pattern among five main assets, which I summarised and named the Pentagon investing method. This is the market cycle that Mr.Cyclic is looking for.

He was thinking on a micro level, trying to find cyclical patterns in individual stocks. I think his method is flawed from the start.

Just as there is no regularity in the direction of stock price movements, no one can guess the direction of a frog's jump, so it is obvious that there will never be a regular cycle pattern in individual stocks.

If he could find a cycle pattern of stock price fluctuations and formulate it in such a way that stock prices always behaved the way they had behaved in the past, then chartists would have been very successful.

But since the stock market doesn't have a regular cyclical pattern, the same pattern will never happen to individual stocks, which is why chartists are doomed. Charts are a thing of the past and can only help us a little bit to figure out where the stock price is at the moment.

In any case, if Mr.Cyclic had found a pattern or regularity in the stock market or in individual stocks, he would have formulated it, just as the author does.

The author took a macro, or macroeconomic, approach and found regularities and cyclical patterns in the cyclical investment cycles among the five asset markets: stocks, apartments, dollars, deposits, and government bonds. He was too late because the author found it first, formulated it, and published it.

But now, he can use the author's original and unique "4-Step Pentagon Investing Method" for U.S residents. People say the financial markets, especially the stock market, are unpredictable.

I used to find it difficult too. But now that the 5-Step Pentagon Investing Method has been created, making money is simple. If you follow the formula, it is very simple to get rich.

Michael James Burry, who made a fortune shorting during the sub-prime, also got the timing of the crash wrong and sold short first, spending three painful years banging his drum every day.

However, the Pentagon Investing Method is the first fintech formula that identifies the cyclical investing cycle patterns among the five major assets markets and the regularity and timing of the cycles, and turns them into a formula. You can even know exactly when to enter and exit the five assets.

To recap,
If you invest in an apartment after six months of investing in stocks, as shown in [Figure 14] ②, you entered the real estate market at the beginning of a major upswing. I have already explained why it is important to enter the apartment market after six months'uprising.

Step 3 of the Pentagon Investing Method is ③ in [Figure 14]. When stocks or apartments are at their most expensive, you swap them for dollars.

Let's look at the actual situation in Korea! If you look at the graph of the KOSPI index in the center of [Figure 13], the KOSPI index is the highest when the vertical dotted line ⓐ or the vertical dotted line ⑤. At this time, the won-dollar exchange rate is at its lowest.

At this point, you can sell your stocks and swap them for dollars. The appropriate dollar selling points are then the vertical dotted line ① and vertical dotted line ③, respectively.

If the stock market crashes as a self-correcting mechanism, if the government raises interest rates because it's worried about overheating, or if there's a sudden economic crisis with an overheated economy, the dollar will soar and stock prices will fall. Or you can watch the stock prices fall first and buy the dollar. This is step 3 of the Pentagon investing method.

It's important to note that as the stock market crashes in a bear market, even if the dollar rises, the price of the apartment will continue to rise for six months from the time the stock market crashes.

You can judge this period by the monthly price of the stock market. You should never miss this opportunity. This is how you can determine when to buy and when to sell an apartment.

If you apply the same six month rule to the third, fourth, and fifth downturns and rebounds, you'll have a 95% success rate in determining when it's time to sell or buy.

Even in the case of a short term bounce, the Pentagon investing method can be used to calculate the exact date of the peak of the bounce by applying the six month lag between stocks and apartments. So, for example, you can accurately calculate the timing of an apartment's decline by using the Pentagon investing method.

In South Korea, the stock index has been in an uptrend for Nomember since October 2022. Therefore, the apartment will have an 11 month uptrend from March 2023, six months later.

This date will not even change in the future because the stock index has already started to decline since August 2023. Therefore, the peak price of an apartment in this rebound will occur in February 2024, 11 months after March 2023.

Over the same period of time, the apartment index will grow almost as fast as the stock index. This is the rate of increase seen in a short term bounce. The date of the end of the rebound is more important.

For investors who were not lucky enough to sell their apartments at peak prices during this cycle, this will be their only chance to dispose of them at shoulder prices. Usually, peak prices are not reached again until about 8 years after the peak. These facts are almost 100% correct, as the power of 33 years of statistics shows.

This is the world's first market-cycle investing formula,

the Pentagon Investing Method. Now, just like math formula, there's an investment formula for fintech.
Even if stocks have already started a major decline, After a six month rebound, apartments start to fall.

This is the phenomenon of the fourth stage of the Pentagon Investing Method, and real estate, i.e. apartments, can be invested accordingly, i.e. if you sell six months after the stock market crashes, you will sell at the highest price.
Next, step ④ in [Figure 14] is to encash your dollars and sign up for a CD when the dollar starts to fluctuate or slowly decline.

By this time, the government has probably raised interest rates three or four times, and the CDs are paying quite a bit more interest than they would have otherwise.

The final five steps of the Pentagon investing Method are as follows. The recession continues and the government now cuts interest rates once or twice to stimulate the economy. When rates go down, you can close your CDs and buy government bonds.

Usually, interest rates are not lowered until after a period of rising interest rates, usually around 11 months, so you should not rush to withdraw your deposits and enter the government bond market. You need to wait for one or two rate cuts before you can safely invest in government bonds.

In other words, the Pentagon investing method is primarily a follow-the-money trade, which means that you watch and follow behaviours such as changes in the international payments, the won-dollar exchange rate, and government interest rate adjustments, so it's clear when to rotate.

Therefore, the five-step investment process of stocks, apartments, dollars, deposits, and government bonds is a perfect way to avoid the painful consequences of bad timing, as physician and investor like Michael James Burry.

Just one thing

While stocks and apartments are the most common investments with the greatest returns, it's important to note that they are only six months apart in best investment timing.

So when you're selling stocks or apartments and Dollar Swapping, it can get a little confusing depending on which asset you're currently invested in. As you know, stocks and apartments have a six month time lag at the right time to buy and sell.

When it's time to Dollar Swap, that is, when the stock is

at its highest price, you should sell the stock and after buying the apartment, and then sell the apartment again six months later, and then you have to decide whether you should skip the apartment purchase and go straight to the Dollar Swap or not.

The main considerations are that there is no capital gains tax exemption for holding for six months before selling, and there are huge costs for real estate transactions. Therefore, it is recommended that you invest your money in a two-track system, i.e., half in stocks and half in apartments, and do not switch between stocks and apartments.

Therefore, I recommend a two-track approach, i.e., investing half in stocks and half in apartments, and not switching between stocks and apartments. This is because the returns on stocks and real estate are roughly the same in market cycle investing fomula.

In other words, even if stocks start to fall, apartments will rise for another six months, so the decision to sell stocks and use apartments as a replacement investment opportunity should be based on the level of greed. If you put aside economic interests for a while, each person's situation may be different.

If you sell your government bonds and start investing in

stocks, you will almost automatically find yourself back in the government bond market again about eight years later. This is the market cycle investing formula exists in the financial markets.

This pattern of cyclical investing becomes a fintech cycle that never changes. This is because money travels the same path, in the same way, every time, chasing profits.

In [Chapter 22], Andre Kostolani's Egg Theory is introduced. He could not have known that people outside the U.S had a golden opportunity to make 8x their money in a short period of time if they swapped stocks or apartments for dollars at the right time,

As I've explained before, the Pentagon Investing Method is just following the money as it water flows, swapping stocks and apartments for dollars.

After that, you should invest in a CD for two to three years. Finally, you should invest your money in government bonds. This is the world's first asset market cyclical investing formula.

For one thing, Kostolani doesn't explain the opportunity to make a lot of money through swaps between assets. There are also a number of problems with his egg theory, such as buying stocks near the bottom of interest rates and bonds near the top of interest rates.

The Pentagon Investing Method suggests that you don't have to make too many difficult interest rate predictions, such as peaks or bottoms, which is what Kostolani wants you to do.

By following the Pentagon Investing Method and rotating through five different types of investments(stocks, apartments, dollars, savings, and government bonds), you can multiply your wealth by 2~8, or even 16 times at the end of one business cycle.

Let's also assume that the stock market has already suffered a major crash and has been exchanged for dollars. The question is, what if you're in step 4 of the Pentagon Investing method, making deposits and waiting to invest in government bonds, and the stock market suddenly starts moving up?

In this case, you shouldn't liquidate your deposits and go back to the stock market.
Since you still have two to three years left to invest in your deposits and an expected time period to invest in government bonds, the rise will either be a trick or the upside will be weak.

Moreover, since the money has not been traded across

the entire market, that is, across the five assets, it will be spread across deposits and government bonds, and the power of the money will also be weak. Also, the annual balance of payments will be still in deficit, not in surplus as it was a year ago, which is the first condition to start investing in stocks.

Therefore, the expansion of money through credit creation is significantly weaker, so it is no wonder that stock prices are weak. So don't be fooled by the mood. Anyone who doesn't want to build massive wealth, up to 16x in a decade or so, shouldn't buy this book and shouldn't waste their time and money reading it.

In the future, Americans will be able to invest successfully if they do not simply invest in stocks or apartments for the long term like Mr.Big Investor Style, but follow the "4-step Pentagon Investing Method", which omits the Dollar Swapping process.

Non-Americans, i.e. investors who do not live in the United States, should be able to use the Dollar Swapping investment technique by following the Five-Step Pentagon Investing Method. This will allow your money to grow up to 16 times in 10 years.

The author's theory is that stocks and apartments should be Dollar Swapped during a major downturn or financial crisis.

If you don't do it, you'll suffer a huge drop in the price of the asset that went up so much during the Great Bubble. According to the Pentagon Investing Method, you must do Dollar Swapping in step 3.

In addition, the economic crisis comes to foreigners who have been enjoying interest rate and market differentials in the last stage of government bond investment.

When an economic crisis hits the country where they invested, foreign investors quickly dumping of their government bonds, stocks, real estate, etc. and they go to their home.

At this point, you should start dumping government bonds with foreigners. You have another opportunity to double your investment. With the money from selling government bonds, you'll be able to buy dollars with foreigners.

Once you've bought back government bonds like a foreigner, you'll need to continue to utilize the huge capital gains and interest from falling long term interest rates.

Fortunately for our readers, this is where step 6 of the Pentagon investing method starts. This is something that happens almost every time in the last six stages of a business cycle.

In the past, there were few opportunities to invest in government bonds because the bond market was underdeveloped and it was almost impossible for investors to buy and sell bonds directly.

However, there are now several ETFs on the market for government bonds, so you shouldn't miss out on this great investment opportunity.

So, strictly speaking, over the course of a single business cycle, the Pentagon investing method could have a normal return potential of 16x, plus about 2x in bond market gains from foreigners selling Treasuries, for a total theoretical return of about 32x.

Since we believe that long term deflation will continue after the government bonds are repurchased, the Pentagon Investing Method's Step 5 will allow readers to enjoy the interest income from holding government bonds for a long period of time, as well as the capital gains from falling interest rates.

As long term deflation progresses, the returns could be even more dramatic, perhaps 2~3x or more again. The time period for investing in government bonds can of course be extended to 2029 in Korea and 2048 globally. The world has been in a long term deflation since January 2016.

The order of cyclical investment in the five major asset markets of stocks, apartments, dollars, deposits, and government bonds is the same in all countries, but the timing of the first investment in stocks and the first investment in apartments will vary depending on the size of each country's economy and its dependence on trade.

If you are a professional investor, you should check with your country's securities research institute or economist analyst to find out how long it takes to invest in your country.

Chapter 12) If you want to get rich, invest all your money in leading stocks!

If you want to get rich, invest all your money in leading stocks! Instead, rotate your investments into the next asset! When you diversify, your returns are also diversified. This is the formula for getting rich.

The Pentagon investing method starts with exchange rate fluctuations. Exchange rates can fluctuate rapidly due to stock market spontaneous technical declines, changes in interest rates, and financial crises etc.

When the exchange rate changes, the amount of exports and imports of each country increases or decreases depending on the trade dependence of each country.

An increase or decrease in the amount of trade leads to an increase or decrease in the amount of money, which in turn causes the economy to fluctuate.

Households, businesses, and governments change their investments in response to these fluctuations. The profit-seeking behavior of economic agents is manifested in economic fluctuations.

Therefore, by investing according to the economic fluctuations, you will naturally be rotating your investments among the big five assets.

The Pentagon Investing method describes the order in which you should invest in each of these five assets, when you should invest, and when you should exit.

So the idea that we should be diversified when investing in stocks is completely wrong. Leading stocks usually go up 4~20x in 3~4 years and end their lives in a crash. We've rarely seen a leaded stock emerge as a next leading stock after a major decline.

The only time this happened was when China became a member of the WTO, opening up a new market of about 1.4 billion people. Studies have shown that there is only a 12.5% chance of a former leading stock becoming a leading stock again. That's right. We should not make a mistake.

We've seen it all the time that whenever a leading stock bearish market crashes, on average, leading stocks drop by 50~90%, not to mention other stocks. They all crash

So the author strongly advise
1) you should not invest in stocks or apartments for the long term. In every business cycle, the leading stocks appear as new industries and start to rise.

In every cycle, leading stock prices start to fall first due to technical declines, rising interest rates, and financial crises etc. and apartments start to fall six months later in Korea

When stocks start to fall, you should sell them immediately. Six months later, you should sell the apartment.
After selling the assets, according to the asset market rotation investment fomula, you should buy dollars.
This is the main point of my explanation in the previous chapter.

The theoretical starting line of the Pentagon investing method is the Diamond Dollar investing method.
As long as the dollar key currency system continues, the big Five asset market rotation investment formula, the Pentagon Investing Method, will continue to work. i.e., the 800% profit from Dollar Swapping alone will not change.

Investment methods that use economic fluctuations and their relationship to the dollar will not change.

This is because it is an investment method for the five investment target assets that reflects both the absolute price change of asset prices due to economic changes and the relative price change to the dollar.

The way to get rich is to swap stocks or apartments for

dollars about once a decade to match each economic change. Therefore, the dollar exchange rate is the most important.

America's "Magnificent Seven" stocks are the world's leading stocks right now. The U.S occupied about 25% of the world's industries and economy.

Therefore, it is not a big mistake for other countries to assume that the leading stocks and leading industries of the United States are the leading stocks and leading industries of their country. If you're having trouble finding a leading stock or industry, consider investing in a thematic ETF composed of leading stocks. This is because each country may have slightly different leading stocks depending on the stage of industrial development.

Let's summarize in a few words!
1) You should never invest in stocks or apartments for the long term.

2) Stocks should not be a diversified investment. Concentrate on leading stocks.
3) When the market crashes, sell all your stocks and swap them for dollars. 6 months later, sell your apartment and buy the dollars, too.

This is the answer.

This is the essence of the Pentagon Investing Method.

Of course, after the Dollar Swap, after sell your dollars at highist price, and next you need to invest in the next rotation asset, which is deposits.

The interest rate on deposits should be quite high because the benchmark interest rate has been increasing. Next, you should invest in government bonds. because the economy has been overly depressed due to excessive control policy. Soon, the government will have to lower the benchmark interest rate, which will cause the price of government bonds to skyrocket.

Savings rates should have been falling for some time now as the benchmark rate has been lowered. If you're still in a savings account, you're a fool. The interest rate will continue to fall, so it's time to close your savings and buy government bonds. Thus, your money should be rotated from stocks to apartments to deposits to dollars to government bonds, in this order. If you don't, you'll lose a lot of money.

The reason for this asset market rotation is the profit motive of human beings. Human greed is always the same in the past, present, and future. So it is same always the big 5 asset market investment cycle.

According to this, if you want to get rich, invest in the leading stocks . Instead, you should follow the rotation sequence of the big five asset markets to get rich.

If you don't believe that I told, invest 50% of your assets in stocks according to the Pentagon investing method.
There are very few books that directly relate the dollar to the real economy, which is where wealth comes from.
Finance technology starts with dollars and ends with dollars. That's why this book is filled with stories about the dollar.

Chapter 13) Diamond Dollars Investing Method

The Diamond Dollar Investing Method is the pricing theory of all goods in the world. All assets in the world, including stocks, apartments, crude oil, and gold, move in the opposite direction to the dollar price under normal economic conditions.

In other words, when the dollar goes down, stocks, apartments, dollars, gold, silver, copper, etc. go up. Conversely, when the dollar goes up, stocks, apartments, crude oil, gold, silver, copper, etc. go down. In this case, the fall and rise rates are about the same.

One common misconception here is that people usually think that an increase in the won-dollar exchange rate will increase exports, but in this case, exports actually decrease.

This can be seen by looking at the movement of the Japanese asset market after the Plaza Accord of September 22, 1985 and the changes in the price of the won-dollar exchange rate and the KOSPI and housing indices during the period of Korea's designation as a currency manipulator(April 1988~October 1989) in [Figure 9]. This can be seen by looking at Japan and China's exports at the time of their designation as currency manipulators.

If you look at the graphs of this inverse relationship, you can see that these two sectors move in opposite directions, like a diamond shape, as shown in [Figure 16] and [Figure 17]. Therefore, investing using this principle, which moves in the opposite direction to the dollar, is always successful, so it is called the diamond dollar investment method.

There are times when the dollar and various commodity prices, which normally move in opposite directions, suddenly move in the same direction. In other words, when the price of a country's domestic assets rise, the price of a country's domestic stocks rise at the same rate.

Also, when the international dollar price increases, the international gold price increases proportionally. This is the moment when long term deflation occurs.

This principle can be used as a great investment opportunity. In this case, unlike the diamond dollar investment method, the dollar price and the price of other commodities move in the same direction, that is, they move in a proportional relationship, so if you apply this to invest, you will have a great investment opportunity unlike others. This can be called the reverse diamond dollar method.

By applying the diamond dollar investment method and

the reverse diamond dollar investment method, you can get 2~8 times the return on your investment in a short period of time. U.S residents can't take advantage of these investment opportunities within their own country.
Because it is not possible in America swapping the dollar for another currency. On the other hand, non-U.S residents can always take advantage of this great opportunity.

On October 13, 2009. the Wall Street Journal(WSJ) reported the news as follows. The explanation is that as the dollar falls, the price of dollar-denominated oil rises, and as the price of oil rises, the dollar is exposed to selling pressure from a widening U.S trade deficit. This is only partially true.

Contrary to the Wall Street article, the author argues that the inverse relationship between the dollar and the prices of stocks, real estate, etc. is always true in countries that are in crisis, whether it is a currency crisis or a political crisis. He also explains that gold prices and crude oil prices have a clear inverse relationship with the dollar in the long run.

As the author originally claimed, if you swap assets, especially stocks and apartments, for dollars, you can quickly make money in a country in crisis. The intersection of the diamond's middle horizontal line is judged to be the value equilibrium line between the dollar and other assets in a normal economy.

The intersection of the lower case letters ⓐ, ⓑ ··· ⓖ in [Figure 17] and the equilibrium line E. These intersections can be thought of as value lines. This is where the intrinsic value of things and the value of the dollar are in balance.

In any country in crisis, except the United States, the price of the dollar fluctuates in a continuous diamond pattern, and there is a clear inverse relationship between the price of the dollar and all other assets.

You can make a lot of money in a short period of time by switching between these two assets. It's Dollar Swapping. Another key point of this book. Recent articles on Wall Street represent the views of a single journalist and may not represent the views of Wall Street firms.

Moreover, they are only reporting on what is happening in the United States. The reporter may not have seen the dramatic price movements between dollars and assets in crisis countries.

In my view, there is always a swapping between the two assets, because only then are the assets of the crisis country properly valued and traded at the right price. Under normal economic conditions, the inverse proportional line between the two assets is shorter, i.e., the diamond is smaller.

But when a country is in an emergency economic situation, whether it's a currency crisis, a financial crisis, a fiscal crisis, or a war crisis, there is a very strong, maximized amount of vertical line, and a direct relationship.

The length of the vertical dotted line increases, just like the diamond in the center. Like the diamond in the center of [Figure 16], the size of the diamond is drawn large.

The size of this diamond will be larger depending on the severity of the crisis. If the crisis is small, it will take the form of a small diamond, and if the crisis is large, it will create a larger diamond.

There is always a symmetrical inverse relationship between the dollar and assets such as stocks, real estate, gold, crude oil, and silver. This inverse relationship between the dollar and assets has never occurred in the United States. It can't happen. Because the dollar is the reserve currency, and to them, the dollar is just cash.

However, the inverse relationship of the dollar to various assets has always occurred internationally. This is why you should always take advantage of Dollar Swapping when the dollar is at its peak, i.e. when stock prices or apartment prices are at their lowest.

A) The first step in creating wealth with the Diamond Dollar Investing Technique is to borrow dollar from a crisis country when the dollar is at its most expensive. You should exchange the loan as soon as you receive it, and then sell your stocks and exchange them to pay it off when the first phase of the dollar's decline is complete. You can play the wealth creation game 4x in a short period of time.

In [Figure 18], points ②, ④, and ⑧ are the optimal borrowing times for dollar financing, i.e., when the dollar price is at its highest. After that, the optimal time to repay is ②, 18 months after(black diamond point 1), ④, 15 months after(black dia mond point 2), and ⑧, 5 months after.

The yields are 53.4%, 38.3%, and 15.6%, respectively, based on the bottom of the first decline. Until the optimal repayment time, stocks and apartments rise sharply in a short period of time because the dollar, which has risen sharply during financial and economic crises, falls sharply.

At this time, you can buy dollars and pay off the dollar loan. This is when the 4x game is completed. It only takes 27, 15, and 3 months, so the interest on the loan is pennies.

B) To get a 4x return on investment, sell stocks and buy

dollars at the time points ⓐ, ⑤, and ⑥ in [Figure 13], i.e. when the KOSPI is at its peak. The subsequent process is the same as A).

C) To earn an 8x return on investment, sell the highest-priced stocks and swap dollars at the time of ⓐ ⑤ ⑥ in [Figure 13], as in B). At the same time, you can borrow a dollar loan and invest as in A) and B).

D) You can also take out a dollar loan at the height of the crisis, exchange it, hold it as cash, and then buy dollars and pay it back when the dollar price comes back to normal.

E) A U.S-based investor who uses the dollar as his or her everyday currency can invest in a crisis country when the dollar is at its most expensive, and then buy back dollars when the price of the dollar starts to fall and calm down and pay back the U.S-based bank.

Doubling on average is a guaranteed investment, and if you can double your local investment, you can easily quadruple your money. Outside of the U.S, the diamond dollar investment method is always the same, so this quadrupling technique is very easy for investors living in the U.S It is a three-step Dollar Swapping investment method of the Pentagon investing method.

There are always financial crises, fiscal crises, and economic crises in the world, and there are always countries at war. Investors who use the U.S dollar as their everyday currency should always look at investment markets around the world with a hawk's eye. There are always opportunities for 2x to 4x returns.

In other words, in Korean standards, when the dollar is at its most expensive, the KOSPI is at its cheapest, so you can take out a dollar loan to buy a KODEX 200 ETF, etc. and then sell it when the KOSPI rises enough, exchange it, pay it back, and quadruple your fortune. Of course, apartments also skyrocket in a short period of time, but it is not recommended to invest in them because there will be nothing left after capital gains tax, acquisition tax, and registration tax.

One of the basic theories of investing is to invest in countries when the local currency is strong. This means that you should not only get investment returns, but also exchange rate gains.

Let's take an example.
Let's say the won-dollar exchange rate was 1,200 won per dollar.

After making a profit on Korean assets(stocks, real estate, bonds, etc.) with the dollar brought in at that time, the foreign investor wants to sell them and leave Korea, but the Korean won has dropped to 1,000 won per dollar.

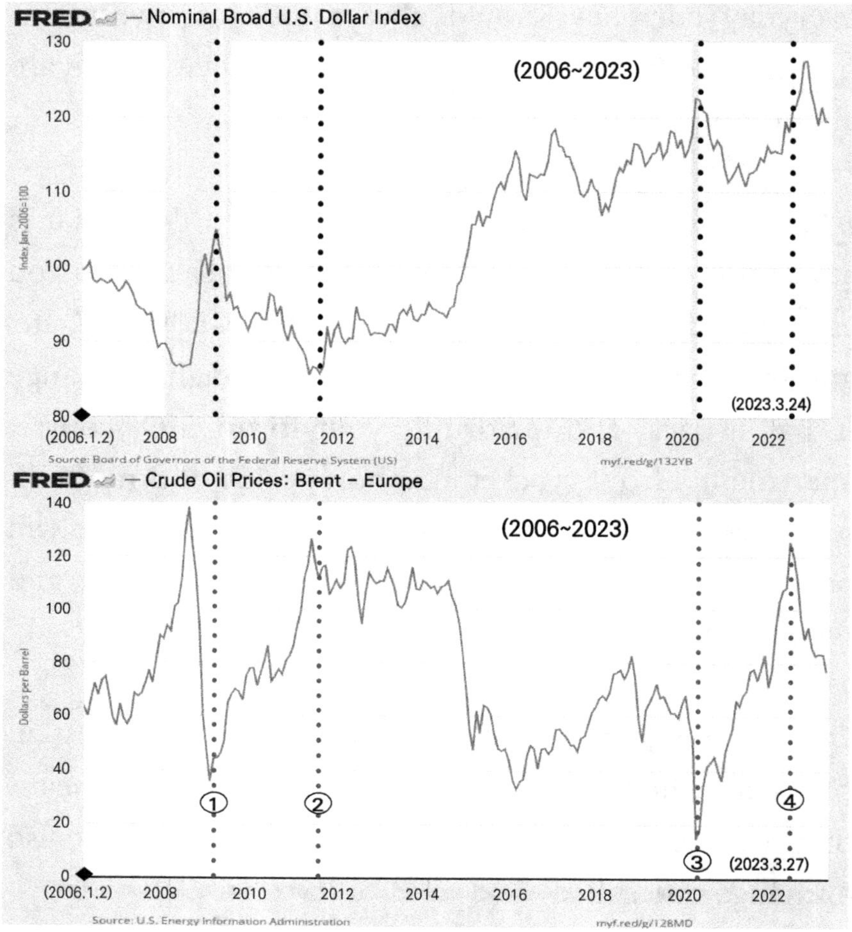

[Figure 15] International dollar(dollar index) and crude oil prices over 18 years(2006~2023)

The foreign investor has already made a 20% exchange gain [(KRW 1,200-1,000)×100%=120%] when they simply sell their domestic investment and get their money back, i.e., when they exchange the dollar. This is why it is advisable to invest in a country with a strong local currency.

Everything in the world(stocks, real estate, bonds, crude oil, gold, silver, etc.) is bought, sold, and compared in dollars when trading and comparing prices internationally. This is the dollar key currency system.

Recently, crude oil has been moving away from the old Petrosystem and starting to trade in yuan, but it's still a small amount. Furthermore, all items in the world are in a trade-off relationship with the dollar price. In other words, all items move in the opposite direction to the dollar index(a price index representing the price fluctuations of the dollar against the currencies of six major countries).

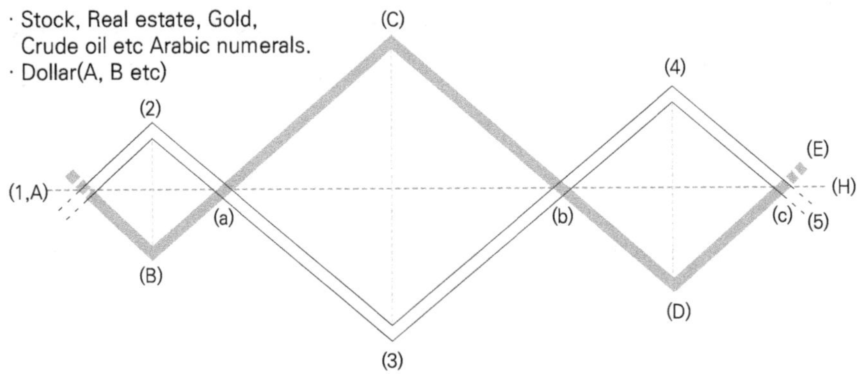

[Figure 16] Diamond-shaped Dollar Replacement Investment

If the oil price rises, the dollar price falls, and if the dollar price rises, the oil price falls. Rather than comparing it with the exchange rate of a single country against the dollar, let's look at the vertical lines ①, ②, and ③ in [Figure 15].

When comparing the dollar index with the oil price, it is clear that there is an inverse relationship with the dollar. So, how should we apply the fluctuations in this dollar price to asset markets when investing in stocks or real estate?

The solution is to replace the spot market with dollars in a diamond-shaped investment.
This method is a technique devised or invented by the author. Again, this exchange investment technique between the dollar and other assets applies only to those residing in the United States

This is because the dollar is their everyday currency and cash. This continuous diamond-shaped dollar investment technique is the author's original method of alternating between the dollar and other assets, which only applies to countries outside the United States.

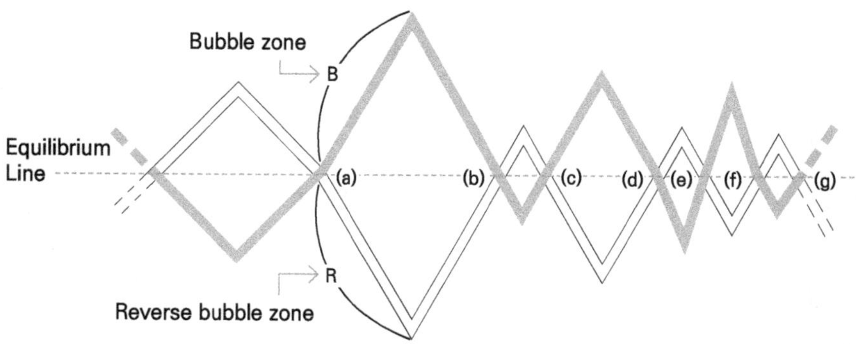

[Figure 17] Diagram of the equilibrium convergence process through bubbles and counter-bubbles

In some cases, the size of the diamond may be larger or smaller than the diamond shape before and after, as shown in the investment diagram in [Figure 17]. However, it is always important to note that there is an inverse relationship between the price of the dollar and other alternative investment assets.

There will be a time lag due to the time required to find the right investment, correct any mistakes, and reinvest.

However, this inverse relationship also applies in normal times, as shown by the vertical dotted lines ②, ⑧ and ⑨ in [Figure 18] for the KOSPI Composite Index. The relationship between crude oil and the dollar is also immediately apparent in the vertical dotted lines ①, ②, ③, and ④ in [Figure 15].

In other words, the highest prices of stocks, real estate, crude oil, gold, etc. are near the lowest prices of the dollar, and conversely, the highest prices of the dollar are near the lowest prices of stocks, real estate, crude oil, gold, etc. The size of the diamond can be thought of as the size of the financial or economic crisis in each country. If a country has a serious economic crisis, the center diamond will be larger, like the bubble and counter-bubble diamond in [Figure 17].

In other words, the dollar surges higher and alternative

assets such as crude oil, copper, and gold plummet. As shown, as stocks, real estate, crude oil, gold, etc. begin to rise, the dollar price begins to fall in response. The Arabic numerals represent the price movements of the assets, such as stocks, which go from 1 to 2, or from 2 to 3.

The dollar price is represented by an alphabet, and as the stock price increases, it starts to decrease gradually from A to B. This is because the price of the dollar has increased. One of the main reasons for this is the increase in foreign investment, including hot money.
Korean apartments lag stocks by about 7 months(the author believes 6 months). This fact is borrowed from Saylor's analysis in The Economics of Illusion. This analysis compares Korea's international payments flows and price changes of stocks and apartments between 1981 and 2013(about 33 years) by lagging the balance of payments graph by one year.

A graphical representation of the relationship these assets is a continuous diamond shape, as shown in [Figure 17].

This process is an infinite iteration of finding a balance point based on the equilibrium line(E), i.e., a picture of many large and small diamonds as shown in [Figure 17].
If we connect them, we can see that the diamonds are linked. This is the diamond dollar investment diagram of the equilibrium convergence process through bubbles

and counter-bubbles.

In other words, it is a useful investment technique for all investors in countries that do not use the U.S dollar as their daily currency.

Non-U.S residents can follow the diamond investment technique when investing in any asset in their country. Sometimes, the correlation between the dollar and other classes does not follow a continuous diamond pattern, but varies for a while. The reason is mainly due to various demand fluctuation factors and people's trial-and-error investment behavior to find the optimal investment asset. In other words, investors seem to be using a trial-and-error method to find the appropriate assets to invest in.

But in the end, they end up with a diamond pattern. The graph from the IMF period also shows that Korean apartments, or residential facilities, lagged the KRW-dollar exchange rate and stock prices by six months, even when the economy was in a major downturn or plunged during a crisis.

In other words, vertical dotted line ① in [Figure 13] is the IMF period, vertical dotted line ③ is the exchange rate during the subprime crisis, and vertical dotted line ⑦ is a dotted line that shows the relationship between the

KOSPI and the housing index during the corona crisis. The exchange rate is always the fastest of the three variables, with peaks at ①, ③, and ⑦.
I.e., the exchange rate is the leading variable. Stock prices fall a little later or even faster than the spike in the exchange rate. At the bottom, you can see that the housing index falls slightly later than the exchange rate each time, that is, 6 months later. So far, we've validated the Diamond Dollar methodology and its results.

This is an investment technique that can multiply your assets 8x in a short period of time by investing in a Dollar Swapping between two assets, stocks and apartments, in a normal economy, i.e. an inflationary economy.

In other words, it can be seen that the investment method for investing in financial assets when the dollar is the most expensive should be completely different from the investment technique when the dollar is the cheapest.

[Figure 13] and [Figure 15] show that there is actually an inverse relationship between the dollar and other assets, as shown in the diamond dollar investment diagrams in [Figure 16] and [Figure 17].

In times of economic crisis, whether it's a general economic downturn, a foreign exchange crisis, or a financial crisis, the dollar always goes up and stocks and apartments go down in response.

Summarizing these facts
"In this book, I derive, theorize, and publish the principles of the Assets Market Rotation Investing Formula, I.e, by using the Pentagon Investing Method, Only Dollar Swapping for 800% Profit."

The subtitle of the book is Tears of Japan 'Why everyone who invests in stocks or apartments for the long term is doomed in the end?' i.e. Long term investment in stocks and apartments ruins everyone.

With this swap investment technique, you can dramatically increase your wealth by up to 8 times by Dollar Swapping between stocks and apartments in 3 steps.

The Pentagon Investing Method's 5-Step Rotational Investment Cycle Pattern is Stocks → Apartments → Dollars → Savings → Government Bonds. Thus fintech process is always the same. This is according to Market Cycle Investing Formula first thing in the world!

It doesn't matter if it's a short term deflation, a long term deflation, or a financial crisis, Pentagon investing Method must always adopted the outside of the United State.

Chapter 14) The Diamond Wealth Dichotomy

Traditionally, the assets trichotomy has been said as a way to protect wealth. The idea is that by dividing your wealth into real estate, stocks, and deposits, you can protect the safety, profitability, and liquidity of your wealth at the same time.

The asset trichotomy is the most popular traditional method of wealth preservation, meaning that dividing your wealth between 33% real estate, 33% stocks, and 33% savings will preserve your wealth because it will remain safe, profitable, and highly liquid.

Currently, South Koreans probably keep more than 90% of their wealth in real estate and less than 10% in stocks or savings.

South Korea is the 7th country to join the 3050 club and is now a real developed country.

In developed countries, the share of financial assets in wealth portfolios increases. This is known as the "Money Move" to financial assets, which usually happens every 10 years or more. Statistics show that people move into financial assets until they have as much as their age.

At the age of 70, 70% of assets are composed of financial assets, which is the asset portfolio of citizens in developed countries. Since Korea is currently in the midst of a prolonged deflationary period, we have a golden opportunity to organize our wealth portfolio in a developed country style. Simply holding on to the old assets trichotomy or dichotomy to preserve wealth only works in an inflationary economy.

It is important to note that in a Long Term Deflation, wealth in real assets such as real estate, gold, silver, etc. will be automatically transferred to holders of cash assets through a process of collapse.
People often talk about whether it's harder to make money or keep money. The new Diamond Dollar assets Dichotomy is a way for someone with $500 billion or trillions to maintain 100% of their assets without no loss and permantly.

There is one more assets dichotomy that the author created by applying the principles of the Diamond Dollar Investing Method and traditional wealth preservation methods.

This is the theory that you can protect your assets by dividing your assets into two equal parts: real estate and cash, stocks, or savings. This traditional assets dichotomy is not a very popular assets preservation method because it is not very useful.

Diamond assets dichotomy:

The author's original assets dichotomy of 50% dollars + 50% other assets requires a different name than the traditional assets dichotomy. To avoid confusion, we'll call it the Diamond assets dichotomy. It is a assetsh preservation method that allows you to keep 100% of your assets forever, no matter what, by splitting your wealth between 50% dollars and 50% other individual wealth or the sum of individual wealth. This method only works 100% of the time in inflationary economies and short term deflationary periods.

It should never be followed in a long term deflation, because in a long term deflation, both the dollar and wealth will collapse.

It is only useful in a short term deflation, i.e., in a normal economy, where you allocate your wealth 50% to dollars and 50% to preserved wealth according to the basic principles of the Diamond Dollar Investing Method. This is because the dollar is inversely correlated to assets such as real estate and stocks.

Preserving wealth, that is, building wealth in both normal times and short term deflation, is very simple and straightforward if you follow the Diamond Dollar

Dichotomy.

Of course, wealth preservation using the Diamond Dollar Dichotomy does not work for people and countries that use the dollar as their everyday currency, so the Diamond Dollar Investing Method does not work in the United States.

Knowing this Diamond wealth dichotomy, it is easy to see that between build and keep wealth, keep is by far the more difficult. This is because keep wealth is so perfectly and simply secured by the Diamond Dollar dichotomy.

The four most common safe havens are gold, the dollar, the franc, and the yen. A safe haven is an asset that investors favor when the value of their wealth is not secure, i.e. when asset markets are unstable. With the price of gold so high right now, people seem to favor it as a safe haven. However, the price of gold will eventually fall sharply in the face of long term deflation.

It is important to note that in an inflationary economy, i.e., in a short term deflationary period, the Diamond Dollar Dichotomy is still applicable, but in a long term deflationary period lasting more than five years, such as in Japan, the Diamond Dollar Dichotomy will not be as powerful, because in a long term deflationary period, the dollar and all wealth will collapse together.

The Diamond Dollar Dichotomy protects 100% of your wealth, but it doesn't increase it, so it's a good wealth preservation method if you're choosing between the build and keep methods.

Whether it's a short term deflation or a long term deflation, cash is the king of deflation. It can be cash itself or cash equivalents. There are cash and cash equivalents, such as the Macquarie Infrastructure Fund and government bonds, that can generate income. Housing annuities are a traditional cash equivalent investment that can be better than cash.

More recently, there have been a number of other inverse ETF products, including KODEX Inverse ETFs, as well as Treasuries, gold, and grains. There are also inverse ETFs for grains, crude oil, and the U.S dollar, which can be utilized to profit from a prolonged deflationary period when all prices fall.

Before the creation of inverse ETFs, there was really nothing to invest in during deflation. Stocks, apartments, gold, crude oil, and anything else of value plummeted in price, and now like institutions, the average person could short sell.

It's no exaggeration to say that there was no way to react in past. The only way to protect your wealth was to sell.

So, let's take a look at some of the best investments to make when deflation hits, whether it was a short or long deflation.

I'm going to introduce you to some goods that are more likely to grow your wealth than preserve it.
These products are useful for investing in short term deflation. They are much more profitable in the long term deflation. This is because interest rates, for example, are expected to fall for a long time.

After "Powell's mistake(the author refers to Powell's expected mistake in dealing with inflation, in reference to Volcker's mistake)", the price of Macquarie Infrastructure Fund and government bonds will spontaneously jump to the sky, depending on the rate of interest rate cut, as interest rates will continue to fall a lot for the next 30 years or more, just like Japan lost 30 years during the long term deflation.

It is important to remember that government bond rates in Japan and other Western countries have even gone to negative rates.

Chapter 15) How to multiply your wealth by 2~8 times in a short period of time using only Dollar Swap Fintech

This chapter introduces the core of the book: a specific investment technique that allows you to invest your dollars for a short period of time and multiply your wealth by 2~8 times. It is a new FinTech technique and the core dollar investment technique of the Dollar Swapping.

By swapping U.S dollars for other assets for a short period of time, you can earn 2~8 times your investment.
It can be done in any country except the United States. Short term deflation, i.e., investing in the U.S dollar during a deflationary period in the normal course of a business cycle, to make 2~8 times your assets in a short period of time.

The following graph [Figure 18] shows the relationship between the Korean won-dollar exchange rate and the Korean KOSPI index over a 42 year period, starting on January 1, 1982.

Since the graphs have the same starting date and are equally spaced in time, you can draw a vertical dotted line anywhere on the graph to find the KOSPI at the same date for the Korean won-dollar exchange rate.

Dollar Swapping fintech tips from an expat:

Let's analyze the two cases separately: a Korean investing in Korea and an American investing in Korea during the crisis. First, let's look at the case of investing in Korea.

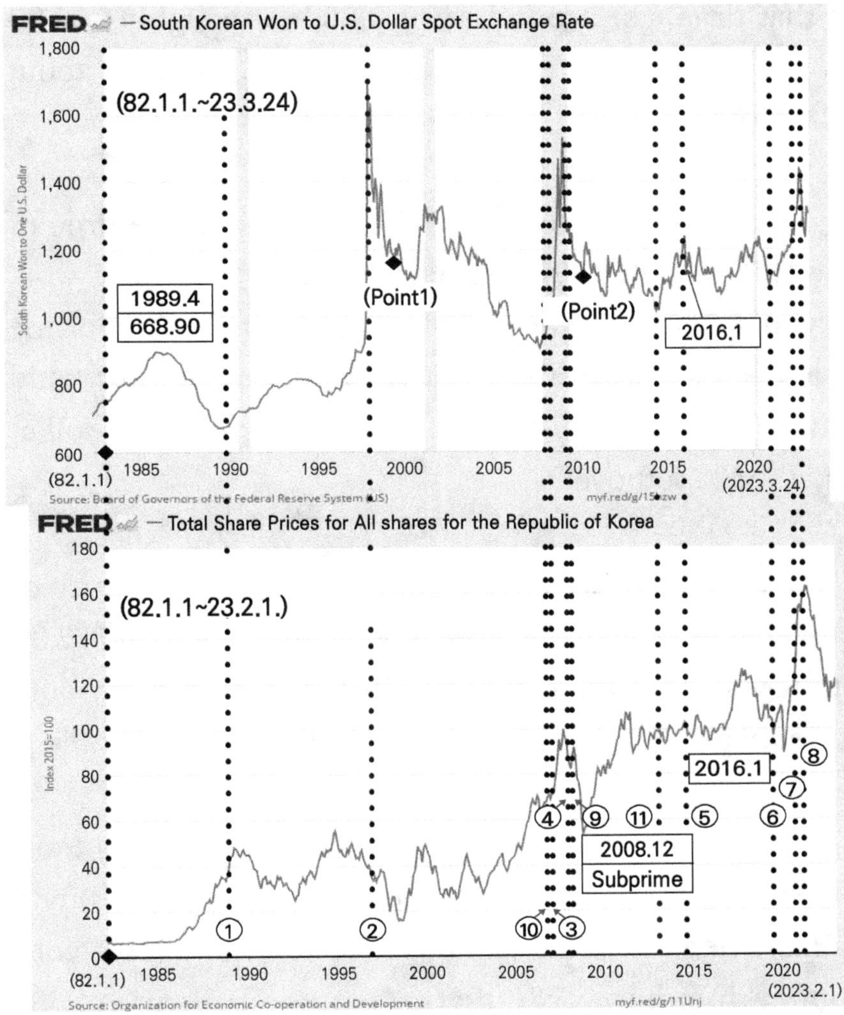

[Figure 18] Relationship between the Korean won-dollar over 42 years(1982.1.1.~2023.3.24.) and the KOSPI index over 42 years(1982.7.1.~2023.2.1.).

1) Buying dollars when they are cheapest and selling them when they are most expensive will usually double your money. The vertical dotted lines in [Figure 18] show the relationship between the dollar price and the KOSPI market on the same day.

Let's look at vertical dotted line ① first. The exchange rate at that time, i.e., around April 1989, was roughly 668.90 won, i.e., the lowest price of the dollar in Korea for about 33 years.

Vertical dotted line ② shows the situation at the time of the IMF in Dec. 1997, when the dollar was at 1,695 won. If you simply bought dollars at the vertical dotted line ① and sold them at the vertical dotted line ②, you would have earned (1,695-669.40)=1,025.60 won per dollar. That's 153% left over.

Next, if you bought a dollar at the October 2007 price of 903.20 at the vertical dotted line ⑩ and sold it at 1,372,30 at the vertical dotted line ⑪ in February 2009, you would have made 469.10 per dollar, or 52% profit.

2) If you take a dollar loan when the dollar is at its most expensive, exchange it in Korean won, and then buy a dollar when the dollar calms down, you can double your money. In other words, if you take a dollar loan at 1,695 won when the dollar is at its most expensive, exchange it,

and make a deposit, as shown in vertical dotted line ② in [Figure 18].

Even if you don't consider the interest on the deposit, you can draw a deposit at the time of vertical dotted line ⑩, i.e. 903.20 won, buy a dollar, and pay it back.

When the dollar is at its most expensive price, ③, you take out a dollar loan and convert it to KRW. Then, when the dollar is cheapest, i.e. at the price of ⑪, you can buy the dollar and pay it back and make a similarly large profit.

3) Naturally, you buy dollars when they are cheapest, i.e. when the vertical dotted line is ① or ⑩, and sell them at the most expensive price as well.

If the price of dollars drops after you exchange them, you only need to buy back as many dollars as you need to repay your dollar loan. This way, you can do Fintech(Financial Technology, financial management) 4 times, and you will have about 4 times the amount of Korean money in your hand.

In fact, this short term dollar investment technique works in any country and in any era. However, it is clear that the country with the best environment to use the dollar investment technique that can multiply your assets by 2~8 times or more in a short period of time is South Korea, which is commonly known as a dollar ATM country.

Investors in Korea, or any country for that matter, can understand investment techniques by comparing the rate of change of the dollar price in your country with the rate of change of your local currency during a financial or economic crisis.

Foreign currency loans are only available in the following base currencies in South Korea: U.S dollar, Japanese yen, euro, Chinese yuan, and British pound, and loans can be made directly in each currency. Loan eligibility may change from time to time.

Sometimes readers complain that their bank won't lend in dollars, but there's always a way to get around this by utilizing dollar ETFs, such as dollar inverse ETFs or leveraged ETFs.

4) Finally, there's the greedier 8x method of investing. In any country, when domestic asset prices are cheapest, the country's stock index is the highest.

This can be seen by looking at the vertical dotted line ① and vertical dotted line ③ in [Figure 18]. This means that buying dollars when the stock index is at its highest is the cheapest way to buy dollars.

If you were a stock trader, you would have been investing in stocks before the vertical dotted lines ① and ③.
By now, you should be investing in government bonds, which is the last stage of the Pentagon Investing method. During this period, the balance of payments is naturally in deficit. However, the economy should now be slowly improving. You can start investing after the economy has gone from a deficit to a surplus in its annual balance of payments about a year ago.

Before investing in stocks, check the reversal day, double-check with the three line break chart, and start investing in the stock market. Investing in Korean stocks or thematic ETFs in industries that are similar to U.S stocks will maximize your returns.

If you start investing after checking these three or four variables, the hit rate is almost 100%. This is because the relationship between the growth of the Korean stock index and the country's balance of payments has been analyzed and compared for about 33 years.

In [Figure 18], we can see that the stock index has risen enough to leave us with about twice as much money as we invested in stocks.

If you sell stocks and buy dollars at vertical lines ① or ③, and then sell dollars at vertical lines ② or ⑨, when the dollar peaks, you will make the most money trading dollars. If you do the math, you'll make about twice as much as the stock index between vertical lines ② and ③.

Again, we can make a profit from the drop in the price of the dollar in the period between vertical lines ③ and ⑨. If we borrow an random amount of money from the vertical dotted line ⑨(we assume the same amount here) and pay it back around ⑪, we can earn about twice as much again. So far, we can see that the total return is 2×2×2=8x.

What would happen if you invested in stocks and apartments for the long term without Dollar Swapping?

1) Since you don't rotate your investments in stocks, apartments, dollars, deposits, and government bonds in five steps according to the market cycle, the leading stocks and leading apartments, which have risen by 4~20 times in about 3~4 years during the great bull market, fall by 50~90% from their peak prices according to the leading stock theory.

Eventually, stocks and apartments return to below par levels. Due to excessive greed, investors often use leverage to invest even more at the peak, resulting in negative returns.

2) The achievable profit, depending on the Dollar Swap,

is giving up about 800%. Therefore, if you do not rotate according to the market cycle cyclical investing formula, but simply invest long term in leading stocks or leading apartments, you expect to get rich, but you will be completely ruined. The outcome varies significantly depending on whether you're a U.S resident or a non-US resident: unless you're swapping with the dollar, you'll be doubly screwed, and almost everyone will be screwed.

Swapping fintech for Americans when other countries are in crisis:

Now let's look at how an American can invest in a crisis in other country for a short period of time.

1) U.S residents who use the dollar as their everyday currency can simply take out a loan in their home country and bring the dollars to the crisis country.
Upon arrival, exchange them for the local currency and sign up for a savings account, which will already have a higher interest rate.

Depending on the degree of the crisis, it's been our experience that the higher dollar prices usually settle down within a year or a few months, or fall back to near normal levels.
At that time, you can withdraw your savings, exchange them for dollars, and send them back to your home country to redeem the loan. This is basically a dollar investment

technique that will give you about a 2x capital gains return.

2) Since the world has been experiencing a long term deflation since January 2016(vertical dotted line ⑤), you can make even greater profits by investing the dollar in crisis government bonds during the long term deflation. This is because interest rates in crisis countries will continue to fall.

Japan's interest rates have a long history of falling to negative rates after a long period of deflation. When a long term deflation begins, domestic asset prices fall steadily. I'll explain later that using this to simply buy and sell dollars can yield between 52% and 153%.
If there is a crisis in another country, a Dollar Swapping fintech for Americans living in the U.S is to bring the dollars into the country when they are at their most expensive and then sell them.

Then, when the dollar price comes back to normal, you can buy dollars and send them back home to redeem the loan.

Alternatively, a very simple investment technique is to borrow in dollars directly from the country in crisis, exchange them, deposit them in a savings account for a couple of years, and then buy back the dollars when the price has normalized. Financial crises come about once a decade, approximately, so you have a chance to make a lot of money once a decade.

In normal times, the dollar is almost unchanged, so it's not an investment for the average person. There are some people who do FX margin trading(a system where brokerages allow individuals to buy and sell dollars with 10x leverage for a small amount of margin), but it is extremely risky and is not recommended.

Next, you need to think about the payback period of your dollar investments, which is very important because if the payback period is too long, it will not be an efficient investment. We will discuss in detail the different recovery periods of the dollar price in different countries and crises in [Chapter 18].

Chapter 16) How to tell when the dollar is rising and when it's falling

The dollar is normally like a calm sea wave. It barely moves, so it's not something you'd normally pay attention to, and certainly not something you'd invest in.

However, in times of financial crisis, the dollar becomes the most attractive asset, i.e., in normal times, the dollar has only a cash function, but in times of crisis, it has an additional and most important property function.

It's not easy to guess when the dollar will surge and when it will crash. No, like stocks, no one can predict it. However, history has taught us that the dollar will surge when
1) When a country faces a foreign exchange or financial crisis, such as the IMF crisis in South Korea. South Korea and North Korea are facing each other. In other words, a war crisis is included.
2) An economic crisis in the U.S, such as the 9·11 terrorist attacks or the 2008 subprime crisis, is large enough to affect the global economy.
3) After a major rise in a country's stock market or apartment market, i.e. when a price bubble bursts.

It is believed that the mainstream uptrend that began in

May 2017 was preceded by a mainstream downtrend that began with the stock market decline in June 2021. The author has applied KTB Investment Securities' nearly 30 years of research into the pattern of the Korean stock market's major rallies and predicted that June 2021 will be the time of the stock market's major downturn. As it turns out, the timing was spot on.

To summarize the findings of our analysis of trend By rising and trend falling patterns in a nutshell, lead stocks rise for about three to four years, with a maximum of 4~20x. Because ETFs have only been around since 2002, the results of thematic ETFs have not been studied separately, but they are likely to perform a bit more weakly than lead stocks.

The last major bull run lasted about 4 years, as the subprime financial crisis in 2008 and the coronavirus outbreak in 2020 unleashed massive amounts of dollar funding.

When a crisis strikes, the price of the dollar, which has been calm, begins to surge. From then on, outside of the United States, in any country and in any time period, it is possible to make a windfall of 2~8x on a dollar investment.

We're used to hearing in the news that being a foreign

exchange dealer is a dream job, the best paying job, etc. The truth is, it's easy to get rich if you're a foreign exchange trader, whether you're working for a bank or an individual investor, as long as you predict the price of the dollar correctly.

Foreign exchange dealers trade billions to tens of billions of dollars every day. Therefore, they are primarily concerned with "today's" exchange rate, which means that their future predictions are weak. They make or lose money in seconds.

But as we know, they are a team that forecasts and trades on a yearly basis. I say "team" because I expect many investors to follow the trading techniques in this book.

Now you just need to know when to buy and sell the dollar. It's not easy to time this, but there are a few tips.
First of all, you should be aware of the usual pattern of rising and falling markets.

In other words, the stock market usually rises for 3~4 years, and then one day something happens, like a financial crisis, that causes stocks to plummet and exchange rates to soar.

The start date of the current bull market was judged to be May 2017, so if the bull market is 3 years old, it will be June 2020, and if it is 4 years old, it will be June 2021. You should always keep a close eye on the stock market in the 3rd or 4th year of a major bull market. In this case, June 2021 is the time for a major bear market due to the money released by the subprime crisis in 2008 and the coronavirus crisis in 2020.

Although the period predicting method has already predicted a major stock market downturn, we need to double-check the time to buy or sell with the reversal day method.

In a nutshell, the reversal day trading approach is to look at the three days or so after a stock's trading volume explodes and a major stock index begins to move more than 1.5% per day as a time to buy or sell.

A reversal day is a day when the stock market begins a major downward trend or a major upward trend, and on this day, there are large fluctuations in stock prices along with large fluctuations in stock indices, indicating that the trend has changed.

This large volume of trading and huge fluctuations in the stock price will tell everyone that this is the day of the reversal(=reversal day).

In other words, you can't predict the reversal day in

advance. Just like you can't predict the price. It's a simple matter of following the market as it notifies you.

The reversal day also tells us when the dollar price will start to rise or fall. Changes in the exchange rate are always the leading variables when compared to stock prices.

Try to identify and analyze the causes of dollar price fluctuations within 1~3 days of the estimated reversal day. Of course, you need to get information from TV news, newspapers, etc. and interpret or synthesize the information yourself.

It's better not to trust the government or experts when it comes to predicting future prices. You should always assume that they have a hidden goal. Also, they always give short term forecasts. What we need is the price in about two years after.

In Korea, this is even more often the case, so you have to rely mainly on foreign sources. In the first place, the so-called experts are there to comment after the fact, they are not forecasters, and in most cases, they have a self-interest in predicting prices.

Therefore, you need to draw your own conclusions, i.e. follow them to their logical conclusion. If you believe that the reason for the price change is valid, you should start buying or selling stocks or dollars within one to three days. This is the day you will sell or buy the stock, and this is the day you will take the dollar loan or repay the dollar loan. By following this tip from the market, you will simply outperform the predictions of all the experts, not just the banks.

This technique can be applied to all asset price movements, including apartments, oil, gold, and more, by identifying the start of a major uptrend in stocks or the start of a major downtrend and the start of a rebound. It has a hit rate of 80~90%. It is especially useful when investing in stocks. Even the world-famous Mr.Big Investor and Goldman Sachs, not to mention banks, can't predict the reversal day . That's because you don't know until it happens, and you can only judge it after it happens. At least this is fair in the market. They're all unpredictable⋯.

The reversal day trading method is very reliable.
On another note, these days you shouldn't make the foolish mistake of running to the bank to buy or sell dollars, because you can buy and sell dollar-related ETFs that are already listed on the stock market and waiting for you. You can do the same by using HTS to trade from the comfort of your home.

These dollar ETFs are brand new funds. When you buy or sell dollar cash from a bank, you have to pay a round-trip fee of about 5% to the bank. With dollar ETFs, the round-trip fee is less than 1%.

However, all ETF products, except for pure domestic equity ETFs such as KODEX200 and TIGER 200, are subject to a 15.4% dividend income tax on profits.

Since they are not regular stocks, they are not taxed on capital gains tax yet. As for foreign ETFs, all but a few are subject to dividend or capital gains taxes of 15.4% to 22%. The decision is a matter of convenience and cost.

I'm not an economist, a former foreign exchange trader, or a securities expert, so some people may not trust what I have to say. But I've been investing for 50 years, and I've been writing books and keeping a close eye on things for about 30 years.

In short, the author is not a celebrity who has made tens of billions in newspaper or magazine ads. However, don't be fooled by the hype. The same goes for auctions. No one should be fooled by all the hype out there.

Chapter 17) Differences in exchange rate movements from country to country and crisis to crisis

We'll look at specific data on exchange rates, interest rates, and stock prices during South Korea's IMF period, as well as how they changed during Japan's June 1996 quasi IMF crisis, Japan's deflationary economy, and the U.K's Brexit to see how much the dollar has risen and fallen.

If you know all these records, you can take advantage of this data in the upcoming crisis. We've already explained in detail how you can earn 2~8x returns by simply investing in the dollar.

Let's take a look at a) South Korea's 1997 IMF crisis and 2008 financial crisis, b) Japan's 1998 quasi IMF crisis and financial crisis, and c) Brexit in 2016 and how long it took for the dollar to recover.

1) South Korea's IMF days

December 3, 1997: South Korea's key economic indicators at the time of the IMF bailout are summarized below [Table 2].

November 22, 1997: The dollar was at 1,060 won, the KOSPI was at 580 points, and the bank's lending rate was 14.85%.

November 30, 1997: The dollar price, KOSPI index, and interest rate are 1,163 won, 407 points, and 17.46% respectively. There is a significant change in the data that someone might have noticed.

November 22, 1997: Over the next week or so, lending rates jumped by about 3%, the exchange rate appreciated by 100 won, and the KOSPI plummeted by 180 points.

December 23, 1997: In just one month, the dollar price, KOSPI index, and interest rate reached 1,950 won, 366 points, and 25.43%, respectively.

Dates	Loan Rates	Base Rate	KOSPI
1997.11.22. (Normal)	14.85%	1,060 won	580
1997.11.30.	17.46%	1,163 won	407
1997.12.23.	25.43%	**1,950** won	366.36
1997.12.24.	27.86%	1,810 won	351.45
1997.12.26.	31.43%	1,490 won	375.15
1997.12.27.	34.43%	1,490 won	376.31
1997.12.29.	36.29%	1,400 won	376.31
1997.12.30.	37.43%	1,600 won	376.31
1997.12.31.	38.86%	1,680 won	376.31
1998.01.31.	29.00%	1,500 won	567.38
1998.02.28.	26.00%	1,630 won	558.98
1998.12.30.	12.14%	1,120.50 won	562.46
1999.06.30.	10.42%	**1,157.50** won	883
*November 22, 1997 was a normal economic day.			

[Table 2] Interest rates at the time of the IMF. Exchange rates. KOSPI index change

June 30, 1999: About a year and seven months after the dollar's peak, the dollar price, the KOSPI, and the interest rate plummeted to near normal values(1,157 won, 883 points, and 10.42%).

Take a look at the table above to summarize that time.

Comparing November 22, 1997, under normal economic conditions, to December 23, 1997, just after the IMF crisis, the dollar appreciated by 83.9% in just one month, while the KOSPI plummeted by 36.8% during the same period.

Although not shown in the table above, the lowest KOSPI value at the time of the IMF was 277.37 on June 30, 1998. Let's take a closer look at the graph in [Figure 18]. The top graph is a graph of the KRW-dollar exchange rate, and the bottom graph is a graph of the KOSPI's fluctuations as the KRW-dollar exchange rate changes.

In other words, [Figure 18] compares the changes in the KRW-dollar exchange rate and the changes in the KOSPI index from the same point in time, 1982.1.1.

The previous vertical dotted lines ②, ③, and ⑩ show the changes in the KOSPI at the same point in time due to the changes in the exchange rate at the time of Korea's IMF in 1997. Since the starting point of both graphs is 1982.1.1., you can draw a vertical dotted line anywhere on the graph to see the KOSPI index corresponding to the Korean won-dollar exchange rate on that day.

Briefly, the first vertical dotted line ② is around the end of December 1997, when the dollar was at its highest price at the time of the IMF.
The KOSPI figure below this vertical dotted line shows the KOSPI index at the end of the month in the same year. According to [Table 2], the dollar price and the KOSPI index were 1,680 won/376.31 points each.

The top graph in [Figure 18], the black diamond(point 1), is around the end of October 2000, when the first sharp decline in the dollar price ended as the IMF crisis calmed down. At the end of October, the dollar price and the KOSPI were around 1,139 won/509.23 points.

The vertical dotted lines ②, ④, and ⑧ show that when the dollar is at its highest, the KOSPI always plummets near its lowest. Conversely, when the dollar price was at its lowest, the KOSPI rebounded sharply to a new high when the dollar is at its lowest.

At the end of October 2007, about 10 years after the IMF crisis and just before the subprime financial crisis, the dollar price was 903 won. This is about the time of vertical dotted line 3 in [Figure 18].

Although the price of the dollar has fallen from the peak of the vertical dotted line ②, when the dollar price surged, there is still a large difference in domestic asset prices from before the IMF crisis. However, it has come down a lot from the peak price.

Without the subprime crisis that started around 2007, the dollar would have theoretically fallen to where it was before the IMF situation. We all know that the subprime crisis sent the dollar back up before it could normalize.

In any case, it took nearly a decade for the dollar to return to its normal exchange rate after the IMF spike.

For about a decade, South Korea went through a process of dollar depreciation to reach a normalized dollar price, during which asset markets responded to the decline in the dollar price by increasing their prices.

The vertical dotted line in [Figure 18] shows that the stock market index is near its peak as the dollar price is almost back to normal. This means that it is safe to invest in the asset market according to the Diamond Dollar Invesing Method.

Next,
The dollar price spike during the 2008 subprime financial crisis lasted about one year and four months,

from October 2007 to February 2009. This is the period between vertical dotted lines ③ and ⑨ in [Figure 18].

After the subprime crisis, the dollar price has returned to its normal price, as shown by the vertical dotted line ⑪, just as the dollar price recovered after the IMF crisis. However, we can also see that the dollar has not yet returned to its pre-crisis price.

This is because the coronavirus outbreak started again in March 2020 before the dollar price could return to normal prices.

Conclusion,
It took 10 years for the dollar to crash and recover from the IMF crisis, and 5.6 years for the dollar to return to its normal price after the subprime crisis.

Korea's IMF situation officially ended after three years and nine months when the last bailout balance of 140$ million was repaid on August 23, 2001. It can be seen that the decline in the dollar price during the subprime financial crisis and the recovery period were smaller and shorter than during the IMF.

2) During the Korean subprime in 2008

Let's take a closer look at the Korean financial market during the 2008 U.S subprime crisis using the graphs of the relationship between the Korean won-dollar exchange rate over 42 years(1982.1.1.~2023.3.24.) and the KOSPI index over 42 years(1982.7.1.~2023.2.1.) in [Figure 18].

In 2008, the subprime situation in the U.S worsened, and by the end of February 2009, the price of the U.S dollar and the KOSPI rose sharply and the KOSPI fell sharply, as shown by the vertical dotted line in [Figure 18].

The graph shows that at the end of February 2009, the dollar was at 1,532.80 won and the KOSPI was at 1,063.03 points.

Also, by August 2014, when the subprime crisis is considered to have subsided, the vertical dotted line ⑪ shows that the dollar, which surged during the subprime crisis, plummeted and the KOSPI surged.

During the 2008 subprime financial crisis, the dollar surged 77.6% in a year and four months, while the KOSPI plummeted 49.5% over the same period.

The vertical dotted line in ⑩ shows that the KOSPI was near its peak at 2,070.86 points at the time, which means that the KOSPI is always at its highest when the dollar is at its lowest.

3) Japan's Quasi IMF days in 1998

In 1998, Japan faced the same IMF crisis as South Korea. In June 1996, the Nikkei and the dollar were at 22,530/109.48 yen, but on June 15, 1998, they were at 15,830/150 yen.

[Figure 19] Changes in the yen-dollar and Nikkei indices between June 1996 and June 1998.

In other words, in about two years, the dollar surged 37% and the Nikkei plummeted 29.7%. The graph [Figure 19] shows the situation in Japan at the time.

This is valuable data because it shows that Japan, the world's second largest economy at the time, saw its stocks rise and fall as the dollar rose and fell.

In 1998, if Japan hadn't worked with the U.S government to hold the yen at 130 yen from 150 yen just before the IMF crisis, Japan would have been in the same IMF situation as us, and the price of the dollar would have nearly doubled.

4) During the Japanese subprime in 2008)

As shown in [Table 3], Japan experienced a 10.6% drop in the dollar and a 51.6% drop in the Nikkei index during the subprime crisis, unlike Korea's surge in the dollar.

Date	Yen rate	Nikkei 225 Index
October 30, 2007	111.02 yen	16,785Point
Early March 2009	99.15yen(10.6%▼)	8,109Point(51.6%▼)
December 2009	93.08yen	10,546Point

[Table 3] Japan during the 2008 subprime financial crisis

What we need to understand from [Table 3] is why the movements of the dollar and the KOSPI index in South Korea and the dollar and the Nikkei 225 index in Japan during the 2008 U.S financial crisis were different.

In other words, in a country like Japan, where there is a long term deflation, the exchange rate and the Nikkei always move in the same direction even during economic crises, which means that the Diamond Dollar investment method does not apply. You should always keep this in mind.

Japan's stock market index, which plummeted in 2008 due to the subprime crisis, recovered to 16,173 points in October 2014, seven years later, and the yen also began to recover after more than seven years, with the full implementation of Abenomics at 112 yen in October 2014.

5) Next, the UK's Brexit(June 23, 2016)

On the day the U.K voted to leave the European Union(Brexit), the pound fell by about 4% against the dollar and the FTSE 100 U.K stock index fell by about 6%. Check out this graph to see how the pound plummeted.

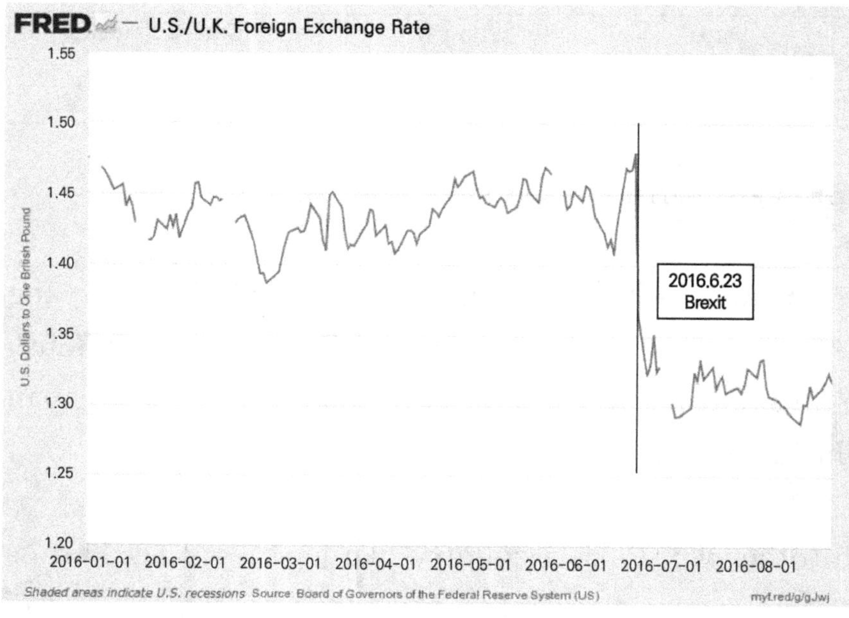

[Figure 20] Dollar-Pound exchange rate plunge on June 23, 2016, at the time of Brexit

Since the Brexit vote, the pound has fallen about 12% against the dollar since the end of 2017.
This means that within the UK, the dollar has surged by 12%, and luxury real estate in the U.K has fallen by an average of 12.5% at the end of 2017.

On average, real estate in global cities has risen about 56% over the past decade, driven by money released by the subprime crisis.

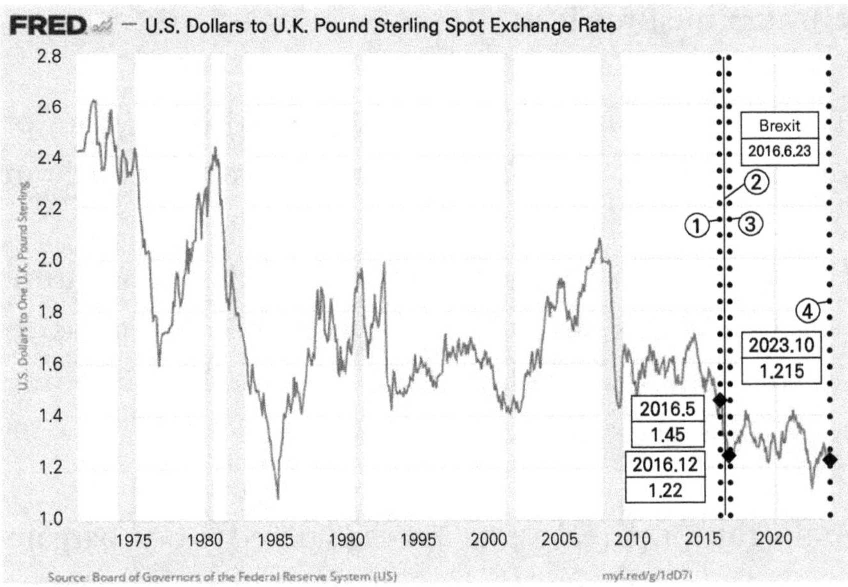

[Figure 21] Brexit and the price of the pound(1971.1.4.~2023.12.29.)

However, only London real estate has been hit by the Brexit shock. U.K stocks have also plummeted in roughly proportion to the dollar's rise.

A detailed graph of the FTSE 100 is not readily available, so we'll just give you the numbers for the day, but you can probably guess from history that it will be inversely correlated to the dollar's movements.

[Figure 21] on the previous page is a long term graph of the dollar-pound exchange rate, which shows how the rate plummeted from 1£=1.45$ in May 2016(vertical dotted line ① in [Figure 21]) before the Brexit decision to 1£=1.22$ in October 2016(vertical dotted line ② in [Figure 21]) after the Brexit.

The vertical dotted line ② in [Figure 21] is the date of Brexit, June 23, 2016. This can be seen more clearly in [Figure 20].
Considering what will happen to the U.K in the future when the crisis subsides and the economy returns to normal, the best investments in the world at that time were U.K real estate and financial assets.

At the time, U.K real estate was considered to be a bargain compared to international prices, down 68.5% on average, based on an expected exchange rate gain of about 12.5%+56%(the average increase in international prices), but we can graphically see that the price of the pound as of October 2023, the vertical dotted line in ③ in [Figure 21], is 1.21$, which has not yet recovered its pre-Brexit price of 1.45$.

In other words, the market may be telling us that the U.K is not a good investment going forward, given the pound's lackluster recovery.

In other words, post-Brexit, the U.K may be viewed less favorably than it once was.
However, given that all currencies except the dollar are weaker now, we believe that the U.K will regain its former position when inflation subsides and the dollar turns lower, making it an optimal investment going forward.

Meanwhile, on August 23, 2001, South Korea's IMF debacle was over. Lonestar's acquisition of Korea Exchange Bank after the country's big assets crashed and before the market had recovered is the same as the U.K real estate situation in the wake of Brexit. Lonestar's trading history in South Korea is discussed in detail in [Chapter 20].

Case studies in several countries have shown that economic crises caused by temporary shocks usually calm down and return to normal within three years.

If the crisis originates from the country's own foreign exchange crisis or economic crisis, such as the IMF crisis in Korea in 1997 and the subprime financial crisis in 2008, the quasi-IMF crisis in Japan in 1998, and Brexit in the United Kingdom in 2016, the phenomenon of plummeting stock prices and surging dollar prices will surely appear.

This is important for everyone because it means that if a country faces a foreign exchange crisis or economic crisis, regardless of whether it is a developed or developing country, the dollar price will surge and the country's asset market will suffer a major crash, just like Korea in 1997 and 2008, Japan in 1998, or the U.K's Brexit in 2016.

More importantly, not only does the price of the dollar spike in crisis countries, but once the crisis subsides, the price of the dollar returns to its original level within a short period of time. This means that you need to take advantage of the ups and downs of the market to find good investment opportunities with Dollar Swapping trades.

There are no research papers by academics or professional research organizations that have analyzed and studied in detail the causes and consequences of the different effects of crises in different countries.

Even in Japan, which was in the midst of a long term deflation when Korea's IMF situation was imminent [Figure 19], the yen-dollar and Nikkei index movements between June 1996 and June 1998 were normal.

However, as we saw above, during the subprime period, the exchange rate and the Nikkei index moved in the same direction, which means that the diamond dollar investment method does not apply.

Even if we are in the middle of the same long term deflation, economic indicators will behave differently depending on the intensity of the crisis. You should always keep this in mind. Depending on the intensity and type of financial crisis, the dollar's resilience and recovery period will vary from country to country.

Chapter 18) Recovery Periods of Dollar Prices by Country and Crisis

The world has been growing through a financial or economic crisis about every 10 years. During these times, the price of the dollar fluctuates.

The international dollar also fluctuates, but the price of domestic assets in countries with small foreign exchange reserves or exposed to crises can rise and fall by up to 80 to 90 percent.

South Korea, in particular, has become a dollar ATM(automated teller machine) country for foreigners due to the abundant liquidity of the dollar and the freedom to move in and out of the country.

Korea is a manufacturing-based country that relies on overseas trade for about 70% of its income and imports and exports almost all of its products, so it can be seen as a reflection of overseas booms and busts.

Short term Dollar Swapping investments, where you swap stocks for dollars, can be a great way to invest your money. It's a simple and straightforward investment technique that's far too reliable to generate 100%+ returns in a short period of time.

It's safe and easy because you're not predicting the dollar's movements in advance like you would with FX margin trading, but rather following the dollar's movements and starting to invest.

To put it more harshly, Dollar Swapping is an investment method in which you don't pay any attention to dollar FinTechs during normal times, but only invest in dollars during crises, and then withdraw your dollar when normal economic conditions come back and wait for the next crisis.

First of all, by checking the recovery of the dollar price in each country during the crisis, you can determine the payback period of the average dollar investment, i.e., how long it takes to realize a profit.

December 3, 1997. The IMF and the subprime crisis in South Korea:

It seems logical that those investing in dollars would be in a good position in the short term. [Figure 18] is a valuable graph showing the relationship between the Korean won-dollar over 42 years(1982.1.1.~2023.3.24.) and the KOSPI over 42 years(1982.7.1.~2023.2.1.).

[Figure 13] is an important figure in which the author

combines three graphs into one so that you can see the relationship between the KRW and the KOSPI and the housing index at the same time for 42 years. Note that the start date of the housing index graph at the bottom is already 6 months lagged.

The author's source for the graph is Federal Reserve Economic Data(FRED) from the Federal Reserve Bank of St. Louis, so it's 100% accurate.

[Figure 13] is a graph that artificially dates the start of the housing index to July 1, 1982, so that the Korean exchange rate and the KOSPI stock index have a six month lag.

This is a very useful graph because if you draw a vertical dotted line anywhere on the graph, you can see the KOSPI index on the date corresponding to the dotted line, the KRW exchange rate on the same date, and the housing index six months later than the KRW exchange rate and the KOSPI index.

Let's have a look at [Figure 18].
The vertical dotted line ② in December 1997 was the IMF situation in South Korea, and the period from then to normal dollar prices took 10 years and 2 months to reach the vertical dotted line ⑩ in October 2007. However, during the first crash in April 2000, the recovery period to the vertical dotted line ① took 1 year and 7 months.

Also, the vertical dotted line in February 2009 shows the situation during the subprime financial crisis. We can see that it took 5 years and 6 months for the dollar to retrace to the vertical dotted line ⑪ in August 2014. The recovery to the point ② in April 2010 took about 1 year and 2 months. As you can see from the graph, there are plenty of profits to be made by closing crosses in the middle of moderate dips.

U.K during the Brexit in 2016:

As shown in [Figure 21], the pound plummeted during the UK's Brexit vote on June 23, 2016, and hasn't fully recovered as of November 2023.

Japan's quasi IMF days in 1998:

As shown in [Figure 19], it took 24 years for Japan's domestic asset prices to return to near normalized prices. We can see that it takes a long time for the dollar price to normalize after a sharp rise in such a short period of time. In Japan's case, it is believed to be the result of long term deflation, which is the result of a long term decline in the price of the dollar.

The results of this case-by-case study show that the impact of a financial or economic crisis will be different for each country, but the period of time for the dollar price to return to normal is roughly one year and two months to one year and seven months.

In other words, the payback period for our diamond dollar investment technique is only about one year and seven months at most. If we allow for a full normalization of the dollar price, the return on investment will be even worse, which means that it is more efficient to withdraw the investment around the first retracement of the dollar price.

In fact, from a bank's perspective, the dollars they hold don't contribute much to their bottom line in normal times. They're just sitting in the bank's vault, like a vendor's inventory, waiting to be exchanged by customers indefinitely.

Not to mention that it's profitable for banks to lend them out. So when banks see that the dollar has already risen quite a bit, and they think it's going to rise further, they start lending it to their customers. [Figure 3] shows that if you invested in dollars in Japan, a country with a long term deflation, you would have lost money, not gained it. The price of the dollar has been falling steadily for nearly 30 years.

In January 1971, it cost 357.56 yen to buy a dollar, and in January 2012, 42 years later, it cost 76.34 yen. During this time, the price of the U.S dollar in Japan plummeted by 78.6%.

Since then, with the implementation of Abenomics, the

price of the dollar in Japan has risen again, jumping 91.5% to 146.20 yen in September 2023. As of November 2023, it is now around 151 yen, meaning that the Japanese economy is back to normal thanks to Abenomics.

To summarize, the price of the U.S dollar in Japan has gone from a 78.6% drop to a 91.5% surge, but it still has 59.1% more to go compared to the 1971 peak. Since all commodities such as gold, silver, crude oil, copper, etc. are also proportional to the dollar during a long term deflation, it is obvious that they will also continue to fall at the same time.

Long term deflation is defined as a decline in prices lasting more than three years. If you know what to expect, you can short stocks, apartments, or any other commodity with confidence.

In Japan's case, the long term deflation lasted about 30 years, and the decline in all assets, including the dollar, was 80~90%, which is unimaginable. By studying Japan's long term deflation and knowing this in advance, the rest of the world can short all assets with confidence after the long term deflation hit in January 2016.

Since we can know in advance how the dollar will behave in the event of a long term deflation, we can not only trade gold on FX margin, but also short apartments, which means that dollar inverse ETFs and commodity inverse ETFs such as gold and silver are also good targets.

By analyzing the relationship between domestic assets and asset markets such as stocks, apartments, and gold in times of long term deflation crisis, we can find new ways to invest. By applying this method, you can easily determine whether or not to enter the commodity market and when to buy or sell.

New FinTech. Multiply your wealth by 2 to 8 times by investing in dollars . The project is simply the fact that you can multiply your wealth by 2 to 8 times by buying the dollar when it is cheapest and selling it when it is most expensive.

The entire world, with the exception of Japan, is currently destined for long term deflation and eventually negative interest rates. In this case, dollar funds from the U.S to a more resilient country like Korea could actually earn two to three times as much by extending the duration of their investment in Korean government bonds.

For reference, interest rates in Japan started falling from 8.3% in 1990 and reached 0% in January 2016. Since then, interest rates have been fluctuating between negative and 0%.

If you're bringing in yen, yuan, pound sterling, etc., you'll have to factor in the exchange rate against your home currency, so your returns will vary. Also, keep in mind that countries like Venezuela, Brazil, and Argentina have little resilience to the dollar's collapse during the crisis.

The United Kingdom has also not yet recovered the value of the pound following Brexit. Combining the results from [Chapters 16~18], we can summarize as follows.

1) At the time of the IMF in Korea

Dollar exchange rate surges 83.9%, stock indexes plunge 36.8%, first recovery period for exchange rate takes 1 year and 7 months

2) During the Korean subprime

Exchange rate surges 77.6%, stock index plummets 49.5%, first recovery period for exchange rate takes 1 year and 2 months

3) Similar IMF situation in Japan

Exchange rate surges 37%, Nikkei plunges 29.7%, first recovery period for exchange rate takes 24 years

4) During the Japanese subprime crisis

Exchange rate plunges 10.6%, Nikkei plunges 51.6%, first recovery period for exchange rate takes 7 years

5) Brexit in the U.K

The exchange rate plunged 15.1%, a rate that has yet to be recovered.

In conclusion,
After analyzing the five cases of the three countries above, the results are summarized as follows. In a normal economy, i.e., a short term deflationary economy, the greater the impact of a financial or economic crisis on the economy, the more the exchange rate surges and the stock price falls less than the exchange rate.

In general, the time period for the exchange rate to recover from a sharp decline to the first recovery period is also longer the greater the impact of the financial crisis on the economy, but about 80~90% of the recovery occurs after one year and seven months.

Therefore
1) In a short term deflationary country, if there is a financial or economic crisis, it is a good investment to sell stocks and buy dollars at the same time as a major decline in stock prices. At the very least, you should sell the dollars and buy stocks again after the first recovery period of the exchange rate, which is one year and seven months.

If you sell your stocks at the start of the secondary appreciation of the dollar, you could realize a total gain of about 4x. If you use dollar fintech to buy and sell, you can get up to an 8x gain, as we explained in detail earlier.

2) In a long term deflation, stock indices fall sharply and so should the exchange rate. In addition, it is important to remember that in a long term deflationary situation, the exchange rate and the stock index are proportional.

Therefore, you should never Dollar Swap stocks or real estate, such as apartments, in a country that is experiencing a long term deflation.

In a long term deflation, the exchange rate, stocks, apartments, crude oil, gold, silver, and bitcoin all go down, meaning there are no assets to invest in, except for government bonds and the Macquarie Infrastructure Fund, which continue to rise as interest rates continue to fall.

Chapter 19) Tears of Japan

The time when the Watanabe women were famous in the world's foreign exchange markets was during the period of yen depreciation, or dollar strength, from 2005 to 2007.

That is, from January 2005 to June 2007, about two and a half years of sustained dollar strength. This is when the yen was continuously weakening from 103.5 to 123.4 yen.

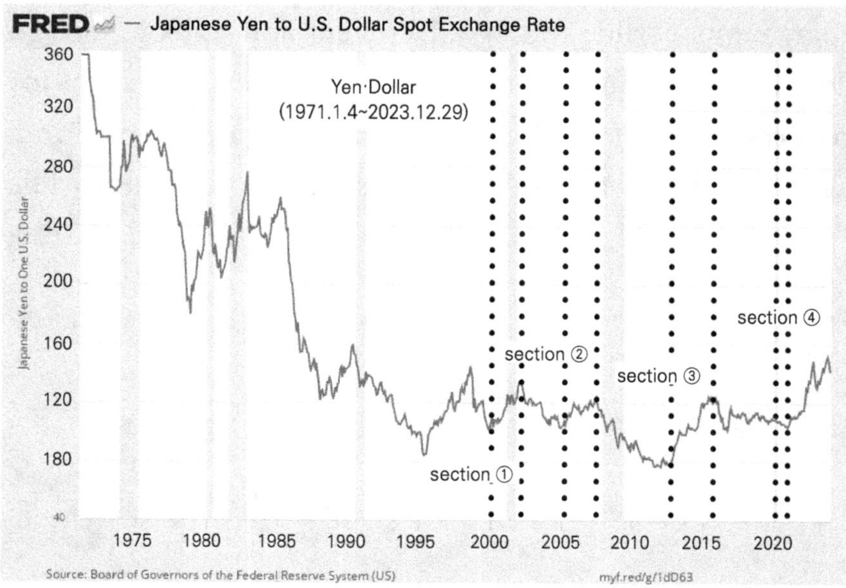

[Figure 22] Yen-Dollar(1971.1.4.~2023.12.29.). Yen-Carry Tradeable Periods ① 2000~2002, ② 2005~2007, ③ 2012~2015, ④ 2021~?

[Figure 22] shows a graph of the Yen-Dollar from January 4, 1971 to December 29, 2023. This shows that the best time to change the yen to dollar was between periods ①(2000~2002) and ②(2005~2007), as well as between periods ③(2012~2015) and ④(2021~?), and while we don't know when the yen carry trade will end, the author believes it will last for quite some time.

Japan was the only country in the world to have a negative government bond rate for eight years until March 19, 2024. In contrast, the U.S. benchmark rate is significantly higher, at 5.5% as of September 2023.

At the time of the Plaza Accord, the price of the yen was around 240 yen. Judging Japan today, we can see that Abenomics has been a great success and Japan has returned to a normal economy. This is discussed in more detail in [Chapter 27].

This is a good time to take advantage of the Yen Carry Trade, which involves borrowing yen with low interest rates and investing in countries with relatively high interest rates and returns.

The first year of these four is the good time to invest overseas. The yen will continue to be more expensive to import than to export. This is because when you bring the yen back into the country, you also make a profit on the exchange rate.

If you also make a profit on your overseas investments during this period, you're in luck.

If you don't invest overseas after converting to dollars and then convert to yen after the dollar drops, you will also make a conversion profit.

On the other hand, if the yen-dollar exchange rate is weak, you will lose money in terms of exchange rate.
In other words, the profit on asset investment and the exchange rate difference will be the total profit. On the graph, this is the four areas above.

During Japan's long term deflation, the yen-dollar exchange rate was almost continuously weakened by Abenomics policies. That's why Mrs. Watanabe's yen-carry trade was possible.

Mrs. Watanabe is the average Japanese investor seeking high yields through cross-border yen carry trades. This time was when the Japanese economy was in the midst of the "lost 20 years," Zero interest rates were long termed, and smart retail investors were looking abroad.

Mrs. Watanabe from Japan, Mrs. Smith from the United States, and Mrs. Sophia from Europe are the protagonists of the Yen-Carry Trade, Dollar-Carry Trade, and Euro-Carry Trade, respectively. And when we say Mrs.

Watanabe, we don't just mean Mrs. Watanabe.

It is a term that is used for both men and women regardless of their actual surname, but mainly because in Japan, like Korea, housewives are responsible for household savings and investments. The word has been around since around 2000. At one point, Mrs. Watanabe's numbered 3 million and accounted for 30% of Japan's foreign exchange market. They mainly sold yen and bought dollars, or U.S Treasury bonds.

This phenomenon can happen anywhere, as long as there is a certain amount of interest rate(yield) differential between countries. After the subprime financial crisis in 2008, dollar carry trades emerged, as well as euro carry trades. However, Mrs. Watanabe's investments, whether they are borrowed from a bank or her own money, are at risk if the yen weakens.

By economic logic, the yen should be weak. It can't be stronger since Japan was the only country to have negative interest rates for eight years until March 2024. Since Abenomics, the yen has remained consistently weak. Abenomics is a success.
In July 2006, Japan held interest rates around 0% while the U.S Fed rapidly raised rates to 5.25%.

The yen-carry trade exploded. The combination of

increased exports to China and a weaker yen against the dollar and a stronger won, like now, caused the exchange rate to plunge to 746.15 won per 100 yen on July 9, 2007.

Right now, as of November 2023, you can still earn more than 5% per year in U.S Treasuries by converting your yen into dollars. However, you should always be aware of the costs involved. The yen-carry trade is still up about 48% from the end of 2021, Bloomberg reported.

As of December 2020, 32 years after December 1988, Japan has emerged from a long term deflation. For 32 years, domestic asset prices fell, meaning that the Japanese yen strengthened over the same period. Will the Japanese yen return to strength in the near future, as many investors predict?

Mr.Big Investor borrowed yen from Japanese banks and invested in the stocks of Japan's five largest conglomerates. Why did he do this? You should think about it before you invest. If the yen strengthen again, the funds invested in Japan will obtain yen-dollar exchange rate profit.

Not surprisingly, the author does not invest in Japan. I think that the Japanese asset market will go up for a long time, but the yen-dollar exchange rate will continue to weaken. I don't think like Mr.Big Investor.

He's not willing to take a loss on the exchange rate to invest in Japan. Let's not forget that the price of the yen went from 260 yen at the time of the Plaza Accord in 1985 to 140 yen overnight.

So why is the yen a safe haven?
I personally disagree. But that's not the reality. Japan has been in a long term deflation for more than 30 years, and even its government bonds had been at negative interest rates.On the contrary, it is the most unstable currency. So the yen should be weak, but the author is, of course, among those who explain its temporary strength in every crisis as a return of Mrs. Watanabe.

The reason for the strength of the yen is that whenever there is even a slight strengthening of the yen due to a financial crisis, these people sell their overseas investments in stocks, bonds, real estate, etc. and come to Japan all at once to buy yen, so that the yen strengthens in times of crisis, i.e., they convert their dollars into yen.

Strong in group logic and groupthink, the Japanese rely on unspoken companionship and word-of-mouth marketing. They flock together in short bursts when profits are made, and they do the same when they get out — the so-called "auntie troops".

At one time they got out of the U.S Treasury market,

returned to their home country, and switched to Japanese government bonds. The price of Japanese government bonds soared. The yen strengthened. At one point, this rendered Abenomics useless.

It is often the case that the yen strengthens out of sync with the fundamentals of an economy. If we look back at the trajectory of the last 30 years since Japan entered a prolonged recession at the beginning of the year 1990, we can see that it was during the Asian financial crisis in 1998 and the global crisis caused by the collapse of Lehman Brothers in 2008.

When there is a global financial crisis, people tend to treat the yen as a safe haven and invest in it, resulting in a stronger yen, and Mrs. Watanabes are at the center of this.

As a result of the strong yen, Mrs. Watanabe , who had lost a lot of money on only the exchange rate, decided to return to Japan with tears in their eyes, taking advantage of the time when the exchange losses were slightly reduced. Japanese who have been unwilling to give up their small gains on overseas investments and have been unable to return home due to exchange losses caused by the continuous strengthening of the yen are returning to Japan.

Since it is money that individuals have earned with their own blood, it is heartbreaking in normal times when exchange losses are large and they cannot return home. It's a pity. This money, which is stained with the tears of the Japanese people, has become a ghost dollar floating around the international financial market because they cannot return home when the yen-dollar exchange rates are low.

Then there's the return of yen-invested funds that companies invested overseas after the 1970s. These funds are always scheduled to lose money when they return home due to the strong yen.

Let's take a look at the long term graph of the Japanese yen-dollar in [Figure 3] for a moment. While Japan's net worth overseas is enormous — over 4$ trillion as of the end of 2021, ranking first in the world — Japanese funds invested since 1970 have never had the opportunity to return home without incurring an exchange loss due to the yen's appreciation.

It is easy to see from the graph that the dollar has been falling and the yen has been rising for more than 30 years. We can see roughly in [Figure 3] that when the dollar was at its cheapest, the yen rose to about 76.34 yen per dollar in January 2012.

However, when Abenomics was implemented in December 2012, the yen depreciated. Take a look at the

evolution of the yen-dollar exchange rate again!
How frustrating must it be for an overseas investor in Japan?

If the same dollar is converted to Japanese yen, it is worth up to 59% (360-146)/360=about 59% less than when it was invested overseas.

This is why Japanese people who have previously invested money abroad cannot even keep their money close to them. Because of the strong yen, the losses are finalized the moment the dollar is brought into the country.

It is irreparable damage. Even if the profitable assets of the overseas investment generate a profit every year, if they are brought back, the profit will be 59% less than the expected return at the time of the previous overseas investment.

Individual investors in Japan must be regret themselves for investing abroad. Because of Abenomics, a dollar can't become 360 yen by spraying money from an airplane over Japan.

If the yen were to clash like this, it would cause a currency war between Japan's competitors and its neighbors due to neighborhood poverty.
Japanese will probably die without ever seeing their

money invested overseas.
Not only will they not be able to spend their money as they please, but they will not be able to keep their invested property close to them, touch it, visit it from time to time, brag about it to their friends, or enjoy it themselves.

We have been watching the tragedy of Japanese overseas investors for more than 30 years, which means the yen has been rising for about 30 years. For about 30 years, Japanese overseas investment money has become a dollar of unknown nationality. This money is the ghost dollar, the tears of Japan.

It is obvious that Japanese overseas investment assets(=ghost dollars) will be eager to bring them into Japan. Even if the value of the dollar increases slightly due to the economic crisis, they will try to bring it back as soon as possible.

This dollar is timid Japanese ant investors who are not aggressive and don't want to accept even a small exchange loss. It is a timid international ghost dollar that will try to enter Japan at the slightest gain or exchange loss.

In addition to Mrs. Watanabe's homing instinct, there is another reason why the yen is the currency of choice in a global crisis. Japan is the world's largest net creditor nation, with more assets than liabilities. It is the least likely country to default. It is ironic that the global economy is in crisis when the yen is considered a safe asset and strengthens.

The yen has rised 59% from its peak of 360 yen in the graph in [Figure 3], so the average Japanese overseas investments are expected to lose up to 2.6$ trillion in only exchange rate losses.

Almost all of it is invested in stocks, bonds, and real estate. They can't even bring them back into the country. Almost all of it is invested by individuals in stocks, bonds, and real estate. You can't even bring them into the country. Is it possible for Japanese retail investors to bring their overseas ghost dollars back home without losing money in yen conversion?

Not surprisingly, Japan is the world's number one manufacturing country, has some of the best technology, and has 29 Nobel Prize winners.

But when it comes to FinTech, or financial technology, Japan is far behind. They're financially illiterate nation. Worse than South Korea. Instead of spending the money earned from exports on the welfare of its people, it has instead blown it on overseas investments. This is how Japan's ghost dollar abroad was born.

The yen strengthens during crises because
1) Ghost dollars, overseas investments made since the 1970s, try to return home.
2) There is a tearful return of individual investors, the Mrs. Watanabe.
3) The aggregation of yen purchases by those who view the yen as a safe haven. These are the causes and consequences of why the yen actually strengthens against the dollar or weakens against the dollar even in times of crisis, unlike other countries.

Of course, this is only true for Japan during normal domestic crises, not foreign currency crises. In this case, i.e. during Japan's quasi IMF crisis in 1998, the dollar surged in Japan as well.

Let's look at a concrete example of a yen carry trade.

Let's say Mrs. Watanabe in Japan borrows 100 yen from a Japanese bank(let's say the interest rate is 1% and a dollar is 100 yen) and goes to a country with a higher interest rate and signs up for a 6% deposit.

Ceteris Paribus, that is, if nothing else is constant except the exchange rate, you are theoretically left with 5%.
1) If the yen-dollar exchange rate drops to 80 yen, you earn 5 yen in interest(6-1=5 yen), but when you exchange it for yen, you lose 20 yen. In the end, you lose 15 yen.

This is how Japan's tearful ghost dollar was born.
2) In the opposite case, let's say a dollar becomes 120 yen. Mrs. Watanabe earns 5(6-1=5 yen) yen in interest income. When she exchanges her money for Japanese money, she earns a 20 yen exchange rate capital gains, so her total profit is(20 yen exchange rate capital gains+5 yen interest income=25 yen). This is how Mrs. Watanabe is born.

During the 2008 financial crisis, FX margin trading became popular in Korea, starting with some aunts in Gangnam. In FX margin trading, you can buy and sell dollars through a futures company or a securities company, and it is like betting with 10x leverage, that is, using 10x leveraged credit.

It's a risky game.
If you really want to get into FX margin trading, you can invest in the listed KOSEF U.S Dollar Futures ETF when the dollar is expected to strengthen, and switch between the two KOSEF U.S Dollar Futures Inverse ETFs when the dollar is expected to weaken. Invest in them, but only when you expect a sharp rise or fall.

Investing in normal times creates an opportunity cost. The dollar is not a good investment because its price rarely fluctuates during normal times.
Predicting exchange rates is a job for experts. No, even the experts are wrong almost every time. It's not for everyone.

But with the help of this book, you can take advantage of the great opportunities(2~8x jackpots) in Dollar Swapping using the market cycle investing formula.

The dollar is not about frequent, short trades, it's about the big picture. You have to see the trees, you have to see the forest, you have to see the mountains, you have to see the mountain range.

If you don't have this big, long view, you shouldn't be investing in dollars, i.e. you shouldn't be investing overseas.
Even if you do make some appreciation gains, you may end up like the ant investors in Japan and suffer irreparable damage from currency exchange losses the moment you bring your money back home.

Since January 2016, the world, including South Korea, has been in a state of long term deflation, and the tears and tragedies of the Japanese should be enough to make you realize that you shouldn't invest overseas. However, Japan's ghost dollar is about to make a glorious homecoming, thanks to the rising yen-dollar exchange rate.

Japan's tears, or long term deflation, are over.
How high will Japanese interest rates go from here?
What will be the impact on the global economy as the

funds Exchange Bank. At that time, the KFB was owned by the Korean government, so the losses came from state-owned property, i.e., the national treasury. Today, big opportunities like this happen all the time around the world.

The problem is financial technology. You have to learn and master FinTech techniques. Anyone who doesn't know how to do this and simply invests long term in stocks and apartments is doomed.

Chapter 20) Dollar FinTech, 8x jackpot investment and analysis of jackpot cases

(Analyses profits of 3.28 trillion won in KEB bank trading and 240 billion won in currency exchange)

Japan has seen a decline in the price of the dollar:
The long term deflation that began in December 1989 devastated Japan's economy as the price of the dollar continued to fall domestically. As the deflation accelerated and prolonged, the price of everything in the country continued to fall, and the salaries of salaried people remained flat for nearly 30 years. As a result, Japan lost its social and economic vitality, leading to Japan's long term deflation.

South Korea has seen a surge in the price of the dollar:
December 3, 1998. A currency crisis in East Asia leads to South Korea's eventual bailout by the IMF. This is the time of the vertical dotted line ① in [Figure 13], which shows that South Korea's foreign exchange reserves, excluding gold, were only $20.3 billion. In response, South Korea's domestic asset prices spiked to as high as 1,955 won.

Faced with the prospect of losing its ability to make external payments in a short period of time, South Korea

sold state facilities and issued foreign bonds to raise additional dollar funds.
According to the author's Diamond Dollar Invesing Method, when the dollar price surges, the price of domestic assets plummets proportionally.

In other words, when the dollar soared to 1,995 won, all assets, including domestic stocks and real estate such as apartments, became the cheapest. In April 1989, the price of one dollar vertical dotted line ⑧ in [Figure 13] was only KRW 668.40.

On the other hand, we have already explained several times in [Figure 13] and [Figure 18] that when domestic asset prices are at their lowest, all assets, including domestic stocks and real estate such as apartments, are at their highest prices. We have explained many times that you can increase your wealth by 2~8 times in a short period of time by utilizing this opportunity as a Dollar Swapping financial opportunity.

A specific example is the dealing of the Korea Exchange Bank. The U.S firm Lone Star made 3.28$ trillion in dealing profits and $240 billion in exchange rate gains from the dealing of Korea Exchange Bank.

The world's top Dollar Swapping success story is the US-based Lone Star, which took advantage of the IMF's financial crisis in Korea in 1998 to buy and sell Korea Exchange Bank in a short period of time.

On August 27, 2003, five years after the crisis, the South Korean government sold the bank to Lone Star for 1.383$ trillion(exchange rate at the time of the sale: 1,175 won).

On February 9, 2006, Lone Star sold the bank to Hana Financial Holdings for 4.635 trillion won(970 won at the time of the buyback) and left South Korea. Lone Star's gross profit from the sale of Korea Exchange Bank was 3.521 trillion won, a return on investment of 254.6%. It took only two years and five months.

When there is a crisis in a country, you can bring in dollar funds, buy assets in the crisis country that have collapsed because of the exchange rate, and then sell the assets when the crisis has subsided and the dollar has regained its value.

In fact, we've already explained many times that this technique can be done by anyone living in the United States. In this case, he increased his wealth by two and a half times in just two years and five months.

Dollar Swapping and Dollar FinTech The core of this technique is based on the fact that stocks, apartments, and other real estate in countries in crisis are inversely correlated to the rise of the dollar.

On August 23, 2001, South Korea's IMF crisis came to an end. This is the same time that Lone Star acquired the Foreign Exchange Bank of Korea, after the country's asset prices crashed and before they recovered.

The sale proceeds alone were 3.282 trillion won and the exchange rate gain was 241.3 billion won(1,175-970=205 won). That's 17.4% of the investment. That's 241.3 billion won in just 2 years and 5 months. The total return from exchange+sale is a whopping 254.6%. In just two years and five months.

For such a large investment, the absolute amount of profit should be more important than the rate of return. That's because it's a full bet. There should be an IB bank in Korea that knows how to make this kind of investment — a post-Brexit UK.

The same type of real estate investment opportunity is waiting for you in the UK, which means you should be investing in the U.K instead of the U.S right now. When you think about it, there are always great investment opportunities around the world.

Crises like the financial crisis used to come in 10 year cycles around the world. Now it's more like a five year cycle.

In fact, there are some conspiracy theories circulating about the acquisition and sale of foreign exchange banks, and the author does not know the truth, but what is clear is that the new fintech techniques outlined by the author are concrete evidence that the dollar becomes a monster asset in times of crisis. It is also a living proof that the diamond dollar investing method still applies.

On December 23, 1997, after Korea's IMF crisis, the highest exchange rate was 1,955 won. In theory, Lonestar should have acquired Korea Exchange Bank on this day, which would have been the cheapest acquisition price and the best exchange rate.

Lone Star acquired KEB on August 27, 2003, six years later, so Lone Star also missed the best time to buy.
However, it's not as easy to coordinate the purchase and sale of a large asset as it is to buy and sell a stock, with due diligence and procedures for timing and payment methods.

In theory, Lone Star did not stick to the basic principle of the author's multi diamond dollar investing method, which is that when the domestic dollar is at its highest price, domestic assets are at their lowest price.

It was later revealed that there were some problems with underwriting qualifications and equity ratios, but the author does not know the details of the situation at the time. It just means that the purchase and sale dates weren't the best ones economically, including the exchange rate. Let's take a closer look!

1) Save on the purchase price

The difference between the highest dollar price and the acquisition date dollar price was 1,950won-1,175won, so we could have saved 775 won per dollar, but we didn't.

2) Sell Funds Max Exchange Rate Failure

The difference between the inbound and outbound exchange rate of 1,175 won to 970 won is not the maximum, but the realized exchange rate gain is 241.3 billion won. If the dollar had been imported at the peak rate of 1,950 won, the exchange rate would have been higher.

If the dollar was imported into Korea at the peak, it would be 1,950- 970= 980 won. The exchange rate gain alone is over 100%. This is what a true investment looks like.

3) Take advantage of the best times for dollar loans

Let's also think about the return on a simple dollar investment using the dollar loan system when the domestic dollar price is temporarily at its highest, not in the case of the IMF in Korea, but in the case of a crisis that comes once every 10 years or so, such as a major economic crisis. If you borrow 100,000$ when the domestic asset price is 1,950 won, deposit it in a bank after conversion, and then buy dollars when the price is 970 won and repay the dollar loan, you will have a 100,000$ dollar profit in less than three years. It's a simple double profit.

Some people have mentioned that it is not easy to get a dollar loan. In this case, buying and selling dollar-related ETFs can have the same effect.

4) As the dollar moves from safe dollars → to monster dollars → to safe dollars, use core fintech investing techniques!

When the domestic economic situation is at a complete bottom due to economic or financial crisis, the domestic stock market is at a complete bottom when the dollar price is at its highest, i.e. 1,950 won.

At this time, if you get a dollar loan and convert it to buy domestic stocks, it is natural that the price of the dollar will fall and the stock will rise sharply in a short period of time, resulting in a trading profit of about 100% in a short period of time.

At this time, the price of the dollar has plummeted, so if you sell the stock and buy dollars to repay the bank, you will repay about 50% less due to the plunge in the dollar again. In an instant, you have a 150% return on your investment(200-50/100=150%).

Technically, the return is infinite. This is because you borrowed all the money and invested it, so your equity was zero.

If you're brave enough, you can increase the amount you buy by 2.5 times on credit and make even more money. From the peak of the crisis, you would have made about 450% in a short period of time.

A country experiences a financial crisis. Financial crisis. Let's say a country is in an economic crisis, or the stock market has started a massive decline and has reached a complete bottom, and you want to invest in it by getting a dollar loan from a bank!

Naturally, the domestic price of a country's currency will be at an extremely low level. Let's say you borrow 100$.

Consider one dollar to one won.
(100$, converted after borrowing → Buy 2.5 times(250 won) on credit → Stock goes up 100% → Cash out(500 won) → Dollar price crashes, reducing the loan by 50%, repaying the full amount(50 won) → Investment return of 450 won(500-50=450 won).

If you trade on credit, you can make a short term profit of up to 450%. The only people who know these FinTech techniques are the author and the reader.

Theoretically, a return of up to 450% is possible in a short period of time. Even if you don't use credit, you can borrow dollars and convert them. You can then buy the stock, sell it, and repay the loan, earning about 100%+50% profit after the dollar crashes, which is about 150% profit in a short period of time.

In the case of Lone Star, the exchange rate gain was actually 205 won per dollar. The exchange rate gain alone was a whopping 17.4% of the total investment. However, as analyzed in 1) and 2), Lone Star's investment was not optimal.

However, Lone Star must have had a very financially literate staff. This is evidenced by the fact that they didn't pass up this golden opportunity.

If you don't take advantage of a great opportunity like this, where you can make a profit on the exchange rate+a profit on the trade, you're a worse IB bank than an individual investor. Recently, people have been using strange words such as financial engineering, quantitative investment, and AI investment to deceive people, but finance is common sense.

You just need to read and invest in the mainstream. If you don't know the principles of the Diamond Dollar Investing Method, which the author summarized several years ago, you'll be too scared to take advantage of this great opportunity.

There are always countries around the world that are experiencing financial or foreign exchange crises, so there are always opportunities to make big money. You can utilize the techniques in this chapter.

Let's take a look at your country's trade dependency: suppose you started investing in stocks a year ago after the annual balance of payments was in surplus, i.e. at the optimal time. Then, after Dollar Swapping, calculate your expected return after paying off the dollar loan!

It's not hard to make a 100% return on a stock investment that started a year ago, after the annual balance of payments surplus, by finding reversal days.

You should always keep in mind the results of 30 years of analyzing Korean stocks, which show that leading stocks go up in 3~4 years, usually by 4~20 times.

Since ETFs were created in 2002, the results of investing in thematic ETFs have not been studied, but they should perform a bit more slowly than leading stocks.

The economy will be good for quite some time after the reversal day, so it shouldn't be hard to make a 250% return on a 100$ investment(assuming a dollar is a won) like the example above by the time the stock market peaks, especially if you buy and sell on credit.

To finance the investment, you can either sell the government bonds you invested in at the end of the last cycle under the market cycle investing formula, the Pentagon Investing Method, or get a bank loan.

The expected return from this point forward would be a minimum of 2x and a maximum of 8x. We have already shown that after a year of balance of payments surpluses, a stock investment started within 2~3 days of the reversal day can provide at least a 250% return by the top of the great bull market.

If you start investing in stocks from the beginning of a major decline, whether it is a spontaneous decline, an economic crisis, or a financial crisis, when the stock market is at its peak, you can earn about 450%. Moreover, if you are a good investor and have access to credit, you can make 700~800% returns with no capital based on credit. In this case, the return is infinite.

In addition, in the long term deflation, the yields on long term government bonds are unimaginably high. They can be as high as 16x as interest rates continue to fall.

In the following sections, we will briefly discuss how to make money by swapping the dollar, the specific and practical methods of dollar FinTech, and the last step of making money by investing in government bonds.

Chapter 21) The ultimate dollar fintech =BONDS=. Eventually 16x is possible.

We've spent our entire lives getting screwed over by banks: they charge us transfer fees to transfer money to our own accounts at the same bank, and they reduce our negative account limits unilaterally. The so-called banks are the king of the kings, the super king of the super kings.
When a crisis occurs, the dollar surges for about a year or two. Let's take a look at the changes in interest rates, exchange rates, and the KOSPI index at the time of the IMF [Table 2].

In the case of Korea's IMF crisis, the time it took for the dollar to rise to its peak was about 1 year and 1 month, counting from the date of the dollar's bottom(estimated to be November 22, 1997), when no one noticed anything wrong. During this time, the dollar jumped 83.9%, while the KOSPI dropped 36.8%.

During the subprime financial crisis, it took about 1 year and 4 months for the dollar to reach its peak from a normal dollar price, and during that time, the dollar jumped 77.6% and the KOSPI dropped 49.5%.
After a short term spike, the dollar usually has one major pullback after a short period of time. After that, it is

common for it to begin a long term, 2~3 year decline.

When the dollar has spiked or is expected to spike, banks want to lend you dollars and earn interest. They also expect the price of the dollar to rise until the loan is repaid. So they're smiling because they want to take advantage of the interest+the exchange rate difference between the price of the dollar at the time of the loan and the price of the dollar at the time of repayment. In other words, it's time to wait for customers who think you're stupid by their standards.

They're probably actively trying to encourage you to take out a dollar loan at a time when the price of the dollar is expected to spike due to the crisis.

But anyone who reads this book and takes out a dollar loan will have chosen the right time to turn the tables on the banks. All you need to do is to take advantage of the opportunity to take out a dollar loan at a time when the price of the dollar is at its highest point. Now, the only question is whether the banks or you can guess when the exchange rate will peak. It's a game of guessing.

You can take out a dollar loan and then sell it to the bank on the spot, which means you can exchange it for KRW and then run to the stock market or apartment market, which will already be falling sharply and hovering at the bottom. But don't go to real estate this time. The Korean real estate market, which already deflated in 2016, is not an investment.

In the foreign exchange market, stocks always start to rebound before real estate when the dollar starts to fall back into its first sharp decline on its own.

In the case of Korea's IMF crisis, it took a year and seven months for the dollar's price to normalize. To summarize what to do after borrowing dollars
1) Stocks will drop sharply for a short period of time until the initial rebound in the falling dollar is over. At this point, you can sell your stocks and pay back the dollar.
2) During the upcoming secondary decline in the dollar, you can sell your stocks, buy dollars, and repay the bank. When the dollar's fall slows to a halt, you can decide that the decline has stopped.
3) As a long term investment, you can redeem your dollars after the dollar has almost completely regained its original value. In other words, you can choose one of three options. If you choose option 3), you will have to pay interest in the meantime.

However, since the dollar loan was taken out at a time when the dollar was already up about 100%, and the repayment will be after the dollar is almost back to where it was before the rise, you'll only need about half the money to buy back the dollar. I.e., you can pay back about 50% less than you borrowed, leaving you with about 50% of the profit.

Also, if you sell the dollars you borrowed and sell the stocks or ETFs you bought at the dumping price at a 100% increase, you can make about 3 times as much money as you borrowed.

In this way, a good investor can triple their money just by borrowing, even if they have no money of their own.
What's more, the return is virtually infinite because it's based on the dollar loan alone, so it's impossible to calculate the rate of return.

This technique is the same in any era, in any country. Let's look at it a little more closely. First, let's say that the dollar spikes from around 1,000$ to 2,000$ in a short period of time. Naturally, stocks in crisis countries are already down 50%.

Real estate usually doesn't start falling until about six months later than stocks. In the early stages of a crisis, real estate starts falling about 6 months later than stocks, meaning that even if stocks are falling for 6 months due to a generalized decline, apartments are rising for 6 months.

Let's summarize this peak dollar borrowing, then peak

dollar repayment investment technique in order.
1) Take a dollar loan from a bank when the dollar has risen almost 100% to 2,000 won(assuming 1 dollar=1,000 won is the normal dollar price). Think of it as borrowing 1$. As soon as you get the loan, you sell it and exchange it for Korean won.
2) According to the diamond dollar investment method, when the dollar price is at its highest, the price of domestic stocks is at its lowest. Since you received the loan when the dollar price was at its highest, you immediately sell the dollar and use the 2,000 won to buy stocks at the bottom of the market or KODEX 200 Leverage, which is a 2x leveraged ETF that moves up or down about twice the average rise or fall of 200 blue-chip stocks on the KOSPI.

The stocks that dropped the most during the dollar's short term spike at the beginning of the crisis will rise the most during the rebound, but it's hard to pick the stocks with the strongest rebound, so you won't be disappointed if you only get twice the average return with this KODEX 200 leveraged ETF.
3) As the dollar rises and stock indices fall, as the crisis subsides or is resolved, the dollar price usually returns to where it was a year or two ago, i.e. close to where it was before the rise.

The KODEX 200 leveraged, or bought stocks that have fallen a lot, so it will rise at nearly double the rate of the index over the same period. In the meantime, the dollar will have fallen sharply, meaning that it will be heading towards its normal price of 1,000$.

4) When the dollar drops to almost even and is around 1,000~1,100 won, it's time to sell your stocks or KODEX 200 leverage that rose sharply in a short period of time.
5) This process also gives you a profit of about 100%, after which you can buy the dollar back to its almost normal price and hand it over to the bank.

It's so easy, isn't it?
6) After selling the KODEX 200 leverage(assuming the purchase price is 1 share=2,000 won), you will have 4,000 won roughly, which means you can sell this ETF when the price of a dollar goes down and reaches 1,000~1,100 won. After this process, you will be left with 4,000 won(total amount)-1,000 won(repayment of the dollar loan)-3,000 won, since you borrowed the dollar loan at 1 dollar=2,000 won, or about 3 times as much.

If you only pay the interest on the loan, you'll have about 3 times as much money left over as if you had no capital, i.e., an all-dollar loan, and the rate of return is infinite. The return is infinite because you didn't put any money out of your own pocket. This is how you can make a lot of money in a very simple way: borrow the highest-priced dollar and repay the lowest-priced dollar. We think we've been getting screwed by banks all our lives, but this is a great opportunity to borrow and pay back bank dollars and give them a headache.

But the banks don't lose anything. They get to keep the interest they've earned, and they get to watch the drama for free. Since the banks lent the dollars instead of investing in the stock themselves, like we do, the profits were monopolized by the investors. They have to be satisfied with just a few percent interest.

So, if you know when the dollar is going up, when the dollar is at its peak, and when it's going down, the money is rolling in, but how do you time it so that you can buy the dollar when it's at its peak?

Judging from the IMF crisis, it seems that neither banks nor governments can do it…. That's right. It's hard for anyone to guess the exchange rate. You can invest in any country except the U.S to take advantage of the rise and fall of the dollar. This phenomenon always occurs in abnormal cases, such as in the event of a major recession or an IMF crisis.

1) If you take a dollar loan from a bank and invest in stocks when the price is at its highest level, you can get about three times the return.
2) Overseas Koreans investing in Korea directly, or those

investing by introducing dollars from relatives overseas, can gain about twice as much if they do not invest in long term government bonds due to long term deflation.
3) If you sell stocks when the dollar is at its lowest and buy dollars in advance and invest in the above order, you will make about 4 times as much money.

This means that when stocks are at their highest, the dollar is at its lowest. It stands to reason that you'll get more than a quadruple return in this case. This is because the returns are cumulative.

Depending on the individual's ability, this return will be a bit jagged, but it's definitely an opportunity that everyone should take advantage of. Keep in mind that this is an investment technique that utilizes market fluctuations between the dollar and stocks that can be applied in any country and at any time, except if you live in the United States!

After reading this far, you might be thinking that the most important thing is to predict the peak of the dollar price. It seems like this is the most crucial point in the game between the bank and me.
That's right.

You might be thinking, how can a private investor beat a bank's ability to predict the peak of the dollar price,

which means that the bank is selling loans because they predicted the dollar price would go much higher?
After all, you might think, what the author is writing about is a dream and only possible in theory. But read on, because your doubts will be slowly dispelled.

What the banks want is to lend us dollars, collect interest, and then expect us to buy back the dollars at a higher price than the price of the dollars when they lent them out. However, as we've seen, even the seemingly endlessly rising dollar has its moments. Typically, it loses more than half of its rise in a year and a few months. The longer we wait, the more we see the dollar fall back to the price of the dollar before it rose.

So we buy dollars when they're cheaper than when we took out the dollar loan and return them to the bank, paying interest but taking advantage of the exchange rate differential. In the end, the bank gets watered down and we get to laugh.

In the case of a long term deflation, the practical methods of Dollar Swapping and dollar fintech are now entering their fifth and final phase as we start investing in government bonds.

So let's see how to invest in government bonds.
After the initial investment has already snowballed about

8 times, the investment amount is quite large because it is invested in government bonds. Therefore, if you increase the investment amount by doubling it again and again by investing in government bonds, the total amount of profit will increase tremendously, so this is the peak investment information.

First of all, the government bonds you should invest in are long term government bonds with a maturity of 10 to 20 years or more. Not ETFs.

In the case of Japan, the country's long term deflation lasted for about 30 years, meaning that government bond holders earned dozens of times more interest than bank deposits during the long holding period. The deflation drove Japan's interest rates down to consistently negative rates.

The price of the bond will increase proportionally, so you will have made a capital gain when you bought and sold. In the case of short term deflation, such as a simple recession, it's actually better to buy short term government bonds(2~3 years) because you can encash your holdings at any time with very little risk.

It's not easy to distinguish whether a deflation is short or long term, but you can do so by determining whether the upcoming recession is cyclical or structural.

In other words, whether in the U.S or outside the U.S, the Pentagon investing method is the same until the second stage, and the U.S does not have a third stage.
The final step, investing in government bonds, is the same. The only difference is the type of government bonds to invest in, depending on whether you are looking for short or long term deflation.

Don't forget that every time there is a major economic crisis in any country, there is always a chance to make a huge 8x investment by Dollar Swapping stocks or apartments for dollars.]

In the case of a long term deflation, interest rates will continue to fall, so on top of the profits from Dollar Swapping, you can make another 2x or so on government bonds.

If the interest rate on a 10 year government bond falls by 1%, it will gain about 7%, the 20 year will gain 14%. The 30 year will gain about 21%. On the other hand, if government bonds increase in interest rates by 1%, government bonds will fall by 7% for the 10 year, 14% for the 20 year, and 21% for the 30 year, depending on the remaining duration. It's a formula. The rate of change is the present value of the total amount of interest to be received in the future.

In the post-COVID-19 era, quantitative tightening and the

U.S FRB raising interest rates to 5.25% led to the failure of SVB Bank in the U.S and the acquisition of Swiss Credit Suisse by UBS.

The collapse was caused by the collapse in the valuation of long term U.S government bonds held by these banks. Therefore, the timing of government bond investments can be a downfall.

Therefore, the best time to buy and sell government bonds is after predicting interest rate changes. If you can't predict it properly, it's best to wait until you actually see the change in interest rates, because interest rate increases and decreases are not a one-time event, but a trend.

Mr.Big Investor is also a poor predictor of interest rates, which is why he only invests in short term government bonds. This is because short term government bonds don't have much of an impact on the price of government bonds.

The author predicts that there will be many more interest rate fluctuations in the future, so the rise and fall of financial companies and businesses has not yet begun in earnest.

In Japan, where long-duration deflation has been ongoing for 32 years, interest rates have consistently fallen to negative rates. The rest of the world, including South

Korea, has been experiencing long term deflation since January 2016. Sooner or later, Korean interest rates will fall to negative rates, just like Japan.

In this case, the 8x return, plus the mark-to-market profit on the govenrn bonds, would total about 16x, which is the final step in the Pentagon investing method. Recalling [Chapter 9], it is theoretically possible to get up to 32x returns. The returns are unimaginable.

During a long term deflationary period, you continue to hold government bonds and earn interest income. You'll also realize a mark-to-market gain as interest rates fall. As the long term deflation comes to an end, interest rates begin to rise.

As interest rates rise, the price of government bonds falls, so it's time to sell them and start investing in stocks again, following Step 1 of the Pentagon Investing Method. Another decade of investing begins.

The best time to invest in government bonds is when a recession is in full swing, because they only increase in price when interest rates go down. Of course, you'll still earn interest during the regular day, but if you don't have any capital gains, it's not a very attractive investment.

In a recession, corporate bonds are at greater risk of

default, meaning that you may not receive interest payments, or they may be delayed. In severe cases, the company may go bankrupt and you may not be able to collect on your bonds.

The corporate bonds may be uncollectible if the corporate issuer goes bankrupt. In the recent case of UBS's handling of the Swiss Credit Suisse M&A, perpetual corporate bonds issued by Swiss Credit Suisse were destroyed at no cost.

Currently, there are perpetual corporate bonds issued by POSCO KEPCO and a few other Korean banks. It is necessary to accurately check the issuance conditions, conversion conditions, and burning conditions of perpetual corporate bonds.

Therefore, corporate bonds are
1) According to the Market cycle investing order of the Pentagon Investing Method's five target assets of stocks, apartments, dollar deposits, and government bonds, corporate bonds are often invested in order to earn interest and capital gains at the same time because interest rates fall at the end of a recession.

2) Coincidentally, bonds, including government bonds, are only suitable for investment during a financial crisis. Bonds, including government bonds, have little price fluctuation during normal times and only earn a small

amount of interest, so they are not a good investment. Therefore, it is recommended not to invest in government bonds during normal times, but only during the fifth stage of the Pentagon Investing Method.

As a result, government bonds and corporate bonds have become investment assets during when the financial crisis is most severe.

Therefore, to avoid various risks that occur during a recession, it is recommended not to invest in corporate bonds and financial bonds other than government bonds. as an investment target.

A 1% decrease in interest rates on a 10 year government bond would result in a capital gain of about 7%, a 14% gain on a 20 year bond, and a 21% gain on a 30 year bond.
On the other hand, if interest rates on government bonds rise by 1%, government bonds will fall by 7% for the 10 year, 14% for the 20 year, and 21% for the 30 year, depending on their remaining duration. The rate of change is the present value of the total amount of interest to be received in the future.

It's a math formula.
In the post-COVID-19 era of quantitative tightening, the U.S FRB raised rates to 5.25%, causing SVB Bank in the U.S to fail and Swiss Credit Suisse to be bought by UBS.

The collapse was caused by the collapse in the valuation of long term U.S government bonds held by these banks. As you can see, the wrong time to invest in government bonds can be disastrous.

Therefore, the best time to buy and sell government bonds is after predicting interest rate changes. If you can't predict it properly, it's best to wait until you actually see the change in interest rates, because interest rate increases and decreases are not a one-time event, but a trend.

Mr.Big Investor is also a poor predictor of interest rates, which is why he only invests in short term government bonds. Short term government bonds

changes in interest rates don't have much of an impact on the price of government bonds.
The author predicts that there will be many more interest rate fluctuations in the future, so the rise and fall of financial companies and corporations has not yet begun in a real way.

In the case of Japan, after 32 years of long term deflation, interest rates have been continuously lowered to negative rates. The world, including Korea, has been in a long term deflation since January 2016. I believe that Korean interest rates will eventually fall to negative rates like Japan.

In this case, on top of the 8x differential return from the Pentagon Investing Method's Step 4, you'll get about 2x the capital gain from investing in government bonds.

Add it all up and you're looking at a stunning 16x return. Recalling [Chapter 11], it is theoretically possible to get up to 32x returns. The returns are unimaginable.

During a long term deflation, you will continue to hold government bonds and earn interest income. You'll also get to capital gains as interest rates fall. As the long deflation comes to an end, interest rates begin to rise.

As interest rates rise, the price of government bonds falls, so it's time to sell them and start investing in stocks again, according to Step 1 of the Pentagon Investing Method. Another decade of investing begins.

The best time to invest in government bonds is when a recession starts in a major way. This is because they only increase in price when interest rates go down. Of course, you'll still get interest during normal times, but if you don't have a capital gains advantage, it won't be as attractive.

In a recession, corporate bonds are at greater risk of default and the likelihood of not receiving or delaying interest payments increases. In severe cases, the issuer may go bankrupt and the bondholder may not be able to collect.

In one case, perpetual corporate bonds issued by Swiss Credit Suisse were burned free of charge as part of UBS's M&A deal with Swiss Credit Suisse.

Currently, there are perpetual bonds issued by POSCO KEPCO and other Korean banks. It is necessary to accurately check the issuance conditions, conversion conditions, burning conditions, etc. before buying and selling.

Therefore, corporate bonds are
1) According to the circular investment sequence of the five investment target assets of stocks, apartments, dollar deposits, and government bonds in the Pentagon Investing Method, corporate bonds are the last investment in the cyclical investment sequence to invest in order to earn both capital gains and interest income because interest rates fall at the end of the recession.

2) Coincidentally, private bonds, including government bonds, are only investable assets during financial downturns.

In other words, you should not invest in government bonds and other private bonds during normal times, but only during the fifth stage of the Pentagon investing method, as they have little price fluctuation and little interest income.

How ironic! Because it's at the peak of a recession that governments and businesses really need money.

Therefore, it is especially important to note that in order to avoid the various risks that arise in a recession, it is recommended that you do not invest in corporate bonds and financial bonds that are not government bonds for the rest of your life. The author does not recommend investing in local government bonds. Only government bonds should be invested in.

3) In normal time, Bonds should not be invested in by individual investors. Do not invest in corporate bonds, district government bonds, etc. and always invest in government bonds, but even then, you should only invest once, at the very end of a business cycle.

Since one business cycle roughly takes 10 years, you should invest in government bonds once every 10 years, at the end of the cycle, as the last investment asset in the Pentagon Investing Method, by closing your periodcal deposit and investing for about 2~3 years. In normal times, government bonds are never an investment.

However, in the case of a long term deflation, you should

hold them for a long period of falling interest rates, enjoying the interest and capital gains. and then you should sell them as interest rates rise at least once or twice.

If interest rates rise by one or two percentage points, it's time to sell government bonds and start investing in stocks, as this is the beginning of a new decade of economic change.

This time, however, long term deflation hit the world in January 2016. The author believes that this long term deflation will continue for 32 years, like Japan.

Therefore, the author believes that Korea will be in long term deflation until 2029 and other countries will be in long term deflation until 2048, so you can enjoy the interest income and capital gains from government bonds alone. There are no other assets worth investing in as long as deflation continues.

4) There is a stock called Macquarie Infrastructure Fund that is similar to government bonds, but only in Korea. It may be better than government bonds.

* One final note: in the wake of the SVB default in the US, U.S Treasury Secretary Janet Yellen has now mandated that U.S government bonds be valued at par, regardless of their current value. This action is in effect until the end

of March 2024.

If U.S Treasuries were to be valued at par, many banks would go bankrupt, as banks are by far the largest holders of U.S Treasuries.

Chapter 22) The Egg Theory should be discarded.

The egg theory without the Dollar Swapping process should be discarded. In the previous chapters, we've seen the principles and phenomena of how stocks and apartments can multiply your wealth 8x by simply Dollar Swapping them, and we've also seen the superiority of the author's Pentagon investing method.

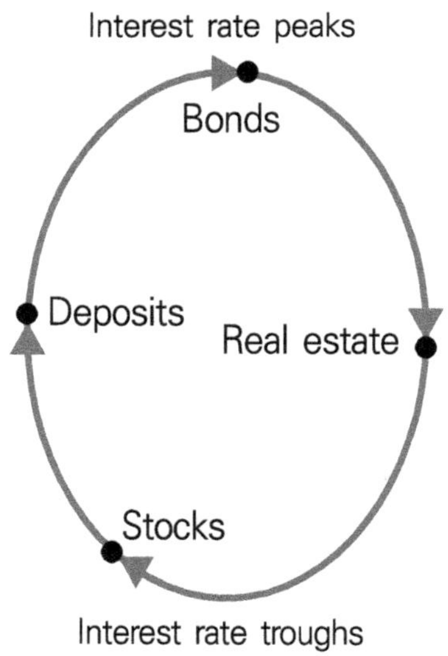

[Figure 23] Andre Kostolany's Egg Theory

We can see that the Pentagon Investing Method, a new cycle investing method, can generate 8x returns by simply Dollar Swapping, and up to 16x returns if you price in a collapse in interest rates at the end of a recession, which is the last stage of the cycle.

So now you know that Andre Kostolani's egg theory is no longer useful or necessary. [Figure 23] is an illustration of Andre Kostolani's circular investing theory, the Egg Theory.

Andre Kostolanyi(February 9, 1906~September 14, 1999), who lived to be 93, was a Hungarian Jewish securities investing theorist and investor.

He has been called the Mr.Big Investor of Europe, the God of Stocks, and was a successful stock investor as well as a theorist.

Anyway, he lived in a closed economy system, so he didn't know the necessity and effectiveness of the Dollar Swapping investing process because he didn't live in a time when the world was open and trade had a huge impact on the economy of each country as well as the world.

This is the biggest flaw in his egg theory. Andre Kostolany's egg theory has many other flaws, but the biggest one is the lack of a Dollar Swapping investing process.

After all, he lived in New York City for many years, so he never experienced or thought about this phenomenon.

Other flaws include the fact that no one knows when interest rates will peak or trough, and the fact that the order of rotation of funds is incorrect.

Chapter 23) Holding Bitcoins Instead of Dollars?

People think that holding Bitcoins instead of dollars will have the same effect as holding dollars.This is complete nonsense. On January 10, 2024, a Bitcoin spot ETF(GBTC) was listed on the New York & Chicago Stock Exchange. Therefore, it will be subject to strict regulation by the US SEC.Bitcoin, which only exists online, is a virtual asset, not a virtual currency.

It is only recognized by SEC as a virtual asset because people buy and sell it for money, just like a "shell currency". Don't misunderstand.Now, there is an infinite supply of Bitcoin because there are both spot and ETFs. Therefore, the price of Bitcoin will eventually converge to zero. This is because now that it is listed as an ETF on the US stock exchange, the anonymity of ownership, one of the biggest advantages of Bitcoin, is gone,too.

In addition, the author believes that the recent discovery of superconducting materials at the Quantum Energy Research Institute in South Korea has been successful. With the discovery of superconducting materials, the price of electricity and crude oil will converge to almost zero in the future. Therefore the production cost of bitcoin will also converge to zero. This is another reason why the price of Bitcoin will converge to zero.

Since Bitcoin is a representative of virtual assetsit is only natural that other digital coin assets will also converge to zero.It is true that bitcoin is beginning to replace some of the exchange functions of the dollar.

However, if this is allowed, it means that governments cannot control the inflow and outflow of foreign currency, and illegal money can be exchanged for free. Since bitcoin converges to zero, holding bitcoin instead of dollars will be suicidal.
Bitcoin fails to fulfill many of the conditions for legal currency. Furthermore, it is a free transfer of power from governments to bitcoin issuers, making it a private monopoly.

Furthermore, it creates the ridiculous phenomenon that anyone can issue a digital currency. Before the Great Depression, central banks were private companies, but it's awkward for a private company to issue fiat currency. Governments can't give away this seigniorage benefit for free.

[Figure 24] Bitcoin price. KRW(Dec. 2024), courtesy of NAVER.

Seigniorage effect is the magic that turns paper into money. A 100$ bill or a 10$ bill costs about the same amount of paper to produce, and the cost is nearly zero in terms of prevailing purchasing power. It's a big business with margins of hundreds of percent.

As such, privately issued bitcoins are likely to disappear in the near future as government digital currencies take over.

Bitcoin does not fulfill the four functions of money: a medium of exchange, a means of payment, a store of value, and a measure of value. In short, Bitcoin can't fulfill the functions of money.

Except for the blockchain function to keep track of all bitcoin holdings and transactions, the role of private bitcoins is likely to end in the future.

However, Bitcoin is likely to be revitalized by being issued in the form of digital currency, digital coins, issued by central banks in each country. "According to an article in [The Newsis], China is at the forefront of issuing and circulating this digital currency. The digital yuan is currently undergoing a forced experiment in China.
The People's Bank of China once said that the "success of the experiment" of the digital yuan will "soon bring about the arrival of cash-digital coexistence".

On Dec. 12, the PBOC teamed up with the government of Shenzhen, Guangdong province, to distribute digital yuan to 50,000 Shenzhen residents at a rate of 200 yuan(about $34,000) each, for a total of 10 million yuan(about $1.7 billion).

During the nationwide trial, payments worth 2 billion yuan(about $340 billion) were made smoothly through 4 million transactions. With the success of the digital yuan experiment in China, the era of coexistence between cash and digital currencies may be coming sooner rather than later.

In the long run, however, private digital currencies like Bitcoin are destined to fade away. It's likely that they will exist as souvenirs.Even a celebrity is heavily invested in

Bitcoin···. In the future, I believe that only CBDC(Central Bank digital currency) issued by the central banks of each country will exist as digital currencies.

This means that people will be able to send money without a bank account or credit card because they will have their own money in a digital wallet. This would make credit cards and payment processors obsolete.

However, government-issued digital currencies combined with blockchain technology make transactions 100% visible to the government. If countries use only digital currencies, black money will be eliminated from the world at once. In other words, bad finance would disappear. Money laundering, terrorist financing, tax evasion, and online gambling would be eradicated.

The U.S dominates international payments through the dollar and uses exclusion from the dollar payment network as a sanction against adversaries.

This means that if it is removed from SWIFT, the dollar payment system, it will be removed from the world's banking payment system for trade finance and remittances of international transactions, and will have to pay in dollars directly in diplomatic briefcases or by separate means of transportation(airplanes, ships, etc.).

The idea is that the global adoption of the digital yuan will inevitably reduce U.S power over China, but there's a big battle underlying this.

China had committed to introducing a digital currency with the goal of having a digital yuan in circulation by the Beijing Winter Olympics in February 2022.

The yuan is also a way to disempower private e-payment systems like Alipay and WeChat Pay. At its core, e-payments are about intermediating consumers' bank deposits and transferring them to merchants.

However, digital yuan, which is itself "cash," does not require intermediation. It can be sent to others online as well as offline. Ultimately, the Chinese authorities' slapdown of Alibaba is intended to reorganize the e-payment market, which is dominated by private companies, in favor of the government through the digital yuan.

It will also work to stimulate the economy through negative interest rates.

So far, negative interest rates have failed to stimulate consumption, but digital money can be left in the closet and the government can spend less money if it is not used.

The dollar accounts for 38.26% of international payments, while the yuan accounts for only 2.42%. If we go further and issue a globally accepted digital currency instead of a country-specific digital currency, it's clear that the dollar will be devalued.

The existence of Bitcoin itself is uncertain, and the idea of holding it as a substitute for the dollar is, in a word, nonsense.

Chapter 24) U.S reshoring policy, a hidden attempt? Trippin's dilemma?

Now that China has become the G2, the U.S is pursuing policies of reshoring and frendshoring, a movement to share key technologies and build supply chains among allies, with the U.S as the centerpiece. In addition, it has imposed high tariffs and import controls on all Chinese goods.

Toys(55%), furniture(38%), plastics(29%), and textiles(20%) were the hardest hit sectors of Chinese exports to the U.S in the second half of 2022. So it's fair to say that the price of everything in this world is going up.

In other words, the international division of labor has been halted by reshoring, and inflation is destined to last longer due to the imposition of tariffs between countries. Of course, other countries may be able to supply the goods that China cannot, but it's more important which country can do it cheaper and in larger quantities.

The U.S is doing the opposite, ignoring one of the most important global economic theories, Trippin's dilemma: the U.S wants to live well alone.

When the U.S current account deficit shrinks, the global economy contracts, which means it grows less, and the price of the dollar rises.
If the U.S deficit grows, the dollar depreciates and the world economy improves. This is the Triffin's dilemma.

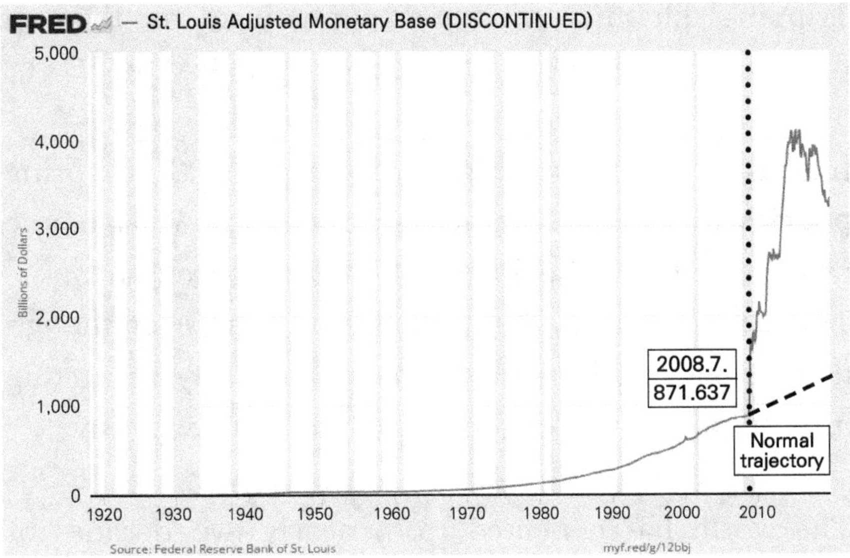

[Figure 25] U.S M1 over 102 years(1918.1.1.~2019.11.1.)

For reference, [Figure 25] is a 102 year graph of M1 supply in the US. You can see how much of the money supply has been post-subprime since September 2008! It's also easy to see how much M1 would have to be reduced to get back to the dotted line, which is the normal base money supply.

In the meantime, what should be done about the contraction and deflation of the world economy due to the Triffin's dilemma?

Going forward, it is correct to say that, given the size of the economy, the amount of money created should be modestly reduced to within the normal rate of money growth to return to normal. Everyone is familiar with Trippin's dilemma, a popular euphemism for the fact that the global economy is trapped in a U.S cycle.

Increased trade restrictions, as well as U.S reshoring policies, mean that Chinese consumer goods will become more expensive. The dollar will naturally strengthen.
The U.S is banning all imports from China, even though they know it will cause more inflation. By restricting imports, all consumer goods become more expensive.

The world has benefited from nearly two decades of inflation-free economic growth since China's entry into the WTO in 2001, and now it's all an illusion. China's integration into the global economy was a short-lived flower!

It is obvious that a shrinking money supply, whether in a country or globally, leads to a cooling economy and a recession. As shown in [Figure 25], the U.S velocity of money is shrinking rapidly, which means that the global economy is entering a recession and the dollar is strengthening. Of course, we know this is to calm inflation…….

The base currency is usually leveraged by 9x through credit creation, which stimulates the economy. We don't know exactly what the monetary multiplier is for the U.S dollar, but we assume it's similar for domestic currencies, since the destruction of credit creation means 9 times less money(credit) in the market.

Is the U.S ignoring the proven Triffin's Dilemma? The theory of the Triffin's Dilemma is that the U.S is always looking out for itself, but in the end, the U.S ends up poorer. How do we solve this conundrum? It seems to me that a second Plaza Accord, like the September 22, 1985, Plaza Accord, will be required to solve the problem.

This may require a wholesale repricing of the U.S dollar and the rest of the world's currencies, i.e., the U.S dollar will be overpriced and then devalued.
With the global long term deflation that began in January 2016, the world will be in a recession, but the U.S will be in a mild recession. Reshoring will reduce the U.S deficit, add jobs, and strengthen the dollar.

Is the U.S reshoring a strategy to manage a slowly declining dollar over time?
As investors, we need to be mindful of fundamentals. South Korea's annualized current account surplus a year

ago should be positive, and then we should enter the stock market. Or the U.S needs to have a higher annualized current account deficit a year ago.

In long term deflation, the U.S dollar is steadily devalued. This indiscriminately lowers the price of all goods around the world, which in turn deepens the global long term deflation.

Reshoring, on the other hand, strengthens the dollar and increases inflation. Reshoring brings companies back to the U.S and brings jobs back home. This causes the dollar to strengthen.

Is this a hidden strategy of the U.S to prevent the international dollar, or the dollar index, from falling? What other hidden attempt does the U.S have?

Chapter 25) After that

Anyone in any country in the world can sell all their stocks or apartments and buy dollars using the Dollar Swapping investment method when the stock market bull run ends or an economic crisis breaks out.

Governments often raise interest rates dramatically to cool an overheated economy, which can lead to a recession and even an economic crisis.

In this case, you can utilize rising interest rates as an investment opportunity with the KBSTAR U.S Long term Treasury Bond Futures Inverse 2X(Synthetic H), which rises as interest rates rise. You can also take advantage of falling stock prices with various inverse products, such as KODEX 200 Futures Inverse 2X, but there are a few stocks that don't work.

Whenever there is a major drop due to an interest rate hike or an economic crisis, the dollar surges and stocks or apartments plummet, and you can utilize this to your advantage and enjoy profits again. In the process, you can easily earn 2 to 8 times your investment in Dollar Swapping.

We discussed in detail in [Chapter 18] how different crises, such as the IMF situation and the 2008 subprime and coronavirus crises, have slightly different recovery times for different countries.

After that, you've done the Dollar Swapping process, and you're done investing in deposits already. A recession is triggered by excessive interest rate hikes that suppress demand. Now, to stimulate the economy, interest rates are lowered and the exchange rate is returned to normal. At this point, as the economy improves, stocks slowly rise first among the five investing assets: stocks, apartments, dollars, deposits, and government bonds.

The length of time it takes for the dollar to recover depends on the strength of the financial or economic crisis.

At this point, stocks slowly rise first as the economy improves. If you look at how long it takes for the dollar to recover during this period, you can see that it depends on the severity of the financial or economic crisis.

When the economy calms down due to rising interest rates, or after the economic crisis subsides, and interest rates on deposits start to fall, it's time to swap to your deposits for a government bond or Macquarie Infrastructure KODEX 200 inverse. Just as there are bubbles in rising markets, there are also reverse bubbles in falling markets in stock, real estate, etc.

In other words, government policies are usually excessive, causing them to rise or fall too much. Therefore, the return is larger than expected, which means that stocks and apartments fall below the equilibrium point or rise too much.As a result, we enter a depression, and interest rates continue to fall.

Government policies and human sentiment will always overreact, so the price of an asset will crash below the equilibrium point, creating a reverse bubble that will continue to bounce back and forth during a recession.

When the dollar of a country in crisis rises sharply, foreign funds rush to sell their stocks, apartments, and government bonds ets in the crisis country to avoid currency exchange losses and leave the country.

That is, the price of the government bond becomes the so-called shit price. They will have been sold, so they will be waiting for us well below the theoretical price.

Again, this is when the dollar spikes and government bonds drop, so you need to be able to use this as an opportunity to cross-trade i.e. Dollar Swap.

If you look at Japan, all you need to do is buy 20+ year government bonds and hold them for the long term, with money that is already 2~8 times your investment.

You can see that you could have easily made another 2~3x or more with the ongoing long term deflation.
This is because Japan's interest rates fell from 8.3% in 1990 to eventually reach negative rates. This is the kind of opportunity that only comes along once or twice in a lifetime for the prepared investor.

Most importantly,
"The Hidden Story of the Creation of Wealth", we believe that a full-blown, long term deflation, this time in South Korea, is expected to last until 2029.

This is because South Korea has about 2.5 times the working-age population than Japan. Korea's long term deflation is likely to progress and end 2.5 times faster than Japan's anyway. This is not the same as Korea's "go-go-go" culture. Despite everything, even if the intensity of the recession is severe, it is better that the long term deflation passes quickly.

Long term deflation is characterized by the fact that all assets, including the dollar, stocks, apartments, gold, and crude oil, continue to fall together for a long time.
In this case, the author believes that the economy will turn around in 2029 for South Korea and 2048 for the rest of the world, and that investors should hold government bonds and enjoy the capital gains and interest from falling interest rates.

If the author is wrong, and Korea returns to a one year balance of payments surplus before 2029 and the world before 2048, and the stock market starts to rise, we can abandon the prediction of the duration of the long term deflation and start investing in stocks with a new entry into the stock market.

A long term decline in interest rates will allow you to enjoy capital gains as well as monthly interest payments on government bonds. Government bonds deposit interest into your account quarterly, but you can spread it out monthly. Government bonds are like cash, and in deflationary times, interest rates steadily decrease, causing their trading price to skyrocket. In any case, government bonds pay surface interest(coupon) every year, so they will show a large gain until the end of the long term deflation.

Cash and deposits also increase in relative value, but government bonds are cash equivalents that pay more interest than cash and deposits, so their relative price increases at a much higher rate than cash.

Japanese government bonds have been rising for more than 20 years to the point where their current value is impossible to calculate. You can't even buy them on the market. No one is selling them. It's also because the Bank of Japan is buying an unlimited amount of 10 year JGBs at a fixed rate.

As explained in detail in [Chapter 21], a 1% decrease in interest rates for a 10 year government bond results in a price spike of about 7%. The price spike is 14% for 20 year bonds and 21% for 30 year bonds. The rate of change is slightly different because future interest is valued at the present value.

The major rally in South Korea's stock market that began in May 2017 is over. In the midst of the deflation, the U.S experienced a devastating inflation rate of 9.1%. After a series of rate hikes to stop inflation, the Fed is likely to respond to the market's impatience by cutting rates too soon.

The so-called "Powell mistake" will be made by the end of 2024. The result will be another spike in inflation and another spike in interest rates. Experience has shown that governments always overreach. After the last bubble burst, the world, including Korea, will now be in a full-blown long term deflation.

The subsequent sharp drop in interest rates is evidenced by the rate cuts in Japan's deflationary economic process. Stocks, apartments, dollars, deposits, and government bonds are all assets that must be rotated at least once during each economic cycle.

After that

The final step of the Pentagon investing method, investing in government bonds to take advantage of additional interest rate reductions, is a fantastic investment method that can return investors as much as 16 times their initial investment. This means that in the medium to long term, you can double your investment by taking advantage of interest rate differentials to exponentially grow your capital.

In most cases, when interest rates are lowered, they are lowered in a short period of time in order to quickly revive the economy, so you can take advantage of the interest rate differential. So, if you are an early investor in a cyclical market that started with a surge in stock prices after the annual balance of payments turned positive a year ago, you can earn about 2~8 times more than you already earned on stocks, plus the profit on government bonds.

Normally, people keep their wealth in some cash or deposits, and most of it in real estate, such as apartments, but not anymore.

As long as deflation continues, it is much better to store wealth in various inverse ETF products such as KODEX 200 Futures Inverse 2X, KODEX Government Bond Futures 10 Year ETF, Macquarie Infrastructure Fund or government bonds.

You only need to sell as you need the money. However, it's important to remember that government bond ETFs have to pay 15.4% in taxes. For government bonds, I recommend buying and selling long term bonds directly through a brokerage firm, preferably HTS.

However, it's not always easy to get the right price when you need it. The Korean government bond market is not active.

In a long term deflationary period, there are no assets to invest in other than the few I've mentioned. Real estate should not be bought within 10 years, no questions asked, whether it pays rent or not.

In the appropriate time to buy back into real estate is after 2029. We're looking at a long death valley of about 7 years or more.

Real estate, stocks, and other commodities are the assets that will continue to decline after this major rise. Deflation is a decrease in the price of things, and a decrease in the price of things means that the companies that make them make less money.
It's rare to find a company that can grow its sales in a deflationary period. It is significant that even during the lost 30 years, Japanese pharmaceutical and biotechnology companies increased their industry index by about 700%

on average.

As real estate prices continue to fall, your monthly rent will continue to fall. That's why investing in rents is a fool's game. The way to make a fortune in a short period of time by investing in dollars is to make a fortune when the recession is in full swing, and the dollar, which was a safe dollar, becomes a jackpot dollar. In other words, the dollar is a monster.

Going forward, when we start to move into a normalized economy, i.e., an inflationary economy, sometime after 2029 for Korea and 2048 for the rest of the world, it's time to sell government bonds, government bond ETFs, and the Macquarie Infrastructure Fund because interest rates will slowly rise.

The Macquarie Infrastructure Fund is another monsterous fund, It's always guaranteed to pay a real dividend, both in inflation and deflation, but if you're just looking at the dividend, it's more favorable in inflation than deflation. Prices don't usually go down very often, but once inflation starts, they go up very quickly, so the impact on Macquarie Infrastructure Fund's dividend is somewhat favorable.

Because all the assets that Macquarie Infrastructure Fund has invested in are all social and indirect capital assets, and when inflation starts, they will raise their fees quickly, and their real revenue will increase, and their dividend will increase because they are destined to always pay out 90% of their profits.

In deflation, the profit system works the same way, i.e., in deflation, you will have to pay less for the use of social and indirect capital, so your dividends will decrease slightly, but all other prices will also decrease, and the user fee will decrease more slowly, so the lower cost will be more favorable in the application period, and the real profit will always be the same.

In short, it's a social indirect capital fund that you don't have to buy or sell. However, the author believes that the U.S rate hike could be 6~8% ahead.
Macquarie Infrastructure Fund, which typically pays a market capitalization dividend of around 6 percent.

At that point, the Macquarie Infrastructure Fund would be down significantly from its current price, as there would be virtually no benefit from the dividend.
This could be devastating for Macquarie Infrastructure Fund, as interest rates will increase significantly during inflation.

Government bonds would also be repriced, with prices plummeting based on their issue rate and current interest rates. Think of the bankruptcy of SVB Bank in the U.S as a result of the repricing of U.S long term bonds. In the end, nothing lasts forever is the answer.

The expected rate hike is 6~8%, which is of course unfavorable for government bonds. It's also worth noting that the Macquarie Infrastructure Fund was set up to close in 2042, but it is increasingly likely to be extended. This is because it is increasingly investing in new SOC facilities.
I see the current inflation as a short inflationary period of 2~3 years in a long term deflation.
Whether it is a short term deflation or a long term deflation, once the economy improves and interest rates start to rise, it is time to gradually sell government bonds and enter the stock market.

If the stock market starts to rise, especially after an annual balance of payments surplus a year ago, the three line break will check for a confirm bullish reversal
Once confirmed bullish reversal, it is very simple and easy to re-enter the stock market and start a new decade of financial growth.

The author originally identified five assets for financial investment: stocks, apartments, dollars, deposits, and government bonds. If you invest in these five assets in order, it will form a circle in the form of a pentagram.
This pentagonal investment method is the market cycle

investing formula and has become the Pentagon investing method.

On average, it takes about 10 years to cycle through the five major assets. This is a cyclical investment cycle that lasts forever, and knowing this is the Mastering the Market Cycle Investing Fomula.

This financial formula was first theorized in Korea, and you can simply enter it into the formula
and it will automatically multiply your wealth by 2~8 times. At its best, it can theoretically increase your wealth by up to 32 times over the course of a single business cycle.

Over the course of a decade, you will have numerous opportunities to invest in these five assets: stocks, apartments, dollars, savings, and government bonds.
How much of the total 32x earnings multiple you earn depends solely on your own determination and risk-taking. If you invest even a portion of your money, say 100 million, under the Pentagon Investing Method, it could grow to 3.2 billion in 10 years. That's 32 times.

The investment formula allows you to earn up to eight times the return on your investment, depending on when you start investing in stocks, when you buy an apartment, and when you swap stocks and apartments for dollars, or Dollar Swapping.

Then, after about 2~3 years of ordinary deposit, when interest rates start to fall, you can move on to the last investment sequence of the Pentagon investing method, government bonds, and the long, long 10 year investment is complete.

Timing is also a trailing trade, so there's little risk of being wrong. If you're actually a little late in the cycle, your returns will be slightly lower, but you won't lose any money.
This is the only market-cycle cyclical investing formula in the world that follows the same cyclical pattern as the Pentagon Investing Method.

Invest according to the Pentagon Investing Method, a cyclical investment formula that follows the market cycle! Now, Koreans will be the best in the world at making money.

Chapter 26) The Dollar Average Method, which can make your child a lifelong stock rich person.

The Dollar Average Method is a method of investing in stocks that consists of buying and selling the same stock, fund, or ETF at a certain time, by a certain amount, at the current market price.

It is based on the theory that stocks will always go up in the long run. Since your investing money is the same every month, if the stock price goes up on the day you buy, you'll buy a smaller quantity, and if it goes down, you'll buy a larger quantity. It's a great way to invest on a monthly timeframe because it removes the human emotion of price.

Specific applications

1) Use this method to get rich even if you start investing in stocks at age 60. People often say that you shouldn't invest anywhere after retirement age because it's too risky.
It's like saying you should live on a pension and a little money for the rest of your life. However, pensions don't even cover the full cost of living, and life expectancy is increasing dramatically every year.

So if you rely on your pension, you'll go broke! Now we

have a world where everyone lives to 90. After retirement age, people live for another 30 years. It is now necessary to invest and build wealth safely in old age using the Dollar Average Method to avoid bankruptcy in old age.

This means that even after retirement, the average person will live for another 20 or 30 years, so you should feel comfortable investing and growing your wealth using the dollar-average method.

2) Use it as a secret weapon to turn kids into lifelong stock millionaires.
If you want to invest in stocks to make your kids wealthy for life, or to have stable investment results after retirement, you need to invest in the long term using the dollar average method.

The reason why most people fail in the stock is because they don't rotate their investments money according to the Pentagon Investing Method. Stocks go up and down too much, and even if you invest in a few blue-chip stocks for the long term, it's dangerous because no company lasts forever. Mr.Big Investor called ETF the best invention of mankind. To invest in ETFs for the long term, you can invest in KODEX 200 or KODEX 200TR in Korea.

It is not easy to determine whether the S&P500 ETF in the United States or the KODEX 200 ETF in South Korea is more favorable, as each country has different safety and growth characteristics, so the choice is up to the reader.

You need to consider growth and safety for each country, but you also need to anticipate long term changes in exchange rates, which is not easy. ETFs are a better way to invest in country-specific portfolios. You can use them if you want to succeed in investing without following the Pentagon investing method.

Stocks should always be invested in growth-oriented stocks to make the most money, which are usually up 4 to 20 times in about three to four years, according to a 30 year analysis of Korean stocks.

Thematic ETFs were created in 2002, so they have not been studied separately, but they will probably grow a little more slowly than lead stocks.

However, studies have shown that lead stocks typically plummet by 50~90% from the end of the leading period. If you invest in the KODEX 200 ETF using the dollar-average method, your purchase price will be reduced to the average price during the subscription period.

Long term investors who don't want to invest in the Pentagon investing method can buy KODEX 200 on a periodic basis every month. In other words, you can buy

KODEX 200 whether it goes up or down using the dollar average method, and you can safely grow your money in your old age.

If you invest in KODEX 200 at once like time deposit, you will lose a lot of money if the stock price plummets due to long term deflation.

If you continue to buy with the dollar average method every month with periodical deposits, you will buy cheaper than the usual price during deflation(recession), so you will end up buying at the average price during the total payment period.

Even if you need money in the middle and sell some, even if the price has decreased or increased significantly, you will always buy or sell at the average price, so you will never lose big money.

This method of buying and selling stocks at an average price is called the Dollar Average Method. Since you are always buying or selling at the total average price of the period you bought, the price of one period does not have a significant impact on the total average price.
Therefore, the longer the time horizon, the greater the effect of almost no price change.

Specific price averaging effects:

Let's look at the specific investment effects of the dollar average method in [Table 4] below. Suppose you invest the same amount of 200,000 won every month.
When a stock is cheap, you buy 100 stocks, like in January, and in October, you buy 143 stocks. The number of stocks you buy depends on the price on the 25th of each month, so the number of stocks you buy each month can vary as shown in [Table 4].

In 10 months, the total purchase amount was 2 million won(200,000×10), and a total of 1,144 shares were purchased at an average price of 1,748 won(2 million won/1,144 shares=1,748 won).

The example is a 10 month investment record, but one business cycle is roughly 10 years, so you can also think of it as 10 years with 5 years of good economic times and 5 years of bad economic times. In other words, you can think of each month as a year.

Since one business cycle is roughly 10 years, and the Pentagon investing method is also based on a 10 year , if you miss a good selling opportunity, it's often not until 8 years later that the stock is back at the buy price.

If you analyze the U.S stock market for 55 years, there are only about 12.5% of cases where a stock that was once a leader stocks becomes a leader again, so I think it's safe to say that a stock that was once a leader stocks will never become a leader again.

Therefore, stocks can rarely be sold without losing money if you miss the opportunity to sell, so if you miss the selling point, you need to hold on to the stock for more than 8 years before you can sell again.

Month	Purchase Date	Purchase Price (won)	Quantity (shares)	Purchase Amount (won)
Jan.	25	2,000	100	200,000
Feb.	25	2,200	91	200,200
Mar.	25	2,150	93	199,950
Apr.	25	1,950	102	198,900
May	25	1,800	111	199,800
June	25	1,700	117	198,900
July	25	1,500	133	199,500
Aug.	25	1,400	143	200,200
Sep.	25	1,800	111	199,800
Oct.	25	1,400	143	200,200
Total		Average 1,748 won	1,144	1,997,450 won

[Table 4] Analysis of the effect of the dollar average method when investing 200,000 won on the 25th of each month

[Table 4] analyzes the effectiveness of the dollar averaging method, which indirectly shows that long term price fluctuations indicate that stocks should not be bought or sold all at once.

So, let's take a look at the reasons and effects of why buying and selling with the dollar average method will never kill you,

1) The difference between the highest purchase price in February(2,200 won) and the lowest purchase price in August or October(1,400 won) is a whopping 36%, but in this case, even if you sell at the lowest price, the average purchase price(1,748 won) is lower, so the loss rate is always 20%(1,748-1,400/1,748×100=20%).

Since the loss rate is 20%(as opposed to 36% for others), the fear is relatively small. You don't sell your entire purchase, just the amount you need to fund it, so you'll never go broke.

If you're investing with a non-dollar-averaging method and you run out of money and sell between August and October, you're not only screwed, but you'll never get your money back.

This is because people usually buy when the stock is higher and think it's going to go higher, so they'll have bought when it's quite expensive.

This is because people generally buy stocks when they are more expensive, and they will buy them when they are quite expensive because they think they will go up more.

Also, in most cases, both institutional and individual investors will hold on until they can hold on, that is, until they really need the money, and then when they really need the money at the end of a recession, they sell the stock at a complete market bottom, which is why it's much more common for long term investors to get completely screwed.

So if you're investing for the long term using anything other than the dollar-average method, you're usually going to sell your stocks at the end of a recession and get completely screwed.

This is because there is always some kind of crisis and everyone needs money, so institutions and individuals alike almost always sell stocks at the cheapest prices.

Even if you sell between August and October(397 shares totaling 600,200 won with an average purchase price of 1,511 won), you can see in [Table 4] that your losses would have been much smaller if you had used the dollar average method. In other words, if we calculate the purchase price and the number of shares purchased through July, we get(747 shares, total purchase price of 1,397,250 won, average purchase price of 1,870 won per share).

The example above is an individual stock, which means that the price can fluctuate a lot. However, the KODEX200 ETF is not as volatile, so you can't go wrong by trading the

KODEX200 ETF or Macquarie Infrastructure Fund using the dollar average method.

This is because, on average, these stocks will always increase in price over a 10 year period as long as the economy or companies are growing.
The KODEX200 ETF is like a small diversified investment in the top 200 companies in Korea, so of course it will grow more than the average growth rate of all listed companies in Korea, and the price will always rise more.

However, the expected return on investment of the leading stocks utilizing the Pentagon Investing Method is 2 to 8 times higher. It goes without saying that this method, the Dollar Swapping investment method according to the Pentagon Investing Method, is the best investment method.

But, the only way to succeed in the long term is to invest in the KODEX 200 ETF, KODEX 200TR ETF, or Macquarie Infrastructure Fund using the dollar average method.

While it seems certain that South Korea will fall into a low-growth slump in the future, the KODEX200 ETF or KODEX200 TR ETF is a collection of 200 companies that are better than the average of all listed companies, so even if South Korea's economic growth rate is lower than the current rate, it will still be much better than the average return of all listed companies in South Korea.

The world is in the midst of a long term deflation, so South Korea needs to realize that, like Japan during the "lost 32 years," it is running out of assets to invest in.

Almost the only investment methods and financial assets that can succeed as long term investments in such times are the KODEX200 ETF or KODEX200 TR ETF, Macquarie Infrastructure Fund and S&P500 ETF.

If you invest in these stocks using the dollar-average method over a long period of time in a regular savings account style, you can turn your kids into lifelong stock millionaires.

What's more, this method of investing can work for anyone, even if you're in your 60s. Non-residents of the U.S must follow the five-step Pentagon Investing Method to be highly successful. However, there is another way to invest that is less successful, but still allows you to accumulate wealth in the long run.

This is the Dollar Average Method of investing in the KODEX 200 ETF or KODEX 200 TR ETF using the Dollar Average Method, or investing in the Macquarie Infrastructure Fund for the long term.

U.S residents are required to follow the four-step Pentagon Investing method, which requires rotating through four different asset classes: stocks, apartments, savings, and government bonds.

If you don't follow the four-step Pentagon investing method and simply invest in the S&P 500 ETF using the dollar-average method for a long period of time, you can still be successful in the U.S, even if you start investing as a child or in your 60s, too.

On the other hand, the author does not recommend that non-U.S residents invest in S&P 500 ETFs in the United States. I believe that the world should experience long term deflation for a significant period of time starting in 2016.
This is because, according to the theory of long term deflation, the dollar's continued depreciation is inevitable, and it will not be able to absorb exchange rate losses, which means that even if the S&P500 ETF makes a profit, the exchange rate losses will offset the profit, making the future unpredictable.

At the end of the day, whether you're a U.S resident or non-US resident, the only way to succeed in stock investing as a long term investment is to invest in the KODEX200 ETF, KODEX200 TR ETF, or Macquarie Infrastructure Fund using the dollar-average method.

You need to rotate through the five asset classes of stocks, apartments, dollars, savings, and government bonds in a market cycle pattern.

During this process, you should never forget to swap stocks or apartments for dollars. This is because you can earn as much as 800%.

Chapter 27) Abenomics is a huge success, now it's time to buy Japan!

If we analyze the events so far, Abenomics was successful in December 2020. The proof of success is that the Yen-Dollar and Nikkei indices have reversed their inverse relationship from a direct correlation to an inverse relationship.

Japan has now been out of long term deflation for exactly 32 years(December 1989~December 2020) since it entered long term deflation in December 1989. and reverted to the normal economic state of short term deflation.

Japanese tears, shed for 32 years, need not be shed anymore. The author is only now realizing that Japan has escaped long term deflation, but Mr.Big Investor is already investing in Japan. What a great guy. How did he know?

Whether it's a hunch or a premonition, or he has proof, Mr.Big Investor is investing in Japan, he's a great guy.
Now you have to buy Japan to make money. Mr.Big Investor first invested in Japan's five major conglomerates(Mitsubishi, Itochu, Mitsui, Sumitomo, and Marubeni) in August 2020, and reportedly did so with loans from Japan.

In the author's opinion, Japan did not escape long term deflation until December 2020, and Mr.Big Investor bought Japan before it was confirmed.

In other words, Mr.Big Investor may have had other means to confirm whether Japan had exited the long term deflation, but he bought Japan on a hunch(?) without checking, and he was right.

Right now, Japanese lending rates are in the 0% range and the average dividend yield of Japanese conglomerates is around 5%, so you've already taken advantage of interest rates.

The reason why Japanese people were not investing in Japanese stocks, even though the math showed a 5% annualized gain, was because the average price of all Nikkei stocks fell by more than 5% per year.

In other words, it was inevitable that the yen-dollar depreciation would lead to exchange losses, turning investments into ghost dollars that would never return home. After more than 30 years of long term deflation, there was nothing to invest in in Japan.

The Japanese had been making rational investments in their own right. Now, Japan has become a normalized economy where financial technology is possible even if they don't invest abroad and invest domestically.

Mr.Big Investor has been increasing his stake in Japan General Trading Company every year. If the shares he already owns hold up, he'll earn about 5% a year.

The Japanese economy is now back in a virtuous cycle. Now is the time to invest in Japan.

Recall that in the author's opinion, Japan is already free of long term deflation, which means that it is much more profitable to invest in exporting conglomerates in the future because of the high exchange rate, which was discussed in detail in the previous chapter on exchange rate policy.

One thing to consider is the yen-dollar exchange rate. In the first place, overseas investments should be made in countries where the local currency is strong.

Only then you can enjoy exchange rate gains. Of course, Mr.Big Investor probably invested in Japan because he believed that the yen-dollar exchange rate is weak now, but will be strong again in a few years.

The economic community believes that Japan's long term deflation began in January 1990. However, the author wrote a few years ago that Japan's long term deflation began in December 1989. This author argued several years ago with the first publication of [Figure 26].

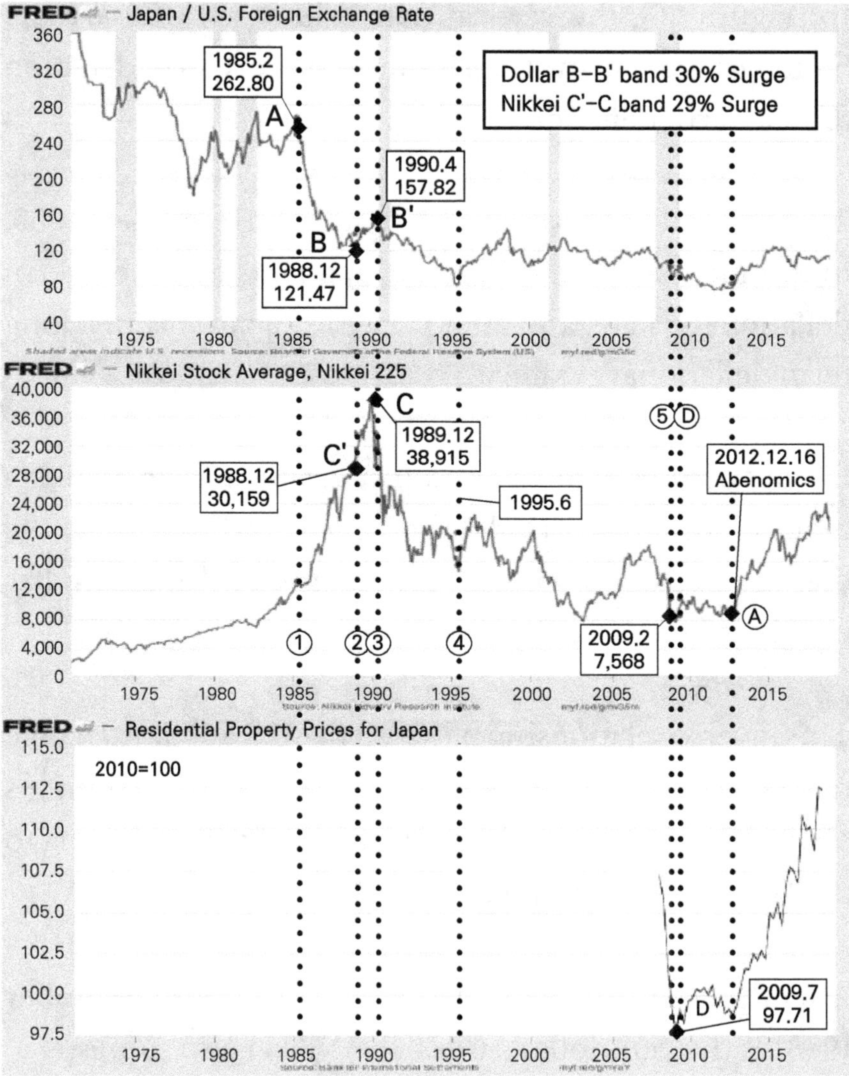

[Figure 26] 48 year change in the price of the yen and the Nikkei and housing indices

The standard for determining whether a country has entered a long-tern deflation is whether the relationship between the domestic exchange rate and the domestic stock index is inversely or directly related.

In [Figure 26], the vertical dotted lines (B)②(C') are the boundaries of Japan's transition from short term deflation to long term deflation.

The vertical dotted line (B)②(C') is December 1989, indicating that before this line, Japan was in a short term deflationary state, and after this line, Japan was in a long term deflationary state.

If you compare the yen-dollar graph and the Nikkei index before the vertical dotted line (B)②(C'), you can see that the Nikkei index is rising sharply as the yen-dollar exchange rate is falling.

This inverse relationship between the U.S dollar exchange rate and the stock index indicates that the country's economy is in a state of short term deflation according to the Diamond Dollar Investment Method.

After the vertical dotted lines (B)②(C'), i.e. after December 1988, as the yen-dollar surges, the Nikkei also surges.
In other words, they start to move in a direct proportional relationship. This is the phenomenon of long term deflation.

From this point on, after (B)②(C'), we can say that the long term deflation has occurred.

If we look at the period between BB' and C', we can see that while the dollar surged by 30%, the Nikkei also surged by 29%, which means that the rate of increase is almost the same.

Let's take a closer look again. The vertical dotted line (A) in [Figure 27] and the vertical dotted line ① in [Figure 27] are the dates of Abe's inauguration as Prime Minister of Japan on December 16, 2020, when Abenomics began to be implemented.

In this time, we can see that the yen-US dollar exchange rate is rising, the Nikkei index is rising, and the Japanese housing index is rising. In other words, Japan was in a state of long term deflation at the start of Abenomics.

The vertical dotted line ② in [Figure 27] is January 2016, when Korea and the rest of the world entered long term deflation. Vertical dotted line ③ in [Figure 27] is September 2016.

Let's take a look at the relationship between these two vertical lines, vertical dotted line ② and vertical dotted line ③. In other words, if you look between the vertical dotted line ② and the vertical dotted line ③, you can see that the Nikkei spikes when the yen-dollar exchange rate falls.

In other words, it is clear that in short term deflation, the yen-dollar exchange rate and the Nikkei are always inversely related. In a long term deflation, on the other hand, the relationship between the yen-dollar exchange rate and the Nikkei is directly proportional. The relationship between the vertical dotted lines ① and ② in [Figure 27] shows that they are directly proportional.

In [Figure 27]①, i.e. January 2016, to the vertical dotted line ②, we can see that the yen-dollar exchange rate and the Nikkei index are directly proportional.

However, from the vertical dotted line ② to the vertical dotted line ③, the movement of the yen-dollar exchange rate and the Nikkei index became inversely proportional.

From ③ to ④, the relationship changes back to a direct relationship, and then to an inverse relationship. This means that from this point on, Japan is showing signs of escaping the long term deflation.

On the other hand, the vertical dotted line (A) in [Figure 5] shows that the world, excluding Japan, entered a state of long-run deflation in January 2016.

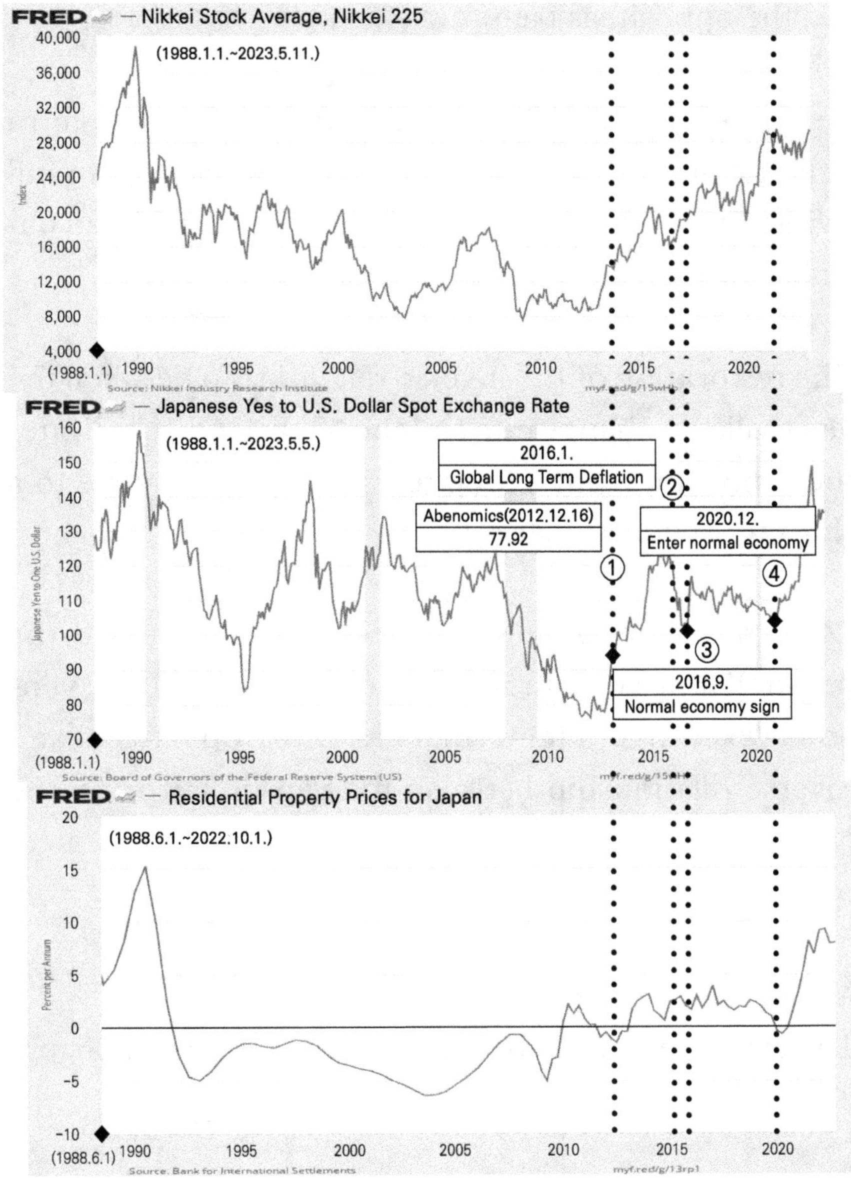

[Figure 27] Japanese Nikkei, Yen-Dollar, and Housing Index over 36 Years

However, since December 2020 (vertical dotted line ④ in [Figure 27], the yen-dollar exchange rate has been rising sharply and the Nikkei has been falling sharply, i.e., the opposite is true.

Since December 2020, Japan's exit from a long-term deflationary state to a normal economy has been in full swing. This is the only evidence that Japan has been out of long-run deflation since December 2020.

The restoration of the inverse relationship between the yen-dollar exchange rate and the Nikkei index indicates the transition from a long term deflationary state to a short term deflationary state.

On September 22, 1985, the Plaza Accord forced the yen-dollar price from 240 yen to 140 yen. Until the yen-dollar exchange rate normalizes, the proportional and inverse relationship between the yen-dollar price, the Nikkei index, and the housing index will be repeated, but the long term deflation is over.

Abenomics was a success.
The evidence is after the vertical dotted line ④ in [Figure 27].

This is the evidence of the success of Abenomics. Japan is now out of long term deflation.
According to the Diamond Dollar Investing Method, in a normal economy without long term deflation, the yen-dollar price and the Nikkei index should move in

opposite directions and even have the same the rate of fluctuation.

This is not a perfect normalization, but the inverse relationship is clear.

Since December 2020, Japan has moved from a long term deflationary state to a short term deflationary state, i.e. a normalized economy.

As shown in [Figure 27], the standard for determining whether an economy is in long term deflation is the inverse relationship between the yen-dollar exchange rate and the Nikkei index, not necessarily the inverse relationship with the Japanese housing index.

In January 1990, Japan entered a long term deflation in December 1988, precisely at line (B)②(C') in [Figure 26]. No matter how hard it tried, there was no way out and no sign of it.

However, after eight years of quantitative easing by Abe, who took office on December 16, 2012, Japan's long term deflation should be considered resolved as of December 2020.

[Figure 27] is a graph showing the relationship between Japan's Nikkei index, the yen-dollar exchange rate, and the housing index over a 36 year period. The middle graph is the yen-dollar exchange rate and the top graph is the Nikkei index.

Both of these two graphics have a start date of January 1988. However, the housing index at the bottom has a start date of June 1, 1988.

The housing index in Japan is always five months behind the Yen-Dollar exchange rate, so the graph of the housing index has a start date of June 1, 1988 for easy comparison. Note that the start date for the Nikkei and the yen-dollar exchange rate is January 1, 1988.

I.e., if you draw a vertical dotted line anywhere on the graph [Figure 27], you can see the relationship between the housing index and the yen-dollar exchange rate on the same date and the Nikkei index on the same date.

Abenomics.
Abe said he would get Japan out of the high yen. With a 2% inflation target, unlimited monetary easing, and a negative interest rate policy, he has now succeeded.

On the other hand, Japan and the rest of the world have been sliding into long term deflation for eight years already. I believe that this process of fighting inflation has brought the world into a long term deflation and a long recession. With the exception of Japan, the world may now be sliding into low growth and negative interest rates.

On the other hand, the Japanese economy starts a virtuous cycle. First, yen that have been invested abroad will return home with their fruits.

The time has come for Japanese overseas investors to stop being ghost dollars and enjoy the fruits of their investment. It's time to buy Japan. No more "Japanese tears" or Japan's long term deflation. The 32 year period(December 1988 to December 2020) of Japanese tears is over.

It was recently reported that Mr.Big Investor has invested in Japan. He must be a savvy investor after all. It's time to invest in Japanese stocks because in any country, stocks move faster than apartments. Japan is a country where stocks start moving five months earlier than real estate.

For any country, it's important to research the order of investment in each asset and the time difference between investments.

Depending on the country's dependence on trade and the type of housing, it is normal for the timing to be slightly different. In South Korea, there is a six month lag between investing in stocks and investing in apartments.

Japan's housing type is mainly single-family houses, while Korea's is mainly apartments. Korea's dependence on trade is about 70%, while Japan's is only 20%. Common sense should tell us that Japan's housing index should move more slowly, but in reality, real estate starts moving five months after stocks in Japan and six months after stocks in Korea.

According to the first market cycle investing formula, the Pentagon investing method, if the U.S has a large current account deficit a year ago, or if a country has a large balance of payments surplus a year ago, its stock index will start to rise.

After that, Japan is 5 months, Korea is 6 months, and it's the optimal time to invest in real estate after investing in stocks 5~6 months ago. For other countries, you can start investing in apartments after the pre-analyzed period.

This is the starting point for the author's other fundamental fintech book, 『The Hidden Story of Wealth Creation: How to Start Investing at 60, subtitled: There's a Secret to Turning Kids into Lifelong Stock Market Riches!』

It is the beginning of the first cyclical investment pattern Dollar Swap fintech formula, Pentagon investing method.

We're in the midst of a long term deflation. In an attempt to cure the brief inflation, Powell may make the "Powell mistake". That is, he may cut interest rates prematurely.

But the revived inflation will then be lowered by a few more rapid rate hikes. Interest rates are high now, too, but that means we could see high rates for quite some time. But after that, we believe the world will enter a true long term deflation. In other words, the world may have to accept a period of high interest rates and 4~5% inflation.

The good news is that the world now has empirical data on how to fight long term deflation with Abenomics: massive monetary easing.

But that doesn't mean that the debt of households, businesses, and governments has been eliminated, and it doesn't mean that the problem of population decline has been solved, so I think we're going to end up with a society where the policy target of 2% inflation shouldn't be achieved. The world is destined for a high-interest rate, high-inflation world in the future.

In the meantime, Japanese people have not been buying stocks and houses in Japan as is customary. Stocks and apartments have been falling steadily for more than 30 years.

But now, to get rich, Japanese people have to buy Nikkei stocks, and they have to buy export conglomerates because it's the age of conglomerates again. This fact will be missed by almost 100% of the Japanese people.

Historically, the yen-dollar exchange rate has favored mid-sized technology companies in Japan.

But now, with the return of the high exchange rate, it's the turn of the export conglomerates.

In August 2022, Mr.Big Investor first bought $6 billion worth of shares in Japan's five largest general trading companies, the country's export powerhouses. Mr.Big Investor is increasing his investment further in 2023. Coincidence or research?

One of the two conditions for successful overseas investments is a strong local currency, and he knows that the Japanese yen is in the midst of a long cycle of weakness.

If the yen continues to weaken, foreign funds invested in Japan will suffer exchange losses when they return to their home countries.

If you invested in Japan by exchanging 110 yen for a dollar, and when you return home after selling your Japanese assets, the yen-dollar exchange rate is 150 yen, you will have an exchange loss of 40 yen per dollar.

Mr.Big Investor didn't invest in Japan by taking dollar funds from the U.S to Japan, but by issuing yen-denominated bonds to Japanese commercial banks to buy stocks of Japan's five largest trading companies.

He borrowed money at an interest rate of about 0.5% or less and bought stocks of Japanese general trading companies with an average dividend yield of about 5%. He already had a 4.5% to 5% return on his investment.

We know some of the reasons, but we need to think about why? From his investment, we can get an idea of the future of Japan.

The Japanese yen hit a low of 76.34 yen to the dollar, and then went up to 151 yen in 2023. It is now around 140 yen. The author believes that the yen will be much cheaper in the future. The goal of the Abenomics policy is to lower the price of the yen.

If you want to invest abroad, you should go to a country where the local currency is stronger.

Right now, Japan is printing money ad infinitum to lower the value of the yen. There are endless ways to weaken the yen.
However, it is an investment that assumes that the Japanese yen will strengthen again in the future, and when it does,

foreign funds will once again rush to buy Japan as the yen strengthens, just like the Plaza Accord of September 1985. At that point, he would sell the rising stocks and buy dollars to get out of the Japanese market.

The fact that Mr.Big Investor began to invest in and significantly increase his holdings in Japan's five largest conglomerates, or trading companies, is also indirect evidence that Japan is out of long term deflation.

Mr.Big.Investor realized that these export-oriented conglomerates would profit greatly from the growing exchange rate differential.

The strategy is to earn an average dividend yield of about 5% per year for the duration of the holding period, and then, when the yen becomes expensive, buy dollars and return to the U.S when the yen-dollar exchange rate is at its lowest, and thus keep all the dividends and exchange gains.

You should invest abroad when you can take advantage of capital gains and exchange rates. Investing abroad is like a hurdle race. The best time to invest abroad is after a stock, apartment, or government bond market crash in a country in the foreign.

I.e., the best time to buy a country's stocks, apartments,

and government bonds is after the local dollar has skyrocketed and the local currency has crashed, and you'll be able to capture both the capital gains and the exchange rate gains. One thing to consider is the recovery potential of the local dollar and how long it will take. I would advise most investors to avoid investing abroad.

But, in Japan, which is coming out of a long term deflation, the author strongly recommends buying export conglomerates due to the rising yen-dollar exchange rate.

Mr.Big Investor invested in shares of Japan's General Trading Company in anticipation of a stronger yen that would eventually return. It's the same reason why he sells yen-denominated bonds to Japanese banks to fund his Japanese stock purchases.

This method completely eliminates gains and losses due to exchange rate differences during the holding period.

It's time for Japanese people to start investing anew in Japanese apartments and other profitable real estate.

If they continue to invest in the same way they did during the long term deflation, they will be on a downward spiral again. As the population of rural areas decreases, the demand for rural real estate decreases, so it is inevitable that rural real estate prices will fall.

However, there is no doubt that people will flock to real estate such as apartments in urban areas, so you should invest in apartments in urban areas.

The era of short term deflation has now arrived in Japan.

I think Japan's long term deflation is over. This is thanks to Abenomics. Abenomics is a huge success. People should start investing in Japan now. Japan's tears, which have been secretly shed for 32 years(1988.12.~2020.12.), are over. It is certain that all asset prices in Japan will rise. The yen is more likely to continue its decline.

The era of the Diamond Dollar Investing method has finally been applied in Japan.

Therefore, I believe that the yen to won exchange rate below 700 won has arrived and the super cheap era is coming.

Will there be a period of strength in the yen-dollar exchange rate in the near future, as predicted by Mr.Big Investor?
The author believes that the yen-dollar exchange rate should be judged by considering the exchange rate at the time of the Plaza Accord in 1985.

For 32 years, the yen-dollar exchange rate was super

strong. From 260 yen to 78.6 yen to the dollar, it was 32 years of continuous yen strength.

Going forward, there will be an era of high interest rates where the world will accept high inflation rates above 2%. And it should be noted that since January 2016, the world, including South Korea, has been in a long term deflation with household debt, corporate debt, and government debt, too.

This is when Japan seized the opportunity. However, Japan's government debt ratio is a whopping 248%. This is by far the highest in the member of the Organization for Economic Cooperation and Development.

The Japanese government cannot afford to choice fiscal policy liberally. Now that Japan has a chance to escape long term deflation with a massive monetary easing program, it should choose a certain way to fully return to economic stability.

This is the sale of Japanese state-owned property.
At a time when real estate prices in Japan are rising, the government should sell off excess and unneeded state-owned assets to Japanese citizens and Japanese companies to pay off the government bonds it has already issued in a short period of time. This is the only way to turn the broken economy around.

Another way is to boost GDP. In the age of AI, dramatic productivity gains can reduce countries' debt ratios. However, the current stagnation in global economic growth is more due to a lack of demand than a lack of productive capacity, so this option has its limitations, too.

In any case, Japan needs to bring its debt ratio back to the average debt ratio of OECD countries. This will bring Japan out of the long term deflation state once and for all.

In fact, it is the only way to get Japan out of a long term deflation state. Keep in mind that all debt, whether it belong to personal, corporate, or government, does not go away until it is paid off.

Japan also should not forget that a persistent and excessive trade surplus is also a long term deflation trigger, too.

Japan is a net creditor country, investing about twice its GDP abroad. This excessive overseas investment also reduces domestic consumption, which can be a source of long term deflation, too.

(This book was completed on January 4, 2024)

Japan's Nikkei 225 Index broke through its all-time high

of 38,915 on January 4, 1990 to 39,156 on February 22, 2024, after 32 years of long term deflation. This doesn't just mean that Japan's economy has revived.

This is the work of the former FED Chairman (Feb. 2006-Jan. 2014), nicknamed "Helicopter Ben," and winner of the 2022 Nobel Prize in Economics. This resolved Japan's long term deflation.

This will be the beginning of the global long term deflation that has already begun in January 2016.too.

Japan's escape from long term deflation was largely due to this celebrity's policies continued to be strongly pushed in Japan, and helped the country escape a long term deflation.

This book was completed on January 4, 2024, and at the time of completion, I had already determined that Japan had already escaped the long term deflation in December 2020. In other words, the Nikkei's record high on February 22, 2024, After that, it is released in March 2024 with only minor modifications, such as Japan's exit from negative interest rates.

2024. 2. 23.
Posted by author Sohn DaeShig

Epilogue

As you can see, there is a big difference between investing as a U.S resident and as a non-resident. It's important to remember that the difference between U.S and non-U.S stock investing methods can make a big difference in terms of investment returns, especially if there is a financial or economic crisis.

I hope that when my beloved grandson, Siyoon, Kim, and my grandson, Hyunbae, Sohn, grow up, they will realize everything in this book. Then both of my grandsons will be rich and live generously for the rest of their lives.

I hope they will never forget that it's a big mistake to think that Mr.Big Investor's long term investments in stocks and apartments will bring them success.

If you don't live in the U.S, I hope you learn from this book that everyone is doomed if they don't rotate their investments through the market cycle between the five major assets: stocks, apartments, dollars, savings, and government bonds.

By the time people reach their early to mid-30s, they usually have some money saved up. This book introduces the first Dollar Swap FinTech method, the Diamond Dollar investing Method, as well as the first market-cycle cyclical investing formula and the Dollar Swap method.

The Pentagon investing method is the author's original creation, the world's first assets market Rotation investing formula. In this book, I derived, theorized, and published the principles of the theory. The book title is "Dollar Swap Fintech make 800% (Assets Market Rotation investing Formula) Pentagon Investing Method. The subtitle : Tears of Japan 'Why everyone who invests in stocks or apartments for the long term is doomed in the end?' i.e. Long term investment in stocks and apartments ruins everyone.

With this Dollar Swap investment technique, you can dramatically increase your wealth by up to 8 times by Dollar Swapping between stocks and apartments when you're in 3 steps. Long term investing in stocks or apts everyone gets screwed.

This book presents the Pentagon investing method, the world's first asset market rotation investing method. I.e. it means that no other book in the world explains the pricing principle between the dollar and other assets, and how to swap the stocks or apartments for dollars. and how to multiply your wealth by 2~8 times in a short period of time.

For people living in the United States, the dollar is the perfect safe assets. For them, the dollar is just cash. However, people living in the U.S cannot use the techniques described by the author to multiply their investments by 8 times in a short period of time.

As long as you factor in a little inflation every year, there's no other asset as safe as the dollar. Of course, we are in a against inflation. It varies from country to country, but for now, it's just a brief period of inflation during a long period of deflation.

The dollar is simply the world's cash, which means it's accepted everywhere in the world, and it's also convenient when traveling abroad because you don't need to exchange currency.

So far, there's not much difference between the American financial theories we've been reading and the non-American financial books that have followed their example. This is because they are either based on American financial books or simply translations of those books.

Therefore, all fintech books are bound to differ significantly from this book. This book is almost entirely original.

This book describes in detail how to make a fortune by focusing on the phenomenon of plummeting asset prices in crisis countries as the price of the dollar surges due to a financial or economic crisis, and the surge in local stocks, real estate, bonds, and other assets as the dollar recovers after the crisis subsides. These are dollar fintech techniques.

Again, if you live in the United States, you can't use the techniques in this book to multiply your wealth by 2~8 times in a short period of time. It's also important to note that the dollar is not always a safe haven for non-US residents. If you don't live in the US, the dollar is a "monster asset".

Even for people who don't live in the U.S, the dollar is a safe haven in normal times, but in times of crisis, it can be the best or worst asset. In other words, it can instantly become a monster asset. Depending on how you use it, it can also be a jackpot.

This book rewrites all existing financial theories from the perspective of someone who doesn't use the U.S dollar as their everyday currency.

It is also the first practical guide to Dollar Swapping, a technique that exploits the fluctuations in the price of the dollar to exponentially multiply your original investment by 2~8 times.

In the United States, this method of Dollar Swapping and dollar FinTech, which uses the fluctuation of the dollar price, is not very useful. However, even within the United States, the order of the cyclical investment cycle patterns of the four assets targeted for financing, namely stocks apartments deposits and government bonds, is a new theory that completely surpasses the egg theory.

But even U.S residents have a chance to win big if they take their dollars to a country where the dollar has risen sharply in the wake of a financial crisis. They can make a fortune in Dollar Swapping, which is called 2~8 times their assets in a short period of time.

Therefore, domestic and foreign readers should read this book two or three times to fully understand it. And investors living outside the United States should be at the starting line to get rich by swapping dollars and stock apartments when the opportunity arises.

Many investors who majored in economics, business administration, accounting, and other supposedly financially related majors have not been able to outperform others in investing.

In other words, neither an economics professor nor an MBA can be successful without studying fintech. It's just that majors are a little faster at picking up financial skills from books.

In the end, only those who study finance technology separately, using books on fintech, will succeed. The problem is that university departments do not teach money-making studies such as stock majors or apartment majors.

Just as there is a real estate major in universities, I think the theoretical foundations are in place for a stock major. Stock major in the university will become an interdisciplinary science. It will be a comprehensive and scientific department.

In the meantime, no one specialization is better suited to make money, and everyone has the same opportunity to make money. This is a great thing for investors with lesser education. A PhD or MBA in economics isn't going to help you make money, either.

Everyone needs to study fintech separately to be good at it. This is why there should be an equity major. In most cases, if you learn a lot, you can get a high-paying job and make a good living. But it's different in fintech: only those who study financial technology separately succeed in investing.

After reading this book three or four times and internalizing it, I hope that all readers will succeed in investing and achieve economic freedom. It is the world's first economic cycle pattern, the Market Cycle Investing Method.

If you've read this bookin detail, you've mastered the Pentagon Investing method. It's a asset market cycle investing fomula. So, You should now be able to use the Dollar Swapping investment technique at your disposal.

Non-U.S residents should follow the five-step Pentagon Investing method, and U.S residents should follow the four-step Pentagon Investing method.

As always, I wish my readers success in investing.

Jan. 4, 2024
Pangyo in Korea

www.ingramcontent.com/pod-product-compliance
Lightning Source LLC
LaVergne TN
LVHW011702200926
848484LV00004B/1046
* 9 7 9 1 1 3 9 2 1 7 3 7 7 *